Older Offenders: Current Trends

ABOUT THE EDITORS

Sol Chaneles, PhD, is Chairman of the Department of Criminal Justice, Rutgers University, New Brunswick, New Jersey, and an elected trustee of the New Jersey Association on Correction. The author of an article entitled "Growing Old Behind Bars" that appeared in *Psychology Today*, September 1987, Dr. Chaneles is presently completing a non-fiction book on art looting during World War II.

Cathleen Burnett, PhD, is Associate Professor of Sociology and Administration of Justice at the University of Missouri at Kansas City. She is founder and President of the Society of Interdisciplinary Research on Elderly Offenders (1985-present). Her scholarly articles have appeared in *Legal Studies Forum, Criminal Law Bulletin*, and the *Journal of Crime and Justice*. She earned a doctorate in sociology from Vanderbilt University.

Older Offenders: Current Trends

Sol Chaneles, PhD
Cathleen Burnett, PhD
Editors

The Haworth Press
New York • London

Older Offenders: Current Trends has also been published as *Journal of Offender Counseling, Services & Rehabilitation*, Volume 13, Number 2 1989.

The Haworth Press, Inc., 12 West 32 Street, New York, NY 10001
EUROSPAN/Haworth, 3 Henrietta Street, London WC2E 8LU England

Library of Congress Cataloging-in-Publication Data

Older offenders : current trends / Sol Chaneles and Cathleen Burnett, editors.
p. cm.
"Has also been published as Journal of Offender counseling, services & research, volume 13, number 2, 1989"—T.p. verso.
Includes bibligraphies.
ISBN 0-86656-806-9
1. Aged offenders—United States. I. Chaneles, Sol. II. Burnett, Cathleen.
HV6791.042 1989
364.3'7'088055—dc19 88-13805
CIP

Older Offenders: Current Trends

CONTENTS

Older Offenders: Current Trends

Introduction

Cathleen Burnett

Elderly Offenders used to be a topic at which respectable criminologists snickered (Cullen et al., 1985). It was considered both a fad that publication-conscious professionals would exploit and a fictional invention that would soon pass from the journals for lack of substantive significance. Neither perjorative accurately describes the current interest in the field. Scholarly attention is continuing to grow rather than diminish, and this volume represents the most recent trends in research that have developed cooperatively out of several disciplines.

In March 1982 the First Annual Conference on Elderly Criminals was held in Albany, New York. Since that time, conferences have been held in Miami (1983), in Kansas City (1985), and in San Bernardino (1987), drawing participants from international as well as national places. These conferences have had the effect of encouraging original research by bringing together those who work independently, often without knowing what research others are developing. In addition, these conferences provide interdisciplinary opportunities that enrich and broaden the scope of all investigations. To further nurture these scattered efforts, a not-for-profit organization was launched in 1985 to serve as a clearinghouse and network for scholars in diverse disciplines: The Society for the Interdisciplinary Research on Elderly Offenders. Members of this society include sociologists, psychologists, police, social workers, architects, correction officials, law faculty, gerontologists, educators, administrators, health professionals, criminologists, federal government researchers, and probation and parole officers.

It should not be surprising that the study of elderly offenders first found fertile soil in the field of gerontology rather than in criminology. Gerontologists by definition focus on age and aging and one of the issues that repeatedly surfaced in discussions of aging and crime was a concern for the increasing fear of victimization among older persons. This solicitude led to observations of other crime-related phenomena, namely, elders committing crimes. Predictions that an "epidemic crime wave" would be sweeping across society as the general population aged were quickly challenged as hyperbole. The concern of advocates for elders was that the socially offensive behavior of a few might manufacture and reinforce a negative image of older persons in general. Traditional gerontological theories were inadequate to serve the policy needs of containing the impact of the older offending behavior that was occurring. Criminologists responded to the alleged elderly crime-wave by identifying the scope of the crime problem through statistical reports, effectively debunking the media depictions as myth.

Thus, most of the early literature addressing crime and older persons focused on victimization issues confronting the senior citizen (Alston, 1986; Chambers et al., 1987). In research and discussion by practitioners and academic alike, concern for the special vulnerabilities of the older person is reflected in the portrayal of the elderly as an ideal victim. Alston (1986) has summarized the factors which influence a person's chances for victimization as attractiveness, exposure and guardianship, applying each to the social circumstances of the elderly. These are lifestyle factors indicating that the elderly will increase their vulnerability to the degree that (1) there is benefit to be gained from them (attractiveness); (2) they are visible and in close proximity to offenders (exposure); and (3) they are lacking some form of protection (guardianship). Others demonstrate that the fear of becoming a victim has not a simple relation to exposure to actual risk (Lebowitz, 1975; Antunes, Cook, Cook, and Skogan, 1977; Yin, 1985; Lindquist and Duke, 1982). The apparent irrationality of high fear found in low risk groups has prompted investigators to explain these inconsistencies (Stafford and Galle, 1984; Akers et al., 1987). Recent research demonstrates that the effects of age, race, and gender on fear of crime are interactive (Ortega and Myles, 1987) and warrant further study of the complexities. In contrast to the research response of experts, society responded to the concerns of fear and risk with protectionism, offering self-help programs to teach potential victims how to prevent or at least to believe in reducing their risk.

Criminologists typically have considered age to be an uninteresting variable, on that does not vary and consequently adds nothing to understanding or the prediction of criminal activity (Hirschi and Gottfredson, 1983). This perspective maintains that "propensity toward crime tends to diminish as one grows older (and) . . . age does not interact with any known causal variables in its effect on crime. Therefore, identification of the causes of crime at one age suffices to identify them at other ages as well" (1983:580). This lack of respect for the age variable is persuasively challenged in subsequent research (Greenberg, 1985; Steffensmeier et al., under review). Variations in the "age distribution for different crime types are inconsistent with the invariancy argument but instead support the traditional sociological view that, although crime rates typically decline throughout life after the initial rise in adolescence, certain crimes peak later, or decline more slowly, or both" (Steffensmeier et al.). The currency of this controversy indicates how recently the age variable has been considered in causal theoretical explanations of criminal behavior.

The conduct of original research on elderly offenders has been slow to develop for several pragmatic reasons. First, a variety of definitions exist for the concept of "old." Not only is there little consensus across disciplines, there is equally little agreement within fields of study as to how to measure or attach meaning to any age designating "old." Definitions are likely to fluctuate, particularly when two disciplines intersect. Criminologists using standard arrest distributions often identify any offender over 30 as "old." Always arbitrarily selected, age delimiters seem to rise and fall with the investigator's sensitivity to sample size. A second problem in the doing of original research on elderly offenders is that relatively few criminal offenders are classified in the upper, "older," categories of official arrest statistics. For many scholars, small numbers suggest lack of significance. However, it is the particularity of elderly offenders which can be intrinsically interesting. The unique, the non-normal, the rare are often much more important to our understanding of the normal than big numbers found in a mathematical curve. Michel Foucault says it this way:

> In a system of discipline, the child is more individualized than the adult, the patient more than the healthy man, the madman and the delinquent more than the normal and the non-delinquent. In each case it is towards the first of these pairs that all the individualizing mechanisms are turned in our civilization; and when one wishes to individualize the healthy, normal and law-abiding adult, it is always by asking him how much of the child he had in him, what secret madness lies within him, what fundamental crime he had dreamt of committing. (1979:193)

In addition to these obstacles, the quality of information about elderly offenders shares the usual data accumulation problems of accuracy and completeness associated with the social and political aspects of decision-making. Issues related to professionalism and institutionalization suggest that an informal bias against identifying or labeling older persons "criminals" likely operates and serves to hide, ignore, or deny illegal behaviors committed by older persons. Police discretion and redefinition of the situation are well-known processes that affect official record-keeping. It would be surprising if such factors did not affect the construction of official records on elderly offenders.

Despite these problems, the study of mature, adult, older or elderly offenders has come of age after an initial and rather traditional examination of statistical reports. Beginning with analyses of national arrest data, these studies inspect sex and racial differences by type of offense (Shichor, 1984; Wilbanks, 1984). Research on offenses covers a wide range in seriousness (shoplifting in Feinberg, 1984; murder in Wilbanks, 1984; embezzlement in Zietz, 1981; alcohol-related crime in Meyers, 1984). Examination of local crime evolves out of the review of national crime statistics. This local focus allows more innovative use of official records in conjunction with background materials, resulting in increasing efforts at conducting original research projects that can have more direct policy implications. Unfortunately, accessibility problems multiply at this level and might deter many scholars from engaging in this sort of inquiry. Official law enforcement agencies are not likely to collect the types of information that researchers require. Verifying the existence of official records according to the age of the violator is only one obstacle. Willingness to provide the information needs to be negotiated, often taking more time than anticipated and consequently frustrating researchers with limited resources. However, none of these problems is unusual for the criminologist. Once obtained, the major challenge in interpreting official records is in overcoming the bureaucratic insensitivity to age. Most criminal justice agents are not aware of their own biases to the ages of their "clients" and fail to recognize the routine usage of classifying persons according to age in normal, taken for granted work perspectives.

WHAT IS IN THIS VOLUME

Arrest rates alone do not tell the story. Courts have increasingly been willing (as well as mandated) to impose longer sentences, sometimes without parole, on offenders and thereby increase the elderly prison population for decades to come. That the numbers will increase is readily accepted and with that social fact comes the public policy debate about what to do with older offenders. This book provides a discussion of many of the issues that will be on the agendas of academic and practitioners as neither field of criminology nor gerontology will be able to ignore the topic. The articles in this collection are offered as a representation of some of the current trends in research on older offenders. They provide a sense of what has been learned and what questions remain. Interestingly, there is no age chosen by the majority of authors to identify older offenders. While one author (Booth) resists choosing any chronological age, the age most frequently chosen is 55 years and over (Sapp, Brahce and Bachand, Burnett and Kitchen, Walsh). The book is organized into three sections. First is a general review of the dimensions of the offenses, along with some discussion of the questions encountered when attempting to explain the behavior. The second section presents empirical research addressing the sentencing alternatives applied to older offenders. The third section provides insight into management and correctional issues that can arise with the incarceration of older offenders.

NAMING THE OFFENDERS

Combinations of strain and control theories are most commonly applied as social explanations for criminal behavior by the elderly (Greenberg, 1985; Rowe and Tittle, 1977; Malinchak, 1980). These theories typically frame the criminality of older offenders in terms of living in a state of drift, relatively free of social controls and responsibilities. Rowe and Tittle (1977) demonstrate that social-psychological processes (integration, moral commitment, fear of sanctions, utility of the crime) do indeed explain much of the age-crime relationship (Greenberg, 1985:10-11). However, in a comprehensive review of the literature, Kercher (1985) compares research results from across a variety of samples and identifies only three variables which demonstrate the expected strong relationship to crime by the elderly: prior criminal behavior, criminal associates and criminal beliefs. More numerous are the factors which are weakly related to elderly crime: physiology, religiousness, sex, race, anomie, marital status (including widowhood), income, occupation, residential mobility, education, unemployment. More often than not factors associated with younger offenders are untested for the older age groups (attachment to friends, retirement, health, prescription drugs). Thus, research into the causes of criminal behavior committed by the elderly generally has not had rigorous or controlled testing of hypotheses. Hirschi and Gottfredson (1983:582) reiterate that "resources should not be devoted to establishing the effects of a variable whose influence on crime is noncontroversial and theoretically uninteresting . . ." The inquiries that have been initiated suffer primarily when focusing exclusively on numbers and rates rather than real people and substantive interdependencies. Most such studies depend on speculative conclusions and interpretations, falling to the methodological trap of ecological fallacy. Improving understanding will require moving beyond available statistics.

Using data gathered by the Federal Bureau of Investigation, Allen Sapp provides an overall view of the patterns and trends in arrests of the elderly, those aged 55 and over. These figures are based on numbers of arrests, rather than how many offenders were charged with the crime or for how many different offenses each offender was arrested. Overall results indicate that while the number of elderly is increasing rapidly, the percentage of all arrests that are arrests of the elderly is declining; dispelling again the popular myth of an elderly crime wave. From 1972 to 1981, the total number of arrests for all ages and all offenses increased by 53%, but arrests of elderly offenders decreased by 3% during the same time period. Although the numbers and percentage of elderly offender arrests both declined for all crimes, there was an increase for the major, or index, crimes reported in the Uniform Crime Reports (UCR). Violent offenses declined slightly, but property offenses increased significantly in the ten year study period. In the violent crimes, arrests of the elderly decline slightly from 2.9% of all arrests for violent offenses to 2.5%. Murder and non-negligent manslaughter declined from 5.8% to 4.6%. Arrests of the elderly for forcible rape increased from 1.0% to 1.8% of all rape arrests, while robbery arrests remained stable at 0.5%. Aggravated assault arrests declined slightly over the ten year period. All of the property offenses showed some increase in percentage of all arrests. Elderly arrests for burglary increased very slightly from 0.4 to 0.7%. Arson, added to the UCR in 1979, reflected a slight increase from 1.7 to 2.0 over three years. Larceny-theft increased from 2.6 to 3.5%, accounting for almost all of the overall increase for major crimes. Not examined by Sapp are the less serious offenses. Others have found that fraud, embezzlement and larceny-theft seem to be the most frequent crimes for which the elderly are arrested, although some authors have found that assaults and sex offenses are relatively common as well (Burnett and Ortega, 1984; Alston, 1986; Inciardi, 1987). Still needing attention are two other types of offenders: female offenders and social/political activists (Ortega and Burnett, 1986; Carpenter, 1985).

One of the problems with national statistics is the inability to distinguish between those older folks who are new to official sanctioning and those who are well-known to law enforcement because of their repeated illegalities. Carl Brahce and Don Bachand are able to compare first time older offenders with "career" offenders in terms of retirement. Brahce and Bachand were able to access criminal history files and found that a majority of retirees were habitual offenders. Their study suggests that seriousness of offense increases with retirement. However, they raise many more questions than they answer in part because of the small number of cases with complete police records. In addition to the need for better record-keeping, more creative gerontological research needs to be applied to understand whether or not retirement *causes* coping strategies which push elders into criminal behavior.

Menachem Amir addresses another problem with aggregate data: the likelihood that unknown offenders are not counted. He suggests that "all elderly offenders are not poor, trying to keep from freezing, living on fixed incomes. Perhaps there are a bunch of guys riding around in cars trying to be inconspicuous and when arrested, they all have heart attacks so they don't have to go to jail; guys that may have big cigars, girls on their arms and the ability to call on the phone and make death come out of the other side of it" (Carpenter, 1985): the Mafia. Amir discusses age and the aging Mafiosa, using an idiographic approach to describe the way normative processes are impacted by aging. Old offenders are not always victims of society—but could be seen as victim-makers; that in the course of achieving success in a career, they ruin lives.

SENTENCING: BLIND JUSTICE?

Part II focuses on the problems of processing the older offender through the criminal justice system. Society labels the older offender a "deviant," a geriatric delinquent; troublesome, but rarely dangerous. What, then, is the Court's response to the older offender? Is it punitive or humanitarian? A major dilemma facing the criminal justice system is how to interpret and apply the various (and often conflicting) goals of the justice system. What does "doing justice" mean when the defendant is an older offender? Should justice be blind to age (Cohen, 1985)? Does fairness demand equal punishment? Or does equity prescribe the discretionary application of age as a mitigating factor? What does a 10 year sentence mean to a 21-year-old and to a 65-year-old? Should punishment fit the offense or the offender for equal crimes? These are questions which expose the need for reconciliation between the legal definition and the public definition of criminal behavior. Examination of the entire criminal justice process demonstrates that elderly criminals are treated more harshly at the front end of the criminal justice system (through conviction) and more leniently at sentencing for felony crimes (Wilbanks, 1985), appearing to quickly dispose of public ethical responsibility for the circumstances of the older offender. The justice system is continually dealing with these issues because society has not had the will to resolve these policy questions. When the offender is old, the legal issues become entangled with aging issues. It is likely the Court's response to these questions will mirror society's manner of fashioning the invisibility of older persons (Jones, 1987). Processing takes the form of exerting control over older persons, thereby increasing the imbalance in social exchange relationships that older persons generally experience (Dowd, 1975). Loss of power, defined as the inability to live independently, intensifies for the older offender. The individual disappears in the web of the Court. Thus, management concerns predominate rather than dignity issues; objectifying the individual rather than addressing subjective concerns.

These kinds of questions lie at the root of the need for research on sentencing. Gary Feinberg and M. David McGriff examine case disposition and judicial sanctions by looking at court records for all defendants with misdemeanant theft charges in Dade County Court in 1985. The findings indicate that judicial recourse to fines relative to probation greatly increases with the defendant's advancing age. Plea seems to be irrelevant in predicting the sanction imposed as is having an attorney present. In addition, Feinberg and McGriff report that racial differences in sentencing are overcome by the strong effect of advancing age. The major exception concerns probation, which even in advanced age seems to be favored for whites over blacks. Sex differences, however, endure as a relevant determinant of sanction.

Gerri Turner and Dean Champion also examine sentencing outcomes by conducting a survey of 166 city and county prosecutors randomly selected in a number of rural counties in Kentucky, Tennessee and Virginia in 1985-1986. official records supplement their investigation. They offer a measure of sentencing severity, the AS/MS ratio, which allows a comparison of the relative severity (or what the judge, by statute, *could* impose) and what sentence is *actually* imposed. Their results raise again the unsettled questions concerning what penalty is equitable or just. Like Feinberg and McGriff, Turner and Champion find that older persons receive lighter sentences for committing the same or similar offense compared with younger persons irregardless of prior record. They suggest that it pays to commit crimes when you are old.

Mark Watson discusses some of the treatment alternatives available for dealing with older sexual offenders. This group of offenders poses particularly grievous problems for whatever domain has control of these men. Without offering solutions, Watson identifies the issues that are typically presented regarding sexual offenders and suggests that all the standard treatments have irreconcilable problems when the offender is old.

Included in this section is a paper which brings probation into focus as one correctional strategy for attending to the older offender. Although the majority of older offenders are, in fact, on probation (see Shichor, forthcoming; McCarthy and Langworthy, forthcoming), very little is known about this group of offenders. Cathleen Burnett and Alice Kitchen interview probationers aged 55 and over, detailing background information from which to begin an assessment of needs and motivations of probation clients. The objective of the project reported here was to develop a social profile of older offenders on probation. In-depth interviews probed four areas: (1) demographic identifiers, (2) social and financial support, (3) legal histories, and (4) attitudes and opinions of life adjustment. Finding that very few public or private organizations recognize the special needs of older persons within their jurisdiction, recommendations for more effective supervision of older offenders were made available to local courts, police and probation officers.

INSTITUTIONS: CUSTODY, CARE, OR THERAPY?

Extending from the inquiry into court management, Part III examines older offenders in institutional settings. Problems faced by any inmate include adjustment to prison life, maintaining physical and emotional health and ultimately accomplishing the return to life on the outside. Older offenders or the offender growing old in prison have additional burdens in regard to these adjustments and accommodations. Typically it is the serious, violent offender who is locked up (Goetting, 1984; Vito and Wilson, 1985) and these men become the "forgotten minority." Older offenders can be classified into three groups based on incarceration history: (1) old offenders, those who were 55 years of age or older at their first incarceration; (2) oldtimers, those grown old in prison, serving at least 20 years on their last offense; and (3) career criminals, those recidivists whose first incarceration had been before the age of 55 and excludes oldtimers. While these types can be identified, almost no prison programs are designed for the older inmate (Goetting, 1984). Issues discussed in this section are problems which face prison officials, correction administrators and indirectly the public at large. Summarized, they represent management issues on the practical level, leaving the more general policy questions to ethical and political decision-makers (Johnson, 1985). "How do you manage the old, how do you prepare them for re-entry into what? Old age? Back into society?" And as the population ages, there is the possibility that management problems will become even worse. The kind of programming and management available generally reflects the level of public (that is, outside) support. If the older offender is indeed a "forgotten minority" then management will resemble a minimal custody approach to incarceration; not likely to respond to the peculiar circumstances of adjustment and vulnerability to victimization faced by the older inmate (Wilson and Vito, 1986). The research reported here offer samples of the type of detailed information necessary to design programs which recognize inmate needs and satisfy the goals of correction.

Patricia Washington describes men 50 years of age or older who are mentally ill and incarcerated in five California county jails. These data are unique in that this is the only available study of mental illness among older men incarcerated in jails based upon a random sample of the entire jail population. She finds a high rate of recidivism, alcohol dependence and contact with the mental health system defines these as men who experience difficulty functioning in society. In addition, the rather high percentage of mentally disordered offenders in small town jails suggests that communities respond in different ways to the problems of these men. Some communities use mental health facilities while others use the criminal justice facilities to deal with them. Additional reports (Jennison, 1986; Rosner et al., 1985) find that alcohol consumption and intoxication explain significant degrees of variance in elderly violence and suggest a "high need for alcohol rehabilitation among elderly offenders; for widespread alcohol screening of older offenders at the judicial level; the need to coordinate alcoholic treatment programs with existing geriatric social services" (Jennison, 1986:64). Thus, elderly offenders can be expected to have chronic mental and physical illnesses, requiring that the existing medical service support network within the criminal justice system be modified to meet their needs (Rosner et al., 1985).

An architectural approach complements and informs the correctional challenges and opportunities for rational management. Professor Moore maintains that older people can have environments which are not only cheaper than typical institutional settings but are able to provide help to the older offenders inside. At any given moment there are likely to be more than 5,000 men over the age of 75 being held in municipal jails around the United States. Simultaneously there will be more than 30,000 men over the age of 40 confined in state prisons in this country. Moore finds a high level of fear permeating the lives of these older prisoners when housed with younger inmates. This fear results in minimizing social interaction with other prisoners as well as staff. The reduction of aggressive behavior among the older prisoners observed strongly recommends a different management strategy be developed for older prisoners which includes the architectural design of housing facilities. In addition, the presence of multiple chronic illnesses suffered by older inmates requiring intensive health care services can be frustrated when interaction with staff is reduced. Moore's findings parallel investigations from two diverse fields of psychology and nursing (Vega and Silverman, forthcoming; Gallagher, 1988).

A repeated concern with older inmates is health care for chronic illness. Dorothy Booth offers criminal justice workers a practical way to assess the health needs of older inmates. Her health instrument is one that takes little training to implement. Protecting and promoting the health of the elderly will serve the dual functions of cost-containment for the jail systems, and humanitarian care for the quality of life during their term of incarceration.

Eamon Walsh places these issues in context with population projections from the New Jersey Correction Department. Taking notice of the sentencing trends, Walsh estimates the number of inmates who will turn 55 prior to parole eligibility. Of particular interest, Walsh separates the young inmate who is in prison for a long term, growing old in prison for special attention. Able to calculate admissions and releases, Walsh has done the kind of analysis that all correction officials need to be doing in order to handle the social, psychological, physical, and educational needs of future populations.

FUTURE RESEARCH AGENDA

As the preliminary questions give way to more knotty issues, only those scholars keenly committed to interdisciplinary work will persevere in this area of study. The benefits of a multidisciplinary perspective have only been introduced in this volume. As yet there is no consensus in the socio-legal domain regarding the implications of aging for criminal justice policy. Any resolution will involve the interface of at least the two disciplines of gerontology and criminology to bring into focus the special problems presented and exposed by the older offender. Most of the papers included in this volume address issues confronting the criminal justice system that relate to the control of the older offender. We must move beyond these management issues to broader and more reflexive policy studies.

An underlying theme throughout these papers is the importance of having dialogue between researchers, policymakers and practitioners. Now is the time to anticipate systemic demands so as to be able to meet the predicted gaps in services. Older persons remain invisible, marginal to society's dominant values, without the skills necessary in a fast changing technologically productive environment to achieve (or maintain) independence. The resulting diminished ability to exchange in the marketplace leaves unresolved who is responsible for those who slip out of sight. It is the legal system which represents authority, a legitimate power which is supposed to take responsibility for the general good order of communities. This responsibility can be our own future.

Clearly, older offenders have real needs for services and supervision. Placing these persons on probation will only be useful to the degree that probation or diversion programs provide the contact necessary to recognize and respond to these needs. The legal power of observation needed to maintain the discipline of the individual is problematic when the elderly are hidden, ignored, and invisible. It is their powerlessness which leaves them vulnerable. We impose discipline to correct but policies which attempt to deter criminality will only be successful as the motivations for committing crime are understood. A lot of the old folks commit crimes right in the face of the police. Political activists are one group who increase their power by discounting the local authorities. But more than empowerment is needed in the long run. A re-definition of what power is can offer a transformation of social reality. Perhaps the present cultural values of instrumental activity, of "doing," can be replaced by the expressive, intrinsic value of "being." Power then can be increased as willingness to live in the moment increases with age.

Emerging directly from the present set of research efforts are several topics for future exploration. On the macro-level, criminology can still make a significant contribution through cross-national and cross-cultural studies. Efforts are underway to provide the data base needed to test the invariancy hypothesis (Bennett, 1988). Early work which identifies the age composition of nations indicates that a general theory of violent crime is appropriate (Ortega, Corzine and Burnett, 1986).

Micro-analyses of crime and criminal behavior through frameworks sensitive to gerontological theory hold rich possibilities for advancing knowledge of older offenders. It would be informative to study the attitudes of the aged vis-à-vis law and proper behavior. It is possible that some groups become less constrained by rules and regulations, perhaps feeling they have earned the right to be free of such restrictions. Those gerontologists identifying and explaining the first time elderly offender will offer insight and understanding of conformity. Moreover, theories of aging can be applied to the individual accounts of illegal behavior. What story does the older person tell others to explain the illegal actions? Is control the problem? Or is need? How do those with prior records differ from first offenders?

Finally, research into criminal activities will be enhanced when age is recognized as a relevant characteristic. Age may have a very significant role for certain types of crimes. For example, the violent aged are more likely to have aged victims who are less likely to survive an assault, thus becoming a murder rather than an assault statistic. Secondly, the role of alcohol and chronic illness in offending suggests it would be useful to know what effect medication can have on criminality.

In this volume we point to the needs and questions now facing society and the criminal justice system. Older offenders, first time or recidivists, young offenders growing old in prison—each group merits a response from a compassionate society. All aspects of the criminal justice system are challenged by these offenders. A civilized society is measured by the way it responds to its marginal members. If any type of justice is to prevail, attention needs to be focused on the elderly offender.

REFERENCES

Akers, R. et al. (1987). "Fear of Crime and Victimization Among the Elderly in Different Types of Communities" *Criminology* 25:487-505.

Alston, L. (1986). *Crime and Older Americans*. Springfield, Illinois: Charles C. Thomas.

Antunes, G. et al. (1977). "Patterns of Personal Crime Against the Elderly: Findings from a National Survey" *The Gerontologist* 17:321-327.

Bennett, R. (1988). "Correlates of Crime: Data Set Documentation," paper available from author, Department of Justice, Law and Society. American University. Washington, D.C. 20016.

Burnett, C. and S. Ortega (1984). "Elderly Offenders: A Descriptive Analysis" in W. Wilbanks and P. Kim (eds.) *Elderly Criminals*. Washington: University Press of America.

Carpenter, G. R. (1985). Comments from Third National Conference on Elderly Offenders. Kansas City, Missouri.

Chambers, R. et al. (1987). *Victims and Deviants*. Athens, Ohio: Ohio University Press.

Cohen, F. (1985). "Old Age as a Criminal Defense," *Criminal Law Bulletin* 21:5-36.

Cullen, F., J. Wozniak, J. Frank (1985). "The Rise of the Elderly Offender: Will A 'New' Criminal be Invented?" *Crime and Social Justice* 23:151-165.

Dowd, J. (1975). "Aging as Exchange: A Preface to Theory" *Journal of Gerontology* 30:584-594.

Feinberg, G. (1984). "Profile of the Elderly Shoplifter," in Newman, et al. (eds.) *Elderly Criminals*. Cambridge, Massachusetts: Oelgeschlager, Gunn, and Hain. pp. 35-50.

Foucault, M. (1979). *Discipline and Punish: The Birth of the Prison*. New York: Vintage.

Gallagher, E. (1988). "Older Men in Prison: Emotional, Social and Physical Health Characteristics," Doctoral Dissertation from Simon Fraser University, British Columbia.

Goetting, A. (1984). "The Elderly in Prison: A Profile," *Criminal Justice Review* 9:14-24.

Gove, W. (1985). "The Effect of Age and Gender on Deviant Behavior: A Biopsychosocial Perspective," in A.S. Rossi (ed.) *Gender and the Life Course*. New York: Aldine.

Greenberg, D. (1985). "Age, Crime, and Social Explanation," *American Journal of Sociology* 91:1-27.

Hirschi, T. and M. Gottfredson (1983). "Age and the Explanation of Crime" *American Journal of Sociology* 89:552-584.

Inciardi, J. (1987). "Crime and the Elderly: A Construction of Official Rates" in Chambers et al. (eds.), *The Elderly: Victims and Deviants*. Athens, Ohio: Ohio University Press.

Jennison, K. (1986). "The Violent Older Offender: A Research Note," *Federal Probation* 50:60-65.

Johnson, E. (1985). "Care for Elderly Inmates: What Can the Prison Do?" paper presented at Third National Conference on Elderly Offenders. Kansas City, Missouri.

Jones, W. Paul (1984). "Gerontheology: Spirituality and Aging" *Quarterly Papers on Religion and Aging* 1:1-7 (Kansas City, Missouri: St. Paul School of Theology).

______ (1987). "Death as a Factor in Understanding Modern Attitudes Toward the Aging: A Symbolization-Avoidance Theory," in D. B. Oliver (ed.) *New Directions in Religion and Aging*. New York: Haworth.

Kercher, K. (1985). "Causes and Correlates of Crime Committed by the Elderly: A Review of the Literature," paper presented at the Third National Conference on Elderly Offenders. Kansas City, Missouri.

Lebowitz, B. (1975). "Age and Fearfulness: Personal and Situational Factors" *Journal of Gerontology* 30:696-700.

Lindquist, J. and J. Duke (1982). "The Elderly Victim at Risk: Explaining the fear-victimization paradox" *Criminology* 20:115-126.

Malinchak, A. (1980). *Crime and Gerontology*. Englewood Cliffs, New Jersey: Prentice-Hall.

McCarthy, B. and R. Langworthy (eds.) (1988) Older Offenders: Perspectives in Criminology and Criminal Justice. New York: Praeger.

Meyers, A. (1984). "Drinking, Problem Drinking and Alcohol-Related Crime Among Older People," in Newman et al. (eds.) *Elderly Criminals*. Cambridge, Massachusetts: Oelgeschlager, Gunn and Hain. pp. 51-66.

Newman, E., D. Newman, and M. Gewirtz (eds.) (1985). *Elderly Criminals*. Cambridge, Massachusetts: Oelgeschlager, Gunn and Hain.

Ortega S. and C. Burnett (1986). "Age Variations in Female Crime: In Search of the New Female Criminal," *Journal of Crime and Justice* 10:133-170.

Ortega, S. and J. Myles (1987). "Race and Gender Effects on Fear of Crime: An Interactive Model with Age" *Criminology* 25:133-152.

Ortega, S., J. Corzine, and C. Burnett (1986). "Female Crime and Modernization: The Impact of Demographic Change" paper presented at the American Society of Criminology. Atlanta, Georgia.

Rosner, R. et al. (1985). "Geriatric Felons Examined at a Forensic Psychiatric Clinic," *Journal of Forensic Sciences* 30:730-740.

Rowe, A. and C. Tittle (1977). "Life Cycle Changes and Criminal Propensity," *Sociological Quarterly* 18:223-236.

Shichor, D. (1984). "The Extent and Nature of Lawbreaking by the Elderly: A Review of Arrest Statistics," in Newman, et al. (eds.) *Elderly Criminals*. Cambridge, Massachusetts: Oelgeschlager, Gunn and Hain. pp. 17-32.

______ (forthcoming). "An Exploratory Study of Elderly Probationers," *International Journal of Offender Therapy and Comparative Criminology*.

Stafford, M. and O. Galle (1984). "Victimization Rates, Exposure to Risk, and Fear of Crime" *Criminology* 22:173-185.

Steffensmeier, D. et al. (under review). "Age and the Distribution of Crime: Variant or Invariant?"

Vega, M. and M. Silverman (1987). "Stress and the Elderly Convict," paper presented at the National Conference on Elderly Offenders. San Bernardino, California.

Vito, G. and D. Wilson (1985). "Forgotten People: Elderly Inmates," *Federal Probation* 49:18-24.

Wilbanks, W. (1984). "The Elderly Offender: Sex and Race Variations in Frequency and Pattern," in Wilbanks and Kim (eds.) *Elderly Criminals*. Washington, D.C.: University Press of America.

______ (1985). "Are the Elderly Treated More Leniently by the Criminal Justice System?" paper presented at the Third National Conference on Elderly Offenders. Kansas City, Missouri.

Wilbanks, W. and P. Kim, eds. (1984). *Elderly Criminals*. Washington, D.C.: University Press of America.

Wilson, D. and G. Vito (1986). "Imprisoned Elders: The Experience of One Institution," *Criminal Justice Policy Review* 1:399-421.

Yin, P. (1980). "Fear of Crime among the Elderly: Some issues and suggestions" *Social Problems* 27:492-504.

Zietz, D. (1981). *Women Who Embezzle or Defraud: A Study of Convicted Felons*. New York: Praeger.

PART I: NAMING THE OFFENDERS

Arrests for Major Crimes: Trends and Patterns for Elderly Offenders

Allen D. Sapp

INTRODUCTION

A child born in 1985 in the United States can expect to live to approximately 75 years of age. As recently as 1920, life expectancy was 54.1 years in the United States. This truly dramatic increase in the life expectancy of Americans has resulted in a rapidly aging society with more and more persons living longer and longer. In response to this aging process of the population, major institutions in American society have undergone, and continue to undergo, drastic changes. Malinchak (1980) points out the stresses on such

---

Allen D. Sapp is an Associate Professor of Criminal Justice at Central Missouri State University. He also serves as Director of the Criminal Justice Research Center at Central Missouri State University. He holds degrees from Sam Houston State University (PhD in Criminal Justice), University of South Carolina (MSEd) and University of Nebraska-Omaha (BGS in Sociology). He previously taught at Sam Houston State University.

diverse social institutions as "economic and tax structures, the labor market, welfare programs, political leadership, and many other concerns, including the criminal justice system" (p. xiii).

Several issues are of direct concern to the criminal justice system where the elderly are involved. A general area of major concern is that of the elderly as victims of crime. A second area of major concern is that of the elderly as offenders. In this paper, an investigation is made into the arrests of the elderly offenders for major crimes.

An operational definition of elderly is needed for any research involving the aged. A number of researchers have agreed that the designation of elderly can most appropriately be applied beginning with the age of 55 years (Keller and Vedder, 1968; Malinchak, 1980; McCreary and Mensch, 1977; Shichor and Kobrin, 1978; among others). For the purposes of this study, those offenders aged 55 or older will be included and labeled elderly offenders. For those who would choose a different age for application of the designation, the data is presented by specific age groups 55-59 years, 60-64 years and 65 or more years of age.

Shichor and Kobrin (1978) and Malinchak (1980) provided results of previous analyses of criminal offense patterns for individuals 55 years of age and older. Shichor and Kobrin (1978) report that during the eleven year period from 1964 to 1974 that arrests of the elderly for major crimes increased 43% as a proportion of all age group arrests. They further noted that arrests for major crimes increased 224% in absolute number of arrests. Shichor and Kobrin (1978) also noted that arrests of the youthful age groups most prone to criminal behavior remained relatively constant throughout the eleven year period, while arrests of the elderly were increasing by 43%.

Malinchak (1980) notes an increase in criminal activity among the aged in St. Petersburg, Florida, of 108% in one year alone. In his analysis of arrests of those aged 60 years or more, he uses absolute numbers drawn from the Uniform Crime Reports (UCR). His conclusion is that crime increased in all age groups but particularly increased among the elderly. Malinchak earlier (1978) pointed out that among the elderly, violent offenses were more likely that property offenses. He indicates that aggravated assault, as a percentage of arrests, was higher for the elderly than for total arrests or for youth groups.

Shichor and Kobin (1978) also identify aggravated assault as the most significant violent offense with 80% of the total arrests for violent offenses by the elderly being for aggravated assault. Malinchak (1978) indicated that in the category of property offenses, larceny-theft was the offense more likely to be committed by the elderly. In a later writing, Malinchak (1980) contends that larceny-theft offenses among the elderly could almost totally be explained by economics. He suggests that larceny-theft may result from the difficulties of living on a fixed income during periods of double-digit yearly inflation.

METHOD OF STUDY

The data for this study are extracted from the Uniform Crime Reports (UCR) produced by the Federal Bureau of Investigation (FBI). The UCR data are published annually by the FBI and consist of crimes known to the police rather than crimes committed. The limitations and shortcomings of the UCR as a source of research data have been thoroughly documented in the literature. (See, for example, Beattie, 1955; Black, 1970; Cressey, 1957; Doleschal, 1972; Hartjen, 1974; Hindelang, 1974; Kamisar, 1972; Kitsuse and Cicourel, 1963; Savitz, 1978; Skogan, 1974, 1976; U.S. Department of Justice, 1973-1982; Wolfgang, 1963.)

Essentially, the major considerations to be understood by researchers who use the UCR include:

1. The UCR is not a complete report of crimes committed. It includes only "selected" crimes and then includes only those occurrences that are known to the police.
2. Participation in the UCR is entirely voluntary and there is no way of mandating reporting.
3. Jurisdictional differences exist in definitions of offenses and varying interpretations affect the data.
4. Drastic changes in numbers or rates of crime may occur because of changes in reporting and communications of known offenses.

5. Reporting is a political process that can have a drastic effect on the data.

With full consideration of the shortcomings and the pitfalls of using the UCR data for time series research, this study extracted pertinent data from the UCR by type of crime, by year, and by age groups. Absolute frequencies were extracted along with percentages where provided. Percentages were computed as necessary. The basis for analysis for this study is percentage. Absolute frequencies are more subject to the fluctuations and limitations than are percentages.

Data were drawn for each year from 1972 through 1981. This ten year period includes an overlap of Shichor and Kobrin's study (1978) of three years (1972-1974). Three age groups are included: 55-59, 60-64, and 65 or older.

FINDINGS OF THE STUDY

Overall, the findings of this study indicate that the percentage of all arrests that are arrests of the elderly is declining, although the numbers of elderly are increasing rapidly. From 1972 to 1981, the total number of arrests for all ages and all offenses increased by 53%, but arrests of elderly offenders decreased by 3% during the same time period. Tables 1 through 10 (Appendix) depict the numbers and percentages of arrests for the ten years included in the study. Total arrests of all ages increased from 6.7 million to 10.3 million, while arrests of the elderly decreased from 413,386 to 400,107. In terms of percentage of all arrests, the arrests of the elderly decreased from 6.2% of all arrests to 3.9%.

Figure 1 illustrates the patterns and trends in total arrests and index crime arrests of the elderly. Although both the number and percentage of elderly offender arrests declined for all crimes, there was an increase for the major, or index, crimes reported in the UCR. Violent offenses declined slightly, from 2.9% elderly arrests to 2.5% elderly, while property offense arrests increased from 1.8% of the total to 2.0%. In absolute numbers, the arrests of elderly for index crimes increased from 26,354 in 1982 and 57,857 in 1981.

Combined arrests of the elderly accounted for 2.0% of arrests for index crimes in 1972 and 2.5% in 1981.

The percentage of elderly arrests for index crimes dipped below 2.5% in 1973, 1974 and 1975, reaching a low of 1.7% in 1974. By 1976, the percentage reached 2.0% and climbed steadily to the 1981 figure of 2.5%. Property offenses reflect a similar dip, dropping from 1.8% of all arrests for property crimes in 1972 to 1.5 in 1974, and increasing to 1.9% by 1976. By the end of the ten year period, 1981, arrests of elderly property offenders accounted for 2.5% of all property offense arrests. Two patterns are noted in the violent offense arrests for 1972-1981.

Arrests of the elderly for violent offenses, expressed as a percentage of all arrests for violent offenses, declined from a 1972 high of 2.9% to 2.3% in 1974. In 1975, the elderly arrests accounted for 2.5%, and in 1976, 2.7% of all arrests for violent index crimes. In 1977, the percentage dipped to 2.6 with another decrease to 2.5 in 1978. The percentage has remained relatively stable since 1978 with 2.5% in 1979, 2.4% in 1980 and 2.5% in 1981.

When individual index crimes are examined, some interesting patterns and trends are evidenced. Figure 2 illustrates the pattern of arrests of the elderly for homicide as a percentage of all arrests for homicide by year and by age group. The term "homicide" is used as a convenient replacement for the more cumbersome UCR terminology of "murder and nonnegligent man-slaughter." Overall, the trend in arrests of the elderly for homicide has been downward, decreasing from a high of 5.8% of all homicide arrests in 1972 to 4.6% in 1981. However, as shown in Figure 2, the pattern has two peaks, one in 1972 with 5.8% and another in 1976 with 5.7% of all homicide arrests. The 1976 peak is an anomalie in a generally decreasing trend. Much of the increase in the 1976 homicide arrests of the elderly is accounted for by an increase in arrests in the 55-59 year age group. Arrests in this age group increased from 1.9% in 1975 to 2.5% in 1976 of all homicide arrests. Actual numbers of homicide arrests for this age group increased 11% in 1976, while total arrests decreased 16.4% for all age groups in the same year. The 55-59 year group had consistently higher homicide arrest percentages than the other elderly groups. Similarly, the 65 and older group accounts for a higher percentage of all homicide rates than does the 60-64 year group.

Figure 3 reflects the general pattern and trend of aggravated assault arrests of the elderly. The trend line depicts the arrests of the elderly for aggravated assault as a percentage of all arrests for this violent offense. Arrest percentages are also provided by year and age group. The overall trend was a slight decrease in arrests of the elderly as a percentage of all arrests. At the start of the ten year period in 1972, elderly offenders accounted for 4.4% of the arrests. By the end of the period of study in 1981, arrests of the elderly for aggravated assault had dropped to 3.5% of such arrests. It is notable that the downward trend was briefly interrupted in 1976 when 3.9% of the arrests for aggravated assault were of elderly offenders. The year 1976 was also atypical for homicide.

Homicide and aggravated assault are sometimes aggregated for analysis since the difference between the two offenses is often the consequence of emergency medical services or emergency transportation facilities. Although such aggregation was not performed for this study, it is clear that the two offenses follow similar trends and have similar patterns for the ten years of study. These two offenses account for the highest percentage of elderly arrests. In both homicide and aggravated assault, the percentages of those arrested who are classified as elderly exceeds 3%.

Arrests of the elderly for the violent offense of forcible rape increased from 1.0% to 1.8% of all rape arrests over the period from 1972 to 1981. (See Figure 4.) Because the actual numbers of such arrests are few, minor peaks and valleys are present in the data. The actual number of arrests in the elderly category ranged from a low of 163 in 1974 to 744 in 1981. Several factors should be considered in evaluating the upward trend in forcible rape.

Forcible rape is consistently the most underreported of all index crimes. Victims are reluctant to report rapes for a variety of reasons. While rape probably is still underreported by a significant percentage, reports of rape have increased dramatically in the recent past. The increase in reports of child sexual abuse and child rape has also been significant. These factors probably contribute to the steady increase in arrests of the elderly.

Robbery arrests increased by 64.8% from 1972 to 1981, but arrests of the elderly remained stable at 0.5% of the total arrests of robbery offenders. As shown in Figure 5, arrests of the elderly as a percentage of all dipped by 0.1% from 1974 through 1978. Thus, the rate has been 0.5 or 0.4% throughout the period. Clearly, robbery is one of the major crimes that does not attract many elderly offenders.

All of the property crimes included in the UCR Index Crimes showed some increase in percentage of arrests of the elderly. Overall, numbers of arrests of the elderly more than doubled from 18,580 arrests in 1972 to 46,260 arrests in 1981, a 149% increase in numbers. Overall, the total arrests for property offenses increased by 74% during the ten year period. As a percentage of all arrests for property offenses elderly arrests increased from 1.8 to 2.5%.

Elderly arrests for burglary as a percentage of all arrests for burglary by year and age group are depicted in Figure 6. The arrests of elderly for burglary increased very slightly from 0.4 to 0.6%. The actual number of offenders aged 55 years or older is low with 1,390 arrests in 1972 and 2,799 in 1981. While it may be only a temporary change, the percentage of arrests for burglary of elderly offenders increased in 1980 and again in 1981 after several years of stable percentages.

Larceny-theft arrests of the elderly increased from 2.6 to 3.5% of all larceny-theft arrests during the period of the study. Larceny-theft reporting was changed in 1973 with all thefts and larcenies being combined under the single category. Despite this change which led to a general increase in the numbers of arrests, the rate for the elderly remained relatively steady. The steady increase in the percentage of arrests for larceny-theft accounted for by elderly offenders began in 1976. (See Figure 7.)

While the percentage of all arrests for larceny-theft accounted for by elderly arrestees has increased, the more significant increase has taken place in terms of the role that larceny-theft arrests play in terms of total arrests of elderly. In 1972 and 1973, arrests for larceny-theft made up 4.0 and 4.6% respectively, of all arrests of the elderly. By 1981, 10.6% of all arrests of the elderly were for larceny-theft. Thus, this offense is the most common of the index crimes committed by the elderly. Further, larceny-theft accounts for almost all of the overall increase for major crimes.

Auto theft reflected a slight rise from 0.4 to 0.7% of arrests credited to elderly offenders. Figure 8 illustrates the arrests of the elderly as a percentage of all auto theft arrests. Actual numbers of arrests of the elderly for auto theft range from 387 to 801 during the ten year period. Minor swings in the trend line with such small numbers can be deceptive.

Arson, added to the UCR Index Crimes in 1979, reflected a slight increase in arrests of the elderly from 1.7 to 2.0% of all arson arrests in the last three years of the study. Since arson is a newly added offense, it is likely that reporting levels are too low to provide accurate trends at this time.

Arrests of the elderly for index crimes as a percentage of all arrests of the elderly have increased yearly throughout the study period. As shown in Figure 9, arrests for index crimes were 6.4% of all arrests of the elderly in 1972. By 1977, such arrests were 9.9% of all arrests of the elderly, and by 1981, 14.5% of arrests of the elderly were for index crimes. Almost all of this increase is made up of increases in arrests for property offenses, although arrests of the elderly for violent index offenses increased from 1.8% in 1972 to 2.9% in 1981 of all elderly arrests. In the same period, arrests for index property offenses increased from 4.6% to 11.6% of all elderly arrests.

Arrests of the elderly for index crimes largely are for one of two offenses—aggravated assault and larceny-theft. Arrests for aggravated assault consistently make up about 80-83% of all elderly arrests for violent index crimes. (See Figure 10.) Homicide contributes 8-12% of the elderly violent offense arrests each year. About 90% of the arrests of the elderly for property index crimes are for larceny-theft. The year-to-year percent remained very stable (from 89.7 to 92.5) during the study period. (See Figure 11.)

SUMMARY AND CONCLUSIONS

This study of Uniform Crime Reports arrest data for the years 1972-1981 has revealed several trends and overall patterns in the arrests of offenders aged 55 years and older. Two major trends are noteworthy. First, arrests of the elderly are generally declining even though the elderly population is increasing. Second, the percentage of elderly arrests for index crimes is increasing with most of the increase in property crimes.

These major trends are not necessarily contradictory nor counter directional. As changes have been made in definitions of minor offenses and decriminalization of many minor offenses has taken place, a number of behaviors are no longer handled by law enforcement and no arrests are made. Vagrancy, public drunkenness and loitering are offenses that have been decriminalized in most jurisdictions. Since these were offenses for which elderly offenders were over-represented, a considerable drop in overall arrests of the elderly resulted. The drop in overall arrests of the elderly, thus, is primarily the result of a drop in arrests for minor offenses. As minor arrests drop, the arrests for major offenses make up an increasing proportion of all elderly arrests.

The offenses of aggravated assault and larceny-theft are the major offenses for which elderly offenders are arrested. Malinchak (1978) and Shichor and Kobrin (1978) both noted that aggravated assault accounted for about 80% of all violent offenses for which the elderly were arrested, a finding confirmed by this study. Shichor and Kobrin (1978) suggest that the level of aggravated assault may be a function of intensified interpersonal relationships. As the elderly retire and become limited in mobility, the range of social interaction decreases. More and more time is spent with increasing age with fewer persons, thus, intensifying the interpersonal relationship and increasing the opportunities for conflict.

Malinchak (1978) also reported that the elderly were much more likely to be arrested for larceny-theft when arrests for index property crimes were made. In his 1980 book, Malinchak contends that the increase in the numbers of arrests of the elderly for larceny-theft is almost entirely a response to present (1980) economic conditions, pointing out the difficulties facing those elderly who are faced with fixed income and double digit inflation. This study has similar findings in terms of the prevalence of larceny-theft in elderly arrests. It will remain for further research to validate or refute this contention.

Overall, the conclusion to be drawn is that there is no epidemic of elderly crime as once predicted. The elderly, although increasing in number and percentage of the population, have not turned to crime in any significantly increased numbers. It is evident that many of the elderly arrestees are in the 55-59 and 60-64 year age groups. What is not known is whether the arrest of elderly are for offenses never before committed or whether many, perhaps a majority, are simply arrests of persons who have led criminal careers and have aged into the study population.

BIBLIOGRAPHY

Beattie, R. H. "Problems of Criminal Statistics in the United States." *Journal of Criminal Law, Criminology, and Police Science*, vol. 46, pp. 178-186, 1955.

Black, Donald J. "Production of Crime Rates." *American Sociological Review*, vol. 35, pp. 733-748, 1970.

Cressey, Donald R. "The State of Criminal Statistics." *National Probation and Parole Association Journal*, vol. 3, pp. 230-241, 1957.

Doleschal, E. *Criminal Statistics*. Rockville, Md.: National Institute of Mental Health, 1972.

Hartjen, Clayton A. *Crime and Criminalization*. (2nd ed.), New York: Holt/Praeger Publishing, 1974.

Hindelang, Michael J. "The Uniform Crime Reports Revisited." *Journal of Criminal Justice*, vol. 2, pp. 1-17, 1974.

Kamisar, Yale. "How to Use, Abuse—Fight Back With—Crime Statistics." *Oklahoma Law Review*, vol. 25, p. 247, 1972.

Keller, O. J. and C. B. Vedder. "The Crimes that Old Persons Commit." *Gerontologist*, vol. 8, pp. 43-50, 1968.

Kitsuse, J. I. and A. V. Cicourel. "A Note on the Use of Official Statistics." *Social Problems*, vol. 11, pp. 131-138, 1963.

Malinchak, Alan A. "The Embarrassing Problem of Elderly Criminals." *Proceedings of the 23rd Annual Conference on Corrections*, Tallahassee, Fla.: Florida State University, 1978.

Malinchak, Alan A. *Crime and Gerontology*. Englewood Cliffs, N.J.: Prentice-Hall, Inc., 1980.

McCreary, C. P. and I. N. Mensch. "Personality Differences Associated With Age in Law Offenders." *Journal of Gerontology*, vol. 32, pp. 164-167, 1977.

Savitz, Leonard D. "Official Police Statistics and Their Limitations," in Savitz and Norman Johnston, eds., *Crime in Society*. New York: Wiley and Co., 1978.

Shichor, D. and S. Kobrin. "Note: Criminal Behavior Among the Elderly." *Gerontologist*, vol. 18, pp. 213-218, 1978.

Skogan, Wesley. "The Validity of Official Crime Statistics: An Empirical Investigation." *Social Science Quarterly*, vol. 55, pp. 25-38, 1974.

Skogan, Wesley. "Citizen Reporting of Crime." *Criminology*, vol. 13, p. 538, 1976.

U.S. Department of Justice. FBI Uniform Crime Reports: Crime in the United

States, 1972-1981 (published annually), Washington, D.C.: U.S. Government Printing Office, 1973-1982.

Wolfgang, Marvin E. "Uniform Crime Reports: A Critical Appraisal." *University of Pennsylvania Law Review*, vol. 11, pp. 708-738, 1963.

Figure 1
Arrests of the Elderly as a Percentage of All Arrests
Arrests for Index Crimes as a Percentage of Index Crime Arrests
by Year

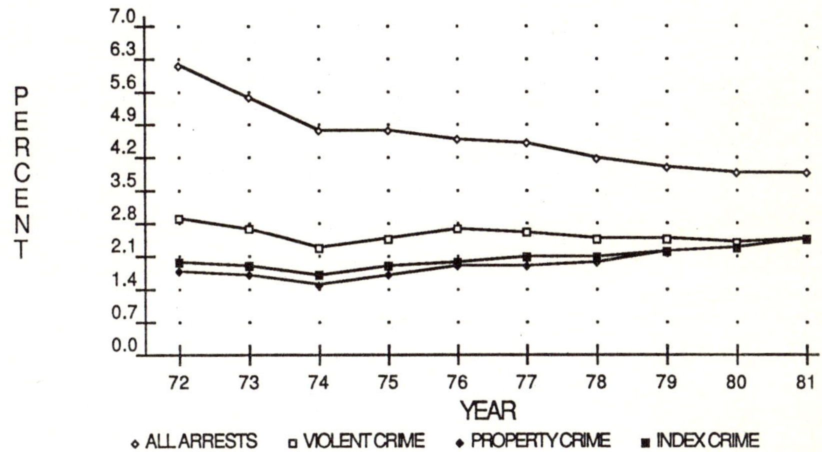

Figure 2
Arrests of Elderly for Homicide as a Percentage of All Homicide Arrests by Year and Age Group

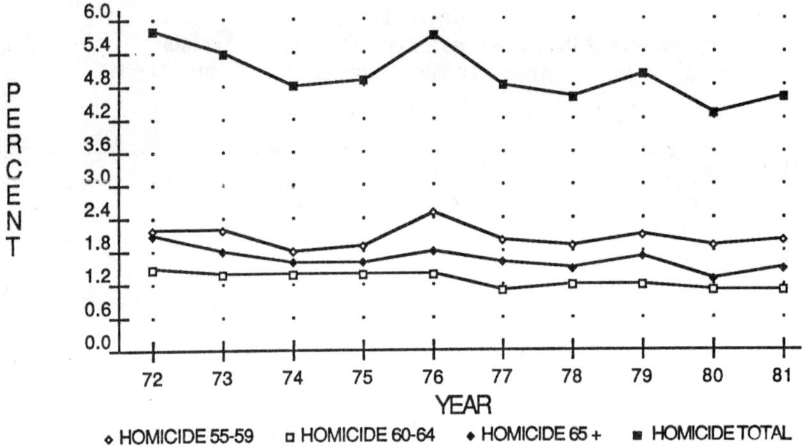

Figure 3
Arrests of the Elderly for Aggravated Assault as a Percentage of All Aggravated Assault Arrests by Year and Age Group

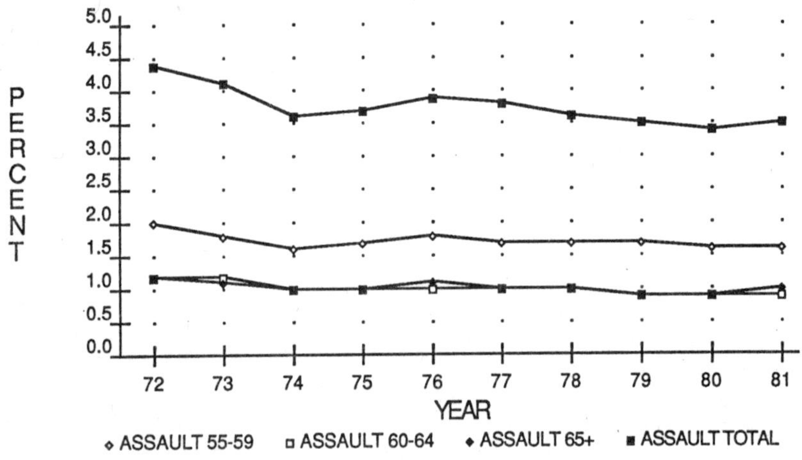

Figure 4
Arrests of the Elderly for Forcible Rape as a Percentage of All Arrests for Forcible Rape by Year and Age Group

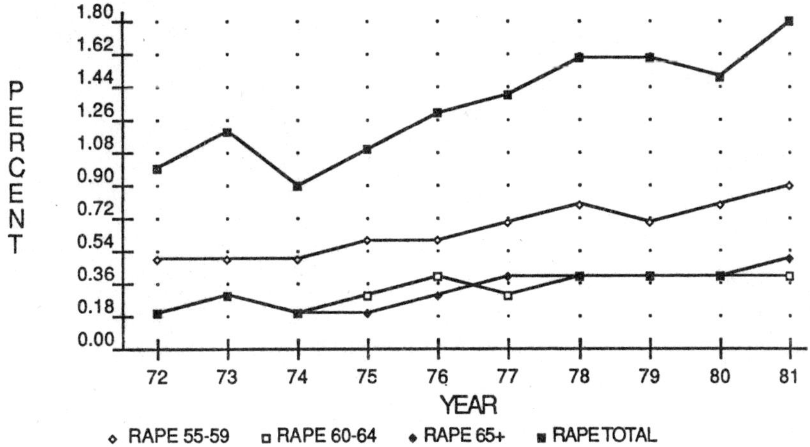

Figure 5
Arrests of the Elderly for Robbery as a Percentage of All Arrests for Robbery by Year and Age Group

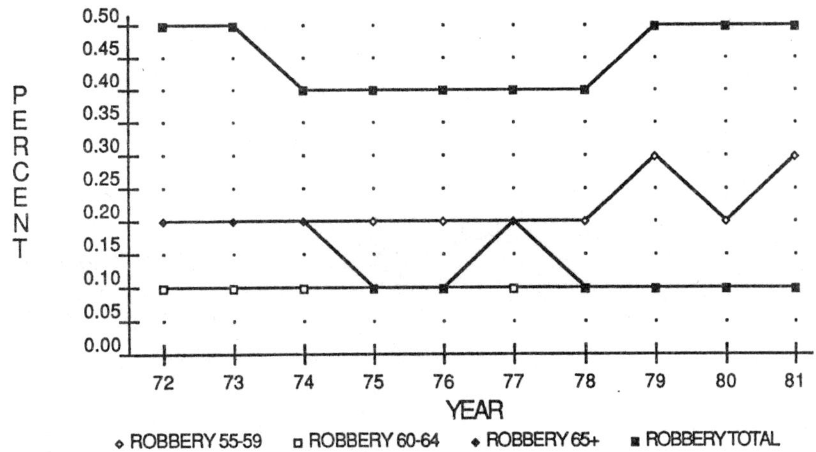

Figure 6
Arrests of the Elderly for Burglary as a Percentage of All Arrests for Burglary by Year and Age Group

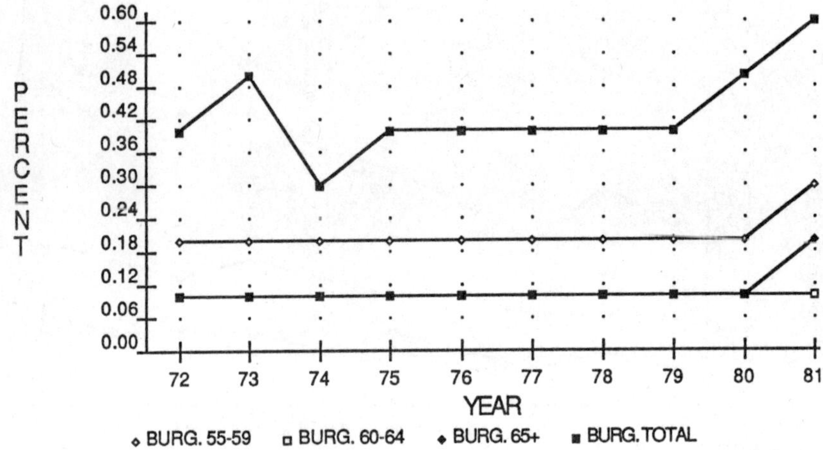

Figure 7
Arrests of the Elderly for Larceny-Theft as a Percentage of All Arrests for Larceny-Theft by Year and Age Group

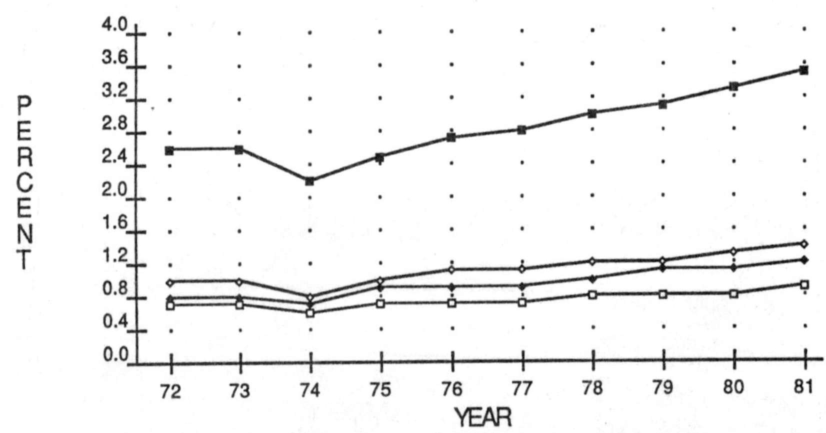

Figure 8
Arrests of the Elderly for Automobile Theft as a Percentage of All Arrests for Automobile Theft by Year and Age Group

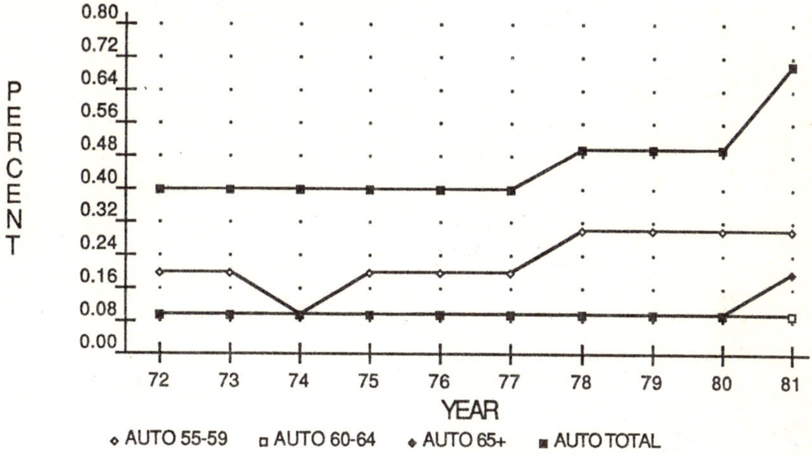

Figure 9
Arrests of the Elderly for Index Crimes as a Percentage of All Arrests of the Elderly by Year and Type Index Crime

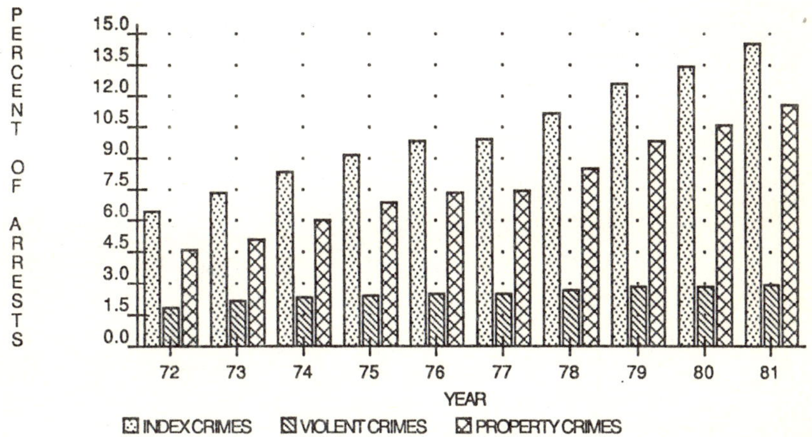

Figure 10
Arrests of the Elderly for Aggravated Assault as a Percentage of Arrests of the Elderly for Index Violent Crimes by Year

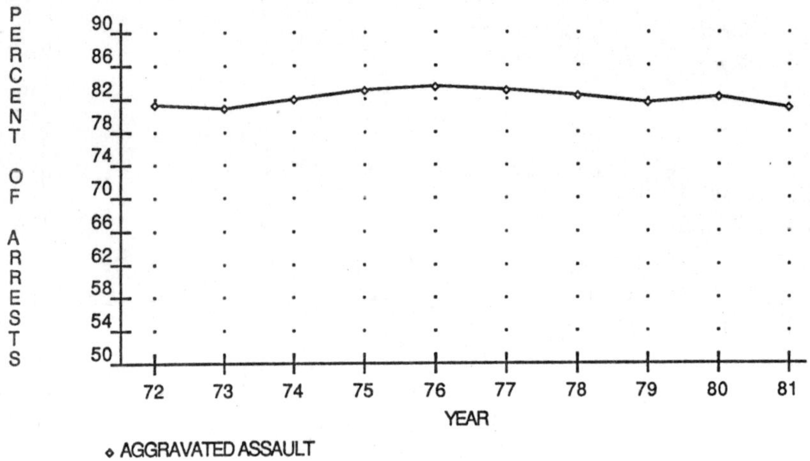

Figure 11
Arrests of the Elderly for Larceny-Theft as a Percentage of All Elderly Arrests for Index Property Crimes by Year

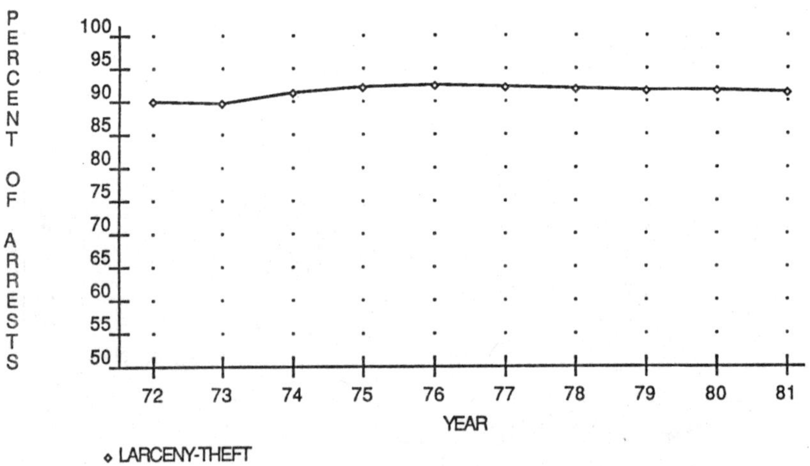

TABLE 1

Numbers and Percentages Elderly Arrested, 1972

	AGE								
	All Age Groups	55-59		60-64		65 and Over		Elderly Total	
	No.	No.	%	No.	%	No.	%	No.	%
Total Arrests	6,706,950	192,189	2.7	119,412	1.7	101,775	1.5	413,386	6.2
Violent Crime	259,837	3,415	1.1	2,040	0.7	2,107	0.7	7,562	2.9
Property Crime	1,048,844	7,525	0.7	5,040	0.5	6,015	0.5	18,580	1.8
Murder and Nonnegligent Manslaughter	16,714	373	2.2	257	1.5	345	2.1	975	5.8
Forcible Rape	17,824	90	0.5	46	0.2	43	0.2	177	1.9
Robbery	89,444	225	0.2	100	0.1	144	0.2	469	0.5
Aggravated Assault	138,763	2,806	2.0	1,703	1.2	1,642	1.2	6,151	4.4
Burglary	296,199	740	0.2	355	0.1	295	0.1	1,390	0.4
Larceny-Theft	642,308	6,526	1.0	4,589	0.7	5,620	0.8	16,735	2.6
Auto Theft	110,337	259	0.2	96	0.1	100	0.1	455	0.4
All Index Crimes	1,311,586	11,019	0.8	7,146	0.5	8,189	0.6	26,354	2.0

NOTE: Percentages may not total due to rounding.

Source: Federal Bureau of Investigation, U.S. Department of Justice. Crime in the United States 1972. 1973, pp. 126-127.

TABLE 2
Numbers and Percentages Elderly
Arrested, 1973

	AGE								
	All Age Groups	55-59		60-64		65 and Over		Elderly Total	
	No.	No.	%	No.	%	No.	%	No.	%
Total Arrests	6,499,864	167,811	2.6	104,547	1.6	87,893	1.4	360,251	5.5
Violent Crime	290,382	3,347	1.1	2,157	0.7	2,331	0.8	7,835	2.7
Property Crime	1,078,842	7,609	0.7	5,006	0.5	5,841	0.5	18,456	1.7
Murder and Nonnegligent Manslaughter	17,395	376	2.2	246	1.4	312	1.8	934	5.4
Forcible Rape	19,198	99	0.5	60	0.3	70	0.3	229	1.2
Robbery	101,894	178	0.2	111	0.1	228	0.2	517	0.5
Aggravated Assault	154,891	2,766	1.8	1,793	1.2	1,782	1.1	6,341	4.1
Burglary	316,272	741	0.2	363	0.1	368	0.1	1,472	0.5
Larceny-Theft	644,190	6,643	1.0	4,546	0.7	5,359	0.8	16,548	2.6
Auto Theft	118,380	225	0.2	97	0.1	114	0.1	436	0.4
All Index Crimes	1,372,220	11,028	0.8	7,216	0.5	8,233	0.6	26,477	1.9

NOTE: Percentages may not total due to rounding.

Source: Federal Bureau of Investigation, U.S. Department of Justice. Crime in the United States 1973. 1974, pp. 128-129.

TABLE 3

Numbers and Percentages Elderly Arrested, 1974

	All Age Groups	55–59		60–64		65 and Over		Elderly Total	
	AGE								
	No.	No.	%	No.	%	No.	%	No.	%
Total Arrests	6,179,406	138,223	2.2	87,473	1.4	72,842	1.2	298,538	4.8
Violent Crime	294,617	2,984	1.0	1,921	0.7	1,954	0.7	6,859	2.3
Property Crime	1,177,584	7,131	0.6	4,811	0.4	5,818	0.5	17,760	1.5
Murder and Nonnegligent Manslaughter	16,044	282	1.8	220	1.4	255	1.6	757	4.8
Forcible Rape	17,804	82	0.5	41	0.2	40	0.2	163	0.9
Robbery	108,481	173	0.2	74	0.1	185	0.2	432	0.4
Aggravated Assault	154,514	2,493	1.6	1,625	1.0	1,515	1.0	5,633	3.6
Burglary	340,697	588	0.2	268	0.1	306	0.1	1,162	0.3
Larceny-Theft	729,661	6,357	0.8	4,454	0.6	5,400	0.7	16,211	2.2
Auto Theft	107,226	186	0.1	89	0.1	112	0.1	387	0.4
All Index Crimes	1,474,427	10,161	0.7	6,771	0.5	7,813	0.5	24,745	1.7

NOTE: Percentages may not total due to rounding.

Source: Federal Bureau of Investigation, U.S. Department of Justice. Crime in the United States 1974. 1975, pp. 186-187.

TABLE 4
Numbers and Percentages Elderly
Arrested, 1975

	AGE								
	Age All Groups	55-59		60-64		65 and Over		Elderly Total	
	No.	No.	%	No.	%	No.	%	No.	%
Total Arrests	8,013,645	179,158	2.2	110,980	1.4	95,391	1.2	385,529	4.8
Violent Crime	370,453	4,012	1.1	2,515	0.7	2,563	0.7	9,090	2.5
Property Crime	1,528,317	10,150	0.7	7,133	0.5	9,087	0.6	26,370	1.7
Murder and Nonnegligent Manslaughter	19,516	367	1.9	282	1.4	320	1.6	969	4.9
Forcible Rape	21,963	123	0.6	63	0.3	55	0.2	241	1.1
Robbery	129,788	220	0.2	111	0.1	155	0.1	486	0.4
Aggravated Assault	202,217	3,373	1.7	2,107	1.0	2,087	1.0	7,567	3.7
Burglary	449,155	790	0.2	397	0.1	398	0.1	1,585	0.4
Larceny-Theft	958,938	9,120	1.0	6,627	0.7	8,566	0.9	24,313	2.5
Auto Theft	120,224	240	0.2	109	0.1	123	0.1	472	0.4
All Index Crimes	1,904,811	14,233	0.7	9,696	0.5	11,704	0.6	35,633	1.9

NOTE: Percentages may not total due to rounding.

Source: Federal Bureau of Investigation, U.S. Department of Justice. Crime in the United States 1975. 1976, pp. 188-189.

TABLE 5

Numbers and Percentages Elderly Arrested, 1976

	AGE								
	All Age Groups	55-59		60-64		65 and Over		Elderly Total	
	No.	No.	%	No.	%	No.	%	No.	%
Total Arrests	7,912,348	175,812	2.2	103,342	1.3	87,801	1.1	366,955	4.6
Violent Crime	338,849	4,188	1.2	2,325	0.7	2,493	0.7	9,006	2.7
Property Crime	1,445,607	10,780	0.7	7,030	0.6	8,978	0.6	26,788	1.9
Murder and Nonnegligent Manslaughter	16,763	412	2.5	239	1.4	309	1.8	960	5.7
Forcible Rape	21,687	139	0.6	81	0.4	67	0.3	287	1.3
Robbery	110,296	189	0.2	80	0.1	125	0.1	394	0.4
Aggravated Assault	192,753	3,521	1.8	1,965	1.0	2,038	1.1	7,524	3.9
Burglary	406,821	806	0.2	385	0.1	359	0.1	1,550	0.4
Larceny-Theft	928,078	9,751	1.1	6,544	0.7	8,489	0.9	24,784	2.7
Auto Theft	110,708	223	0.2	101	0.1	130	0.1	454	0.4
All Index Crimes	1,787,106	15,041	0.8	9,395	0.5	11,517	0.6	35,953	2.0

NOTE: Percentages may not total due to rounding.

Source: Federal Bureau of Investigation, U.S. Department of Justice. Crime in the United States 1976. 1977, pp. 181-182.

TABLE 6

Numbers and Percentages Elderly Arrested, 1977

	AGE								
	All Age Groups	55-59		60-64		65 and Over		Elderly Total	
	No.	No.	%	No.	%	No.	%	No.	%
Total Arrests	9,029,335	198,077	2.2	113,788	1.3	97,454	1.1	409,319	4.5
Violent Crime	386,806	4,647	1.2	2,606	0.7	2,852	0.7	10,105	2.6
Property Crime	1,596,304	12,551	0.8	7,793	0.5	10,141	0.6	30,485	1.9
Murder and Nonnegligent Manslaughter	20,096	416	2.0	225	1.1	325	1.6	966	4.8
Forcible Rape	25,800	180	0.7	91	0.3	101	0.4	372	1.4
Robbery	122,514	244	0.2	76	0.1	193	0.2	513	0.4
Aggravated Assault	221,329	3,872	1.7	2,245	1.0	2,278	1.0	8,395	3.8
Burglary	454,193	947	0.2	392	0.1	438	0.1	1,777	0.4
Larceny-Theft	1,006,915	11,279	1.1	7,310	0.7	9,562	0.9	28,151	2.8
Auto Theft	135,196	325	0.2	91	0.1	141	0.1	557	0.4
All Index Crimes	1,986,043	17,263	0.9	10,430	0.5	13,038	0.7	40,731	2.1

NOTE: Percentages may not total due to rounding.

Source: Federal Bureau of Investigation, U.S. Department of Justice. Crime in the United States 1977. 1978, pp. 180-181.

TABLE 7

Numbers and Percentages Elderly Arrested, 1978

	AGE								
	All Age Groups	55-59		60-64		65 and Over		Elderly Total	
	No.	No.	%	No.	%	No.	%	No.	%
Total Arrests	9,775,087	199,119	2.0	113,311	1.2	99,564	1.0	411,994	4.2
Violent Crime	446,122	5,143	1.2	2,905	0.7	3,080	0.7	11,128	2.5
Property Crime	1,723,140	14,106	0.8	8,950	0.5	12,045	0.7	35,101	2.0
Murder and Nonnegligent Manslaughter	18,755	360	1.9	224	1.2	285	1.5	869	4.6
Forcible Rape	28,257	224	0.8	104	0.4	126	0.4	454	1.6
Robbery	141,481	304	0.2	107	0.1	212	0.1	623	0.4
Aggravated Assault	257,629	4,255	1.7	2,470	1.0	2,457	1.0	9,182	3.6
Burglary	485,782	1,054	0.2	433	0.1	572	0.1	2,059	0.4
Larceny-Theft	1,084,088	12,637	1.2	8,357	0.8	11,279	1.0	32,273	3.0
Auto Theft	153,270	415	0.3	160	0.1	194	0.1	769	0.5
All Index Crimes	2,169,262	19,249	0.9	11,855	0.5	15,125	0.7	46,229	2.1

NOTE: Percentages may not total due to rounding.

Source: Federal Bureau of Investigation, U.S. Department of Justice. Crime in the United States 1978. 1979, pp. 194-195.

TABLE 8

Numbers and Percentages Elderly Arrested, 1979

	AGE								
	All Age Groups	55-59		60-64		65 and Over		Elderly Total	
	No.	No.	%	No.	%	No.	%	No.	%
Total Arrests	9,506,347	186,336	2.0	104,507	1.1	94,264	1.0	385,107	4.0
Violent Crime	434,778	5,183	1.2	2,794	0.6	2,980	0.7	10,957	2.5
Property Crime	1,728,524	14,857	0.9	9,689	0.6	12,915	0.7	37,461	2.2
Murder and Nonnegligent Manslaughter	18,264	379	2.1	225	1.2	304	1.7	908	5.0
Forcible Rape	29,164	214	0.7	125	0.4	130	0.4	469	1.6
Robbery	130,753	359	0.3	137	0.1	157	0.1	653	0.5
Aggravated Assault	256,597	4,231	1.7	2,307	0.9	2,389	0.9	8,927	3.5
Burglary	468,085	1,124	0.2	509	0.1	460	0.1	2,093	0.4
Larceny-Theft	1,098,398	13,179	1.2	8,915	0.8	12,223	1.1	34,317	3.1
Auto Theft	143,654	407	0.3	176	0.1	147	0.1	730	0.5
Arson	18,387	147	0.8	89	0.5	85	0.4	321	1.7
All Index Crimes	2,163,302	20,040	0.9	12,483	0.6	15,895	0.7	48,418	2.2

NOTE: Percentages may not total due to rounding.

Source: Federal Bureau of Investigation, U.S. Department of Justice. Crime in the United States 1979. 1980, pp. 196-197.

TABLE 9
Numbers and Percentages Elderly Arrested, 1980

	AGE								
	All Age Groups	55-59		60-64		65 and Over		Elderly Total	
	No.	No.	%	No.	%	No.	%	No.	%
Total Arrests	9,703,181	180,724	1.9	103,684	1.1	93,985	1.0	378,393	3.9
Violent Crime	446,373	5,030	1.1	2,796	0.6	2,930	0.7	10,756	2.4
Property Crime	1,751,704	16,053	0.9	10,376	0.6	13,632	0.8	40,061	2.3
Murder and Nonnegligent Manslaughter	18,745	349	1.9	201	1.1	248	1.3	798	4.3
Forcible Rape	29,431	238	0.8	108	0.4	107	0.4	453	1.5
Robbery	139,476	333	0.2	170	0.1	151	0.1	654	0.5
Aggravated Assault	258,721	4,110	1.6	2,317	0.9	2,424	0.9	8,851	2.4
Burglary	479,639	1,187	0.2	551	0.1	527	0.1	2,265	0.5
Larceny-Theft	1,123,823	14,314	1.3	9,574	0.8	12,857	1.1	36,745	3.3
Auto Theft	129,783	377	0.3	138	0.1	164	0.1	679	0.5
Arson	18,459	175	0.9	113	0.6	84	0.5	372	2.0
All Index Crimes	2,198,077	21,083	1.0	13,172	0.6	16,562	0.8	50,817	2.3

NOTE: Percentages may not total due to rounding.

Source: Federal Bureau of Investigation, U.S. Department of Justice. Crime in the United States 1980. 1981, pp. 200-201.

TABLE 10
Numbers and Percentages Elderly Arrested, 1981

	AGE								
	All Age Groups	55-59		60-64		65 and Over		Elderly Total	
	No.	No.	%	No.	%	No.	%	No.	%
Total Arrests	10,293,575	187,143	1.8	111,945	1.1	101,019	1.0	400,107	3.9
Violent Crime	464,826	5,319	1.1	3,083	0.7	3,195	0.7	11,597	2.5
Property Crime	1,828,928	18,140	1.0	12,185	0.7	15,935	0.9	46,260	2.5
Murder and Nonnegligent Manslaughter	20,432	404	2.0	230	1.1	310	1.5	944	4.6
Forcible Rape	30,050	262	0.9	134	0.4	143	0.5	539	1.8
Robbery	147,396	369	0.3	177	0.1	198	0.1	744	0.5
Aggravated Assault	266,948	4,284	1.6	2,542	0.9	2,544	1.0	9,370	3.5
Burglary	489,533	1,328	0.3	728	0.1	743	0.2	2,799	0.6
Larceny-Theft	1,197,845	16,242	1.4	11,172	0.9	14,847	1.2	42,261	3.5
Auto Theft	122,188	388	0.3	180	0.1	233	0.2	801	0.7
Arson	19,362	182	0.9	105	0.5	112	0.6	399	2.0
All Index Crimes	2,293,754	23,459	1.0	15,268	0.7	19,130	0.8	57,857	2.5

NOTE: Percentages may not total due to rounding.

Source: Federal Bureau of Investigation, U.S. Department of Justice. Crime in the United States 1981. 1982, pp. 171-172.

A Comparison of Retiree Criminal Characteristics with Habitual and Nonhabitual Older Offenders from an Urban Population

Carl I. Brahce
Donald J. Bachand

INTRODUCTION

As more attention is given to the serious criminal acts committed by older persons, sociology, criminal justice and gerontology researchers are probing deeper into the individual circumstances and social aspects of these illegal behaviors. Investigators are examining the older offender and the judicial system (Feinberg, 1982; 1984); type of offenses (Newman, Newman and Gewirtz, 1984); relationships between victim and assailant in homicides (Kratcoski and Walker, 1986); as well as trends and circumstances of criminal behavior (Rubenstein, 1982; Shichor and Korbin, 1978; Goetting, 1984).

This paper presents findings from a sample of older men, aged 55+, who were arrested for law violations in a large, industrialized, midwest city. Criminal histories and arrest records are con-

Carl I. Brahce is Director of the Gerontology Center and Professor of Education at Kent State University and Professor of Gerontology at Northeastern Ohio Universities College of Medicine. He received an MA from Eastern Michigan University and a PhD from the University of Michigan. He has taught at the University of Michigan.

Donald J. Bachand, PhD, is Professor of Criminal Justice at Saginaw Valley State College, Saginaw Valley University, University Center, MI 48710.

This research was supported by a grant from the Northeastern Ohio Universities College of Medicine Office of Geriatric Medicine and Gerontology.

trasted for the "career" or habitual violator and the "new" or first-time offender. These data are analyzed with special attention given the variable of retirement.

Researchers have shown that the increasing trend of criminal activity among older persons, 55 and above, is continuing. Bachand (1984) compared the number of older adults arrested in Michigan with population growth of the older population in Michigan and in the United States. Most categories of crimes increased far beyond increases that could be attributed to population change: Bachand found a 124% increase in felony larceny and 56.5 % increase in violent crime. Studying larceny arrests in Florida between 1971 and 1979, Feinberg (1984) reported an 80% increase in the arrest rate for persons aged 60 to 64. Increased participation by older persons in professional, organized crime, white collar offenses, alcohol-related and violent offenses has been documented by several studies (Kratcoski, 1987; Newman, Newman and Gewirtz, 1984; Bachand and Brahce, 1984). Kratcoski (1987) notes that the research on older offender behavior indicates a significant increase in both crimes against persons and property crimes by the elderly.

The indications of greater participation in crime by older persons of age 60 and above and the parallel observation as to the serious nature of that participation suggest the likelihood of an even greater problem in the future. The number of potential older criminals is going to increase. Older persons constitute the fastest growing segment of the population increase. Those 65 or older reached 28.5 million, or 12% of the U.S. population in 1985. By 2030 there will be 65 million older persons or two and a half times their number in 1980 (U.S. Bureau of the Census, 1986). At the same time, life expectancy also continues to increase. In 1985, persons reaching age 65 had an average life expectancy of an additional 16.8 years (18.6 years for women and 14.6 years for men).

Ironically, at a time when more persons are living longer in relatively good health, the trend toward earlier retirement continues. American Association of Retired Persons (AARP) (1987) reports a trend that could result in increased dissatisfaction with retirement for many – the corporate trend of downsizing, that brings careers to an unexpected stop. (Downsizing refers to the current practice in industry of trimming the work force to effect a reduction in operating costs.) The forced exodus brought on because of consolidations, buyouts, mergers, restructuring and foreign competition, results in forced retirement for large numbers of employees. Especially hard hit in this downsizing are the nonunionized employees, especially managerial and professional workers. Although Atchley (1987) found that most individuals held positive views of their new leisure retirement status, he reported a negative attitude by those who would have liked to have continued on the job. Compulsory retirement for these persons was unfair and bad. Negative attitude toward retirement, poor health and concern with lower income have been correlated with dissatisfaction with retirement (Thompson, Streib, and Kosa, 1960; Beck, 1982). When retirement does result in an identity crisis it may lower an individual's self-esteem, and may inhibit activities and social participation (Miller, 1965). A recent study that examined retirement as a critical life event by Mathews and Brown (1987) correlates the findings of previous research that unexpected or involuntary retirement leads to lower satisfaction with retirement.

In a study of role loss and coping resources, Elwel and Maltbie-Crannel (1981) found relationships between stress and disruptive change, role loss and satisfaction relating to personal income and health.

Researchers also have studied what the social scientists refer to as the person's supportive network. The person who is satisfied with being older and retired is that individual who maintains a strong support system. If the person experiences stressful or difficult situations, his or her physical and mental well-being will be enhanced by such a network (Cassell, 1974). Pihlblad and Adams (1972) found that among small town elderly, satisfaction is most affected by participation in formal organizations, by friendship associations, and least by family contact.

Other studies have found that women are more extensive users as well as providers of social support than are men (Sarason et al., 1985). Traditionally, it is considered unmanly for men to seek comfort from others, it is also socially unacceptable for men to provide comfort or participate in the nurturant role. Therefore, although a man may need the guidance of someone who has experienced the trauma of retirement, he is not likely to seek such solace (Sarason et al., 1985).

In her review of literature, Schorr (1987) found very little research on adjustment patterns for those actually experiencing the situation of retirement—at the time of occurrence. A number of unplanned events, however, can occur at retirement; a spouse or the individual may experience serious illness or accident that is debilitating; the sudden burden of becoming a caregiver for an older parent; change in one's financial situation; death of spouse, friend or close associate.

Another situation that can contribute to dissatisfaction with retirement is that many corporations are offering early retirement plans as both a legal and possibly more humane way to avoid widespread layoffs. These incentive plans to induce older workers to retire early (called "golden handshakes") can create unforeseen financial problems for many employees since pension values will not be the same as if the person had worked to age 65. One barometer of dissatisfaction is that the number of age discrimination complaints being filed with the Equal Employment Opportunity Commission by older workers has increased dramatically (AARP, 1987).

THE DISENGAGEMENT THEORY

The theory of disengagement and retirement was postulated by Cumming and Henry (1961). They suggested that as individuals disengaged from key roles, such as work, they become preoccupied with self and will actively withdraw or disengage from society. At the same time, society recognized the individual's withdrawal and withdraws opportunities for the person to be actively engaged in activities. Disengagement considers the individual's work role to be the primary source of satisfaction and pride. Ekerdt (1986) replaced this notion with a busy ethic theory—to be a good retiree, one must be busy at something.

Most Americans don't consider leisure pursuits to be useful activities. This suggests that those experiencing retirement feel guilty and are forced to take part in leisure or useless activities. Taking part in such forced activities reinforces a sense of loss or dissatisfaction with the retirement role (Hooker and Ventis, 1984).

A hypothesis explored in this study is that there are comparable differences in the criminal orientations of habitual older offenders and nonhabitual older offenders. A second hypothesis is that the condition of being retired, for some individuals, increases the likelihood that they will become involved in criminal activity. A third hypothesis is that those individuals who are retired, dissatisfied with their leisure retirement situation, will exhibit criminal behavior characteristics that can be compared with those of habitual and nonhabitual older offenders.

DATA FOR THE STUDY

The data used in this study were drawn from the arrest and criminal history files of the Flint, Michigan, Police Department (FPD). The sample (N = 491) consists of the histories of all persons aged 55 and above who were arrested in Flint, Michigan from June 1981 through January 1984. The sample was then stratified by age, i.e., 55 to 59; 60 to 64; and 65+.

The computer printout of arrested subjects produced a sample (N = 491) of which 88.8% were males and 11.2% were females. Blacks accounted for 59.9% of the sample, while whites represented the remaining 40.1%. Distribution by age revealed 51.7% of the sample were aged 55 to 59; 27.3% were aged 60 to 64; and 21.0% were aged 65+ (Table 1).

The subjects accounted for 662 arrests during the study period. Of these, 13.3% were for violent crimes; 14.0% for property crimes; 31.7% for alcohol-related crimes; 21% for narcotics-related crimes. The other category of miscellaneous misdemeanors accounted for 37.8% (Table 2).

The mean arrest rate among the sample (N = 491) during the study period was 1.4 arrests, of which 22.4% were for felony offenses and 77.6% were for misdemeanor offenses. There were 662 arrests during the study period (Table 2).

Table 1

Elderly Offender Sample: Age, Race, and Sex

Subjects Arrested--Flint, Michigan

June 1981 to January 1985

Sample Description

N=491 (55+)

Variables	Number	Percentage
Male	436	88.8
Female	55	11.2
Black Male	269	54.8
Black Female	25	5.1
White Male	167	34.0
White Female	30	6.1
Black	294	59.9
White	197	40.1
Age Groups		
55 to 59	254	51.7
60 to 64	134	27.3
65 and over	103	21.0
		100.0

FINDINGS: NONHABITUAL OFFENDERS

For this study, nonhabitual or new older offenders are defined as individuals aged 55 and above not having an arrest record prior to June 1, 1981. As seen from Table 2, 415 or 84.5% of the sample were classified nonhabitual using this criterion. Further analysis reveals that 83.3% of the males and 95.5% of the females in the total sample showed no previous arrest history. New elderly offenders were most likely to be arrested for Part II (less serious offenses) (85.4%). New elderly offenders were most often arrested under the "other/miscellaneous misdemeanor" category (44.8%), followed

Table 2

Distribution of Arrests

	Total Offender Sample N=491		Non-Habitual Offenders N=415		Habitual Offenders N=76	
Offense Type	Arrests	Percentage	Arrests	Percentage	Arrests	Percentage
Violent [1]	88	13.3	40	7.5	48	37.8
Property[2]	93	14.0	46	8.6	47	37.0
Alcohol-Related[3]	210	31.7	198	37.0	12	9.4
Narcotic-Related[4]	21	3.2	11	2.1	10	7.9
Other[5]	250	37.8	240	44.8	10	7.9
	662	100.0	535	100.0	127	100.0
Part I[6] (Index)	148	22.4	78	14.6	70	55.1
Part II[7]	514	77.6	457	85.4	57	44.9
	662	100.0	535	100.0	127	100.0
Mean Arrest Rate:	1.4		1.3		1.7	

1. Select categories from Parts I and II, i.e., murder, rape, robbery, aggrevated assault, and offenses against family and children.
2. Burglary, larceny, motor vehicle theft, fraud, arson, embezzlement, and stolen property.
3. Drunk while intoxicated, liquor law violations, drunkenness and disorderly conduct.
4. Drug abuse, possession, and distribution.
5. Prostitution, vice gambling trespassing, and city ordinance violations.
6. As defined by the *Uniform Crime Reports.*
7. As defined by the *Uniform Crime Reports.*

by alcohol-related offenses (37.0%), and property crimes (8.6%) (Table 2).

FINDINGS: HABITUAL OFFENDERS

The second group selected for analysis consists of those older offenders having previous arrest records, the habitual or career criminal. The career offenders (N = 76) differ dramatically from the crime orientation of the new offender group (Table 2).

Part I crimes accounted for only 14.6% of the new offenders, while they totaled 55.1 % for career offenders. The arrests for violent crimes for new or nonhabitual offenders totaled 7.5%, while violent crimes accounted for the highest category 37.8% for the habitual or career offender. Similarly, serious property offenses were only 8.6% for the new offender, compared with 37.0% for the career criminals. Looking at arrests for possession or delivering narcotics, the new offender arrests accounted for only 2.1%, while they were 7.9% of career offender arrests (Table 2).

In order to better understand differences between the habitual (career) criminal and the nonhabitual (new) offender, arrest record patterns were reviewed. Total arrests for the habitual group were 1,266, with a mean arrest rate of 16.8 (Table 3). Of the sample of 76 persons, 44 or 57.9% had served at least some time in jail or

Table 3

Arrest History Data of Habitual Elderly Offenders

Total arrest for sample (history)	1226
Mean arrest rate (per N)	16.8

67 or 88.1 percent of N had at least 1 previous arrest for an alcohol-related crime.

338 or 27.6 percent of the 1226 arrests recorded were for alcohol-related offenses.

44 or 57.9 percent of the sample (n=76) had served at least some time in jail or prison.

72 or 94.7 percent of the sample had at least 1 prior conviction.

prison. Many began their criminal activities early in life. The number of total arrests ranged from 17 to 72, with one habitual offender having nine arrests for violent crimes, and another seven arrests. Three men had spent from eight to 16 years of their lives incarcerated.

For both groups, alcohol was a major factor. Of the total arrests for the habitual or career offenders, 338 or 88.1% had at least one previous arrest for an alcohol related crime. And the new or nonhabitual offenders also were seriously involved with alcohol, accounting for 37.0% of their arrests. Alcohol-related offenses were the second highest category with miscellaneous misdemeanors accounting for 44.8% of the arrests (Table 3).

FINDINGS: RETIREES

The third group of older offenders to be analyzed in this study includes those individuals known to be retired. Only those persons, all men, for whom the arrest records clearly indicated retirement (most often also noting place of previous employment such as the Buick automobile plant) are included in this group. The age distribution of this retiree group is as follows: 56-59 = 5; 60-64 = 9; and 65-69 = 4.

This analysis will draw upon previously discussed findings from the gerontological and criminal justice literature as well as compare the offense patterns of the retired group with those of both habitual and nonhabitual offenders. For comparison purposes, the retirees' arrest records are shown with regard to age of first offense, the latest charge and age as an older offender, and the total arrests (Table 4).

Looking at the age of first arrest, it is noted that seven of the 18 retirees were in their 20s and 30s when first arrested. Their numbers of arrests totaled 117, or a mean arrest rate of 17.6. This compares with a mean arrest rate of 17.8 for the habitual offender group. Thus, these retirees could be considered to be habitual offenders. What obviously distinguishes them from the other habitual offenders is the fact that they had been able to have working careers and had not spent years in incarceration. Three of this group, with arrest records totaling 24, 24, and 29, were last arrested for a violent

Table 4

Arrest Characteristics of Retiree Offenders

Age of First Offense	43	63	62	60	62	21
Age of Last Arrest	60	63	62	60	62	61
Latest Charge	Assault w/Dang. Weapon	Deliv. Drugs	Poss. Deli. Drugs	Assault I to Murder	Larc. Bldg.	Larc. 0/100
Total Arrests	9	1	1	1	1	12

Age of First Offense	20	21	51	30	43	52
Age of Last Arrest	58	56	66	62	59	59
Latest Charge	Poss. Deliv. Drugs	Arson	Murder	Fel. Assault	Assault I to Murder	Fel. Assault
Total Arrests	4	13	6	29	2	2

Age of First Offense	69	33	40	23	23	53
Age of Last Arrest	69	69	69	59	62	60
Latest Charge	CCW Fel. Assault	Assault I to Murder	Fel. Assault	Poss. Drugs	Assault I to Murder	Larc.
Total Arrests	1	24	10	11	24	3

crime, i.e., assault to commit murder. Two of this group who, first arrested at age 21, were last charged with Type II crimes, arson and larceny. And two were last arrested for possession of drugs (Table 4).

Seven of the retiree group had no previous arrest, or only one for a misdemeanor. These can be considered to be nonhabitual offenders. Of these, four were last charged with a violent crime, i.e., assault/murder; one with committing larceny, and two for drugs possession.

Of the retiree group, four men were in their 40s and 50s when they committed their first infraction. Three of these men were last arrested for serious offenses: assault with dangerous weapon, felonious assault and murder and one was charged with larceny.

DISCUSSION

The above findings point to several observations. First, the criminal activity of the older arrestees involve serious infractions. Both those who were involved in some criminal activity early in life and those who only were first arrested in their later years after retiring were charged with violent crimes. Those who first were arrested in their 40s and 50s also were involved in serious activity after retirement.

Secondly, although alcohol was a common factor in arrest patterns of both habitual and nonhabitual older offenders, it was not found in the arrest patterns of the retired group.

Ten of the 18 retirees were charged with violent crimes against other persons. In their study of homocides, Kratcoski and Walker (1986) discovered that homicides committed by elderly persons were likely to occur in the home, to be intraracial in nature and to be committed primarily by males. Victims of elderly homicide offenders were less likely to have been involved with alcohol consumption than victims of offenders in other age groups. Rubenstein (1982) reported a consensus in the literature that the older first offender will be found to have more often engaged in crimes against other persons than that these crimes will be violent crimes of passion.

In addition to crimes against other persons, retirees were arrested for possession of drugs, arson, and larceny. Although the numbers of this group are too small to draw conclusions about specific offenses, it is clear that all infractions were serious. Despite the fact that nearly half of the charges were first arrests, they did not typify the usual charge for the nonhabitual offender of less serious crime.

Two of the subjects were arrested for drug offenses after retirement at ages 62 and 63. Neither had a previous record of any consequence. Another retiree who had several previous arrests was charged with a narcotics violation at age 58.

CONCLUSION

These findings suggest several questions that require further investigation. Can the nature of serious criminal activity after the work role ceases be related to dissatisfaction with a leisure role? Does the pattern of apparent violent behavior for some retirees against other persons suggest that the individual is so dissatisfied with retirement that frustration and stress can lead to criminal behavior?

Researchers have established that disengagement from work roles can effect one's adjustment to a leisure role (Allmer and Kutner, 1969). They report substantial evidence that disengagement among the aged can be predicted to occur as a concomitant of physical or social stresses which profoundly affected the manner in which the life pattern of the person is redirected. Miller has postulated an identity crisis theory to account for losses of self-concept and identity when retirement results in adjustment problems (Miller, 1965).

Investigators have shown that there is a relationship between one's social class and propensity to assume meaningful leisure time activities. Other studies have shown relationships between stress and disruptive change, role loss, and satisfaction upon retirement (Elwell and Maltbie-Cranel, 1981). These findings point to a need for further investigation of the nature of criminal activity and its causes and circumstances for retired individuals.

The following research questions are suggested:

- What social supports are evident for those retirees who enter into criminal activity after retiring from work?
- What relationships, if any, are evident between a reduced social network, stress, depression and dissatisfaction with the leisure status for the retired individual who commits a criminal act?
- What are the relationships, if any, between reduced income,

sudden change in life situation, i.e., illness of self or spouse, and propensity for criminal behavior after retirement?

– What variables in retirement, such as acceptance of leisure status, ability to establish social supports, assumption of new roles to replace those of work, can be found between men and women in retirement and propensity for criminal behavior?
– What evidence can be found for determining whether persons who have had previous problems with the law are more likely to commit violent offenses than others who have never been law violators in retirement?
– What demarcations of time can be established for those retirees who commit criminal acts after ceasing work, such as violations in the first year, third year, five years or more? What other factors can be found related to criminal activity in specific time periods after retirement?
– What relationships, if any, are evident for individuals for whom disengagement from meaningful work roles results in a negative perception of self-worth, and criminal activity that threatens the well-being of other older persons including the retiree's spouse and friends?

As previously noted, there is little information as to the actual event of retirement and its immediate effects on individuals in terms of coping strategies for dealing with changes they cannot foresee. The potential lure of criminal activity and its substitution rewards for retirees is an area that requires further study.

REFERENCES

Aday, R. H., "Institutional Dependency: A Theory of Aging in Prison." Ph.D. dissertation, Oklahoma State University, 1976.

Atchley, R.C. *Social Forces and Aging* (rev. ed.). Belmont, CA: Wadsworth Publishing Company, 1977.

Bachand, D. J. Increased Criminal Behavior by the Elderly: Concerns for the Justice System. American Society of Criminology. Cincinnati, OH, November 7, 1984.

Bachand, D. J. and Brahce, C. I. The Elderly Offender; Factors That Influence Prosecution Outcomes. The Gerontological Society of America. San Antonio, TX, November 1984.

Beck, S. H. "Adjustment to and Satisfaction with Retirement," *Journal of Gerontology* 37, September 1982 pp. 616-624.

Cassell, J. "Epidemiological Perspective of Psychosocial Factors in Disease Etiology." *American Journal of Public Health*, 64, (1974) 1040-1043.

"Corporate Ideas for Effective Work Force Management—Retirement," in *Working Age* Vol. 3, No. 3, November/December 1987 pp. 1,5.

Cumming, E. L. & Henry, W. E. *Growing Old; The Process of Disengagement*. New York; Basic Books, 1961.

Elwell, F. and Maltbie-Crannel, A. "The Impact of Role Loss Upon Coping Resources and Life Satisfaction of the Elderly." *Journal of Gerontology* 36 (March 1981): 223-232.

Federal Bureau of Investigation. *Crime in the United States*, 1984. Washington, DC: U.S. Government Printing Office, 1985 pp. 172-33.

Feinberg, G. White Haired Offenders: An Emergent Social Problem. The Gerontological Society of America. Boston, MA, November 1982.

Goetting, A. The Elderly in Prison: A Profile. American Society of Criminology, Cincinnati, OH, 1984.

Krajick, K. Growing Old in Prison. *Corrections Magazine*, March, 1979.

Kratcoski, P. and D. Walker, "Homicide Among the Elderly: Analysis of Victim/Assailant Relationships." Paper presented at the Annual Meeting of the Academy of Criminal Justice Sciences, Orlando, FL, March 1986.

Kratcoski, P., Brahce, C. I. and Walker, D. Final Report on the Findings of the Study, Violent Crime of the Older Offender. Northeastern Ohio Universities College of Medicine, Rootstown, OH, 1987.

Matthews, A. M. and Brown, K. H., "Retirement as a Critical Life Event," *Research on Aging* Vol 9/Nov. 4 December 1987, pp. 548-571.

Miller, S. "The Social Dilemma of the Aging Leisure Participant." In *Older People and Their Social World*, edited by A. Rose and W. Peterson. Philadelphia, PA: F.A. Davis, 1965.

Newman, E., D. Newman and M. Gewirtz. *Elderly Criminals*. Cambridge, MS: Oelgeschlanger, Gunn & Hain, 1984.

"Older Workers Are Bearing the Brunt of Most Downsizing Programs," AARP *News Bulletin*, Washington, D.C. Vol. 18, No. 11, December 1987, pp. 1, 4-5.

Panton, J. *Characteristics of Aged Inmates*. Raleigh, NC: North Carolina Department of Correction, 1974.

Pihlblad, C. T. and Adams, D. S. "Widowhood, Social Participation and Life Satisfaction." *Aging and Human Development* 3 (1972): 323-30.

Rubenstein, D. The Elderly in Prison: A Recent Look. American Society of Criminology Meeting. Toronto, Canada, 1982.

Sarason, B., Sarason I., Hacker, T. and Basham, R. "Concomitants of Social Support: Social Skills, Physical Attractiveness and Gender." *Journal of Personality and Social Psychology*, 49 (2) (1985) 469-480.

Schorr, E. L. Retirees: An Analysis of Social Support Networks. Unpublished Masters Degree Thesis, Kent State University, 1987.

Schuckit, M. A. Geriatric Alcoholism and Drug Abuse. *The Gerontologist* Vol. 17. No. 2, 1977.

Shichor, D. and Kobrin, S. "Note: Criminal Behavior Among the Elderly." *The Gerontologist* 18 April (1978) 213-218.

Tallmer, M. and Kutner, B. "Disengagement and the Stresses of Aging" *Journal of Gerontology* 24:70-75 (1969).

Teller, F. E. and Howell, R. J. *Criminal and Psychological Characteristics of the Older Prisoner*. Salt Lake City. Utah Division of Corrections.

Thompson, W., Streib, G. F., and Kosa, J. "The Effects of Retirement on Social Adjustment." *Journal of Gerontology* 15, (1960) : 165-169.

Aging and Aged in Organized Crime

Menachem Amir

I. INTRODUCTION

Every aged is like all the rest of the aged. He will be studied mainly in terms of the physiological changes in his body.

Every aged is like someone in the aged population. He will be studied in terms of the cultural, social and organizational environment that gives significance to the physiological changes which he undergoes, i.e., provides definition of aging and its consequences to his life and his relationships with his milieu. Every aged is like no one, he is unique. He will be studied in terms of his past and present personal experiences which shaped his process of aging and his adjustment to it. These distinctions determine also the theory of aging as either a personal or social phenomena. I shall dwell on the problem of the aged in one specific social organization—in organized crime. Remember that in the recent arrests in Italy and in the United States, of organized crime criminals, the age of those arrested was between 68-72. They were the type of "Bosses" on whom I found most of my data. Also, the age of those who participated in the Organized Crime Conventions in Atlantic City, in Miami, in Appalachia, New York in 1957—they were all bosses and under-bosses, and "Dons," within the age range of 60 and above. And lastly, the commission of organized crime—like the Russian Politburo and the English House of Lords—are alike in the sense that their members are old, and often very aged.

Thus, I shall combine two phenomena: the aged, or aging and Organized Crime. But alas, because of the nature of the available

---

Menachem Amir is Professor of Criminology, Institute of Criminology, Faculty of Law, The Hebrew University, Jerusalem, Israel.

data, I shall have to generalize from data on individual aged persons. This is not very scientific because of the social, cultural, and personal variations in the life of the studied persons. But because of the dearth of research, I had to make do with biographies, or autobiographies, with some anthropological and sociological studies on Mafia, Organized Crime and family businesses, in Sicily Italy, the United States and material I gathered on Organized Crime in Israel (Amir, 1985).

II. DEFINITIONS

Old Age and Aging

There are various definitions of aging and old age which depend on the discipline of the scholar: the biological-physiological definition attends to changes in the biology of the body cells; the cultural sociological definition regards changes, voluntary or enforced, in social roles. Culture and society define what to expect from the aged in terms of his style of life, but also how he is expected to react to the conferred status of an "older person." It includes bureaucratic decisions that will define the lower age limit of being "old" or various gradations of aging. Social definitions contain the social reactions to aging—including various policies and regulations with regard to those defined as "aging persons," or "senior citizens."

Individual personal definitions are those in which the person defines himself and shapes his life accordingly. This self-definition is anchored in his cultural and social environment.

The operational definition in this paper is a bureaucratic, arbitrary definition, i.e., those of 60 years of age and older—a definition likely to be found in any public and corporate economic institution.

Organized Crime

Organized Crime does not refer to professional criminals who usually work alone, nor to organized criminality, that is, any organized group, of robbers or burglars. Organized Crime refers to the economic activity of an organized group which aims to draw profit from criminal activities, mainly by supplying goods and commercial social and political services to "black markets" or through the activities of brokerage and mediation in the legitimate and the illegitimate economic worlds. With the persistent and planned use of violence and corruption, all aim to establish a monopoly in the business or in geographical areas (Abadinsky, 1983; Amir, 1985).

III. THE NORMATIVE SYSTEM

For the aged in Organized Crime, normative systems are sources of problems and thus deserve special attention. Most explicitly discussed in the literature are the Italian group set of values, emanating from the Mediterranean background (Davis, 1977) but more specifically from the Sicilian (Blok, 1974; Dolci, 1960; Hess, 1973) and the Italian cultural imperative (Barzani, 1974; Blok, 1974; Boissevain, 1974; Gambino, 1974). This set of values is upheld by the elders who are also the first generation of immigrants to the United States. They collide with the second and third generation already absorbing the American normative system. If the first normative framework is important to explain the emergence of Italian Organized Crime and some of its basic features, the second set can explain the nature of Organized Crime among second generation Italians, among the Jewish group, and the development of Organized Crime among other ethnic groups.

And there is another set of values which make all organized criminals, regardless of their ethnic origin, follow certain defined rules, the code of Organized Crime (see Cressey, 1964; Homer, 1974; Salerno and Tompkins, 1969). As we shall see later the intergenerational conflict between the young and the elders stem from the different adherence to one or the other set of values or part of it.

The traditional "central" Italian normative system for which there is a basic consensus is characterized as family-oriented, emphasizing male dominance centrality. The male orientation emphasizes the character traits of courage, coolness, patience, social and economic initiative, the ability to manipulate people and circumstances. Also stubbornness in upholding the traditional values pertaining to the family and its honor, but with flexibility in the economic sphere.

These characteristics are the gist of the most coveted status of the male – "honoured," "respected" – that can be converted into economic and social resources, and by transforming social and economic networks into authority and power (Gambino, 1974; Ianni, 1972).

In Italy, Sicily and Russia (Georgia, see Amir, 1985) "honour" is conferred for economic entrepreneurship, the seizing of opportunities for diversity and expansion in the legitimate or the criminal economic enterprises. What is emphasized is an active entrepreneur. This is what they call "work." There is an inherent disdain for manual labor. The aim in life is to live like a "gentleman." Thus in this kind of work, age is not a limitation. It can give the person a sense of being indispensible in spite of aging. It allows him, together with the norm of "honour," to achieve added respect and continue his social and also his economic exercise of authority.

These implications of the traditional normative set of values, and the capitalist normative emphasis on activity and achievements, partly explain why from the biographical literature it is observed that the aged in Organized Crime almost never rests. To rest would be to live in social limbo.

Another aspect of the old and the new American value system is the orientation for satisfying basic hedonistic desires and passions. Thus we learn about their penchant for good food, women and other male pleasures.

And lastly, for the Italians, and the Georgian Jews in Israel, the special attitude toward the elder is important – respect and authority defer to his rule in the family, even when he is no longer involved in economic matters, when his respect and authority can no longer be translated into resources. When this deference demands only ritual humility, obedience without the conviction that the "respected' person is deserving, the deference he commands will foster intergenerational struggle.

IV. THE AGED

The literature on Organized Crime and the chronicles of the periodic "wars against Organized Crime" describe the members and leaders who are old, even aged. It was said (Salerno and Tompkins, 1969: 191-193) that members of Organized Crime almost never retire. Many do not reach old age. Either they were pushed out, made to retire or literally annihilated within their own group because of peer struggle, intergenerational conflict, or violation of the "code" (Gage, 1971: 97). They may have also perished in the wars between groups over the monopolization of an economic activity or for gaining exclusiveness in a geographical area (Fustenberg, 1969: 199). Thus, recently we were informed (Abadinsky, 1985) that Giancano, an Organized Crime boss in Chicago, was murdered at the age of 67, or that Angelo Bruno perished in Philadelphia at the age of 69, and another boss in Chicago was shot to death at the age of 70.

Also the government, in its continuous war against Organized Crime drives the aged to leave "willingly," or most often after experiencing imprisonment (Demaris, 1981: 915; Kobler, 1971; McPhaul, 1970). Even in their old age, when they have left (seemingly or actually) their active membership in Organized Crime (DeMaris, 1981), they are harassed and persecuted by the government.

Such vendettas also exist in Organized Crime as those who left are still haunted by those still in. Thus, it is very hard to retire from organized crime.

Various types of "survival" in Organized Crime can be distinguished from types of continuous active role, including social leadership and/or economic management. From the literature we can distinguish between:

A. those aged who are still active in social (ethnic and familial) systems, but also in the economic organization connected with the social system (e.g., Ianni, 1972; Talese, 1971);
B. those who are in their old age still active in the economic, criminal or legitimate organization, but have no bases or affiliation to a family system. They serve as leaders or in expert positions in the corporation they developed (e.g., McPhaul, 1970; Messick, 1972; Teresa, 1963);
C. those who have left the economic arena but are only active in the family system as the authority—patriarchal figure, ruling family life within and its relations with the outside world (Anderson, 1979; Ianni, 1972);
D. there are those who did not rise to any important position and aged in Organized Crime remaining as small hustlers or run-

ners of small businesses for the criminal corporation (Mass, 1968). Others in this category are those who did not amass wealth and are supported by the organization, and live comfortably as if on pension (Salerno and Tompkins, 1969: 197);

E. there are those who survived and are still active in the legitimate economic organizations which they found before retiring from criminal involvement. Often these supposedly legitimate businesses are only a front, a facade for their continued criminal operations (Fried, 1980; Messick, 1972; Zeiger, 1971); and

F. some are absentee owners, just reaping thc profits of their business while others operate it for them (Abadinsky, 1981: 163).

In the Italian Mafia we find more aged in categories (A), (C), (E) and (F), while in the Jewish group, most of the leaders who survived can be found in groups (B) and (F). This is because the Jewish criminal organizations did not develop on a family basis; nor on ethnic affiliation (Fried, 1980; Toby, 1958). In the Georgian group in Israel the aged are in the same categories as the Italians, again groups (A) and (C).

Still another distinction can be made between those who climbed up from the bottom into important positions because of talent to use force or to manipulate situations. They became experts, e.g., "money movers," as judges (Zeiger, 1971: 22, 31; Abadinsky, 1983: 167; Cressey, 1969) or as power brokers (Blok, 1974; Hess, 1970: 129-139). Others climbed more readily because they belong to the social group that established the business and still controls it (Anderson, 1979; Ianni, 1972). This type is found more often in the Italian family because there it is also connected with the tradition, already existing in Italy, of "honour" and respect for the aged (Albini, 1971; Boissevain, 1974; Davis, 1977; Emrich, 1967; Gambino, 1984; Hess, 1970). This is so, especially if he has proved himself by his economic achievements. It allows him to maintain his authority and power in the social system and in the economic organization, legitimate or criminal. (See Ianni, 1971; Gambino, 1974; Hess, 1973 on the distinctions between these terms.)

If he is divorced from the economic sphere, he still maintains his social control within the family, and his decision-making role as to the family relations with the outside world. Tradition gives him power to be the guardian of the family, upholding its cohesiveness. If the family is also the social base for a business enterprise, the elder will use his power to continue the family rule over the business. Moreover, he is to be considered a stabilizing force, as a paragon of tradition in an organization which is in the midst of change.

The second group is of those who reach important positions, even leadership and management roles, but without the support of a social base, for example, a family. They fought their way up on the basis of social skills, organizational ability and the temperament for manipulation of people and circumstances, of adaptation to emerging conditions, and of calculated violence. They were able to weave social networks of mutual aid and support, based however, on pure economic interests (DeMaris, 1981). They are what we may call the real "Boss." (See Abadinsky, 1981: 162; Anderson, 1979; Cressey, 1969: 221-2; Kolberg, 1971; McPhaul, 1970; Messik, 1972.) They survived in the business of crime so long that they can maintain respect with force, or are economically strong and able to fend off greedy competitors. They leave when they lose the support of their social base—within the organization or the support of social bases outside the organization (Cressey, 1969). In both groups, the elders are demoted or annihilated when they relax the traditional code of Organized Crime like the "Omerta," or when they allow themselves to be in the public view, such as with Columbo or Bonano. What is interesting about the Columbo story is that he attempted to change the image of the Boss in the Mafia (Gage, 1971: 97). Both he and Bonano forgot that they were not the heads of a legitimate corporation, but the executive leaders of a Criminal Economic Syndicate, that has its own rules of secrecy and anonymity, and has its special measures to deal with violators: to demote them, to exile them or to execute them (Cressy, 1973).

However, in the case of the Italian family business, it is possible either to demote the elderly to secondary role in the business, or to allow him to function in the family system, even as a titular head based on the old age tradition (Block, 1974; Hess, 1970: 54-67; Ianni, 1979). And those who seemingly retire to enjoy life and maintain a small business never cease to be compulsively active, with the drive for expansion and monopolization (Salerno and Tompkins, 1969: 191-193). In this way the elders who survive in Organized Crime resemble the elder in the top or middle position in legitimate corporations, who also are reluctant to leave the field, and strive to maintain relations with their peers (Evan, 1976).

Whenever the elders (or when they were younger) directed the economic organization, they managed an organization, a partly or wholly criminal firm. (See Finney and Lesieur, 1982; Gross, 1980; and Vougham, 1982 on the nature of white collar type criminal economic firms. On criminal firms of the Organized Crime type, see Amir, 1985; Anderson, 1979; Ianni, 1972; Rubin, 1968.) As managers or directors of their businesses they display the entrepreneurial type of management rather than the fiduciary one (Evan, 1976: 90). That is, they rule the social and economic structure of the business on behalf of the owner only, directing his behavior exclusively toward profit maximization. His counterpart, the fiduciary manager, does not make such self-servicing decisions.

The activities of organized criminals are often characterized as brokers or mediators in providing goods and services (Boissevain, 1974: 133; Smith, 1978). It involves social and economic entrepreneurship. These roles do not depend on age unless health impairs judgment and mobility. They were also able to convert their personal authority and organizational and economic talents into resources. They were able to transform their style of life into a career that does not have to be terminated in old age (Boissevain, 1974: 174-9; Hess, 1973: 124-127). Thus, even without the basis and the support of a "family" they can survive economically while often they become absentee owners of businesses.

From the literature and from my study in Israel (Amir, 1985), we can learn about another set of roles which allows the elder not only to survive, but to remain active within the organization. I refer to judicial and mediation functions which they exercise alone, or as members of a "commission."

In these roles, old age has traditional positive value and function in the accumulation of experience and wisdom. There is a belief (so often betrayed) that they lost the lust for power and of advancing individual or group interests. However, their very career in Organized Crime, demonstrated in their high position, negates such an assumption.

In summation, most of the aged in Organized Crime fade away; like their counterparts in the legitimate world, depending on their health and wealth. But few, and the pyramid has a place only for a few at the top, do not retire. It is these few who serve in a paradoxical role. While they can be considered a stabilizing force, change can lead to the loss of their importance, as for example, the weakening of the kin and affinity group and the overriding importance of economic considerations – all these processes make the mere presence of the aged in the family and economic organization a source of intergenerational tension as well as other conflicts.

V. INTERGENERATIONAL PROBLEMS

The problem of the aged in any economic corporation is connected, among other variables, to the multi-age structure in that organization (e.g., Eva, 1976; Foner, 1984). Such is also the case in the economic organization of Organized Crime. There, the problem is more complicated, since some of these criminal corporations are based on traditional, cultural and social sets of rules which bestow ascendancy and importance to the elder.

Thus, in the literature I reviewed (see Homer, 1984; Ianni, 1972; Salerno and Tomkins, 1969), the young often accuse the elders of conservatism is business, with the unwillingness to take risks and to be what they think is more efficient. The battles are waged when both groups belong to a common social system – the family which is not only a business organization. This age difference or actually intergenerational conflict evolves from value differences and conflicts between the old world view and the new; between the Italian or European normative map and the American way of life (Cressey, 1969: 241-2). It is often the conflict between first generation immigrants and succeeding generations. Often the conflict is about style of life or over the deference that the young are compelled to accord the elders as well as submission to traditional values in social, economic family or even individual life. Thus, when business expansion calls for decentralization and independence, the elders tend to centralize and personalize their authority (Cressey, 1969: 246).

While the young aspire for quick gains by any means, the elders halt the young until "they will prove themselves" (Gage, 1971; Gambino, 1974; Talese, 1971). The elder who subscribes to gradual economic growth and the surrendering of rational economic decisions to the traditional social and cultural norms, regulated by patrifocal-patriarchal authority vested in the hands of the elders. All this while the status of the aged decreases with modernization (Foner, 1984: ch. 2).

This situation of intergenerational tension is more common in the Italian Mafia, since it often integrates a social (family) system with an economic organization.

Moreover, with or without the social system base of the economic organization, these are criminal processes that operate both in legitimate business organizations like those observed from the studies on corporate white collar crimes (e.g., Clinard, 1983; Finney and Lessieur, 1982; Ermann and Lundman, 1982; Gross, 1980; Vaugham, 1984) and those pertaining to criminal enterprises (Anderson, 1972; Ianni, 1972).

The problem of how to contain in one group both the economic-rational element based on the accumulated achievements of the whole age structure, that is, the horizontal level, and the lateral level based and originating from the multi-aged structure of the organization is common. This problem of intergenerational conflict is absent in the syndicate form of Organized Crime, where the economic organization is divorced from a social system, like a "family." Thus, such a dilemma is not observed in Jewish Organized Crime groups. First because Jewish "Mafiosi" rose to leadership and executive positions by their own efforts not based on a family group, but relied on peers—albeit mainly Jewish partners. Also the Jewish "Mafiosi" did not have a second generation in their family to follow them (Toby, 1958); they were spared from conflicts with younger groups about ways of doing business, approaches to life, to crime and from the demands of the youth to replace the old leadership positions in the organization (Block, 1980; Fried, 1980).

In the Italian groups, this kind of conflict and intraorganizational tension is most observed when the Organized Crime Commission refuses the elder Bonnano to set his son as the leader of the family and its business organization (Talese, 1971; Zeiger, 1971).

Organizational theory recognizes this as the "age-lump problem" (see Downs, 1966: 20), most likely to occur under two conditions: first, in any aging economic organization when the "founding fathers" still occupy central positions; secondly, when the organization, legitimate or criminal, is also a family business or connected with a social system, which accords the aged a special role or decision-making power also in the economic organizations. Thus, many young refuse to stay in the criminal organization; not only because the aged rule it, but, ironically, groomed by the elders for command posts which they did not vacate, they no longer function as frontmen to shield and support the organization (Cressey, 1969).

Organizations attempt to solve the problem of intergenerational conflict in the following ways: to confer on the aged symbolic roles in the economic organization, while maintaining their authority in the family system. Or, to allow the young to develop their own economic entrepreneurship, outside the family business, in the legitimate or criminal business world. It is also possible that the elder will accept modernization, accommodate new demands even in the illegal economic sphere, like dealing with drugs, or to cooperate as the head of the "family" system, with the business organization (Ianni, 1972). But even then, new intergeneration conflict can arise. In Zeiger (1971) "Sam the Plumber" represents the elderly in Organized Crime, and constantly admonishes the young for their proclivity toward violence, for their penchant to disregard traditional values, and for being irresponsible and careless: "they don't grow up" says Sam (Zeiger, 1971; p. 213).

But the young members are restless. They are not impressed anymore by the old guard, who often only through them have access to the outside economic and political world. They are fed up with the elder fighting old rivalries, endangering the social and economic stability of the organization (Zieger, 1971).

The old are left to maintain discipline by using the "Mafia Code" of compliance (Cressey, 1973) and by demanding obedience to their personal authority stemming from the traditional value given to "Respect and Honor." It is, by the way, not a baseless obligation. These aged dons, without education and out of misery, did establish economic empires.

Thus, so long as the elders remain active in the social and economic arena, the intergenerational tensions will persist. But if pushed out, or retired, new tension will arise in the struggle to fulfill the position left by the elders.

VI. STANDARD OF LIFE

From the popular media the impression is given that the aged in Organized Crime do not have to worry about their economic well-being. The media and biographies (e.g., Anderson, 1979; DeMaris, 1981; Messik, 1972; Talese, 1971; Teresa, 1983) and more rigorous studies (e.g., Ianni, 1972) tell about those who succeeded to accumulate fortunes and to retire, or semi-retire to comfortable lives, some to mansions or estates. They refrain from occupying apartments in order to continue the style of life of secrecy, seclusion, and maximum avoidance of publicity. Those who prefer to lead this way of life often choose to live in their ethnic neighborhood.

This standard of life is typical of corporate executives, with individual variations of personal and subcultural taste. Many of the Italians spend time with their families describing themselves as devoted fathers with demands for family rituals of respectable family life. For leisure they play golf. We discover (Talese, 1971) that Bonnano also reads books on the mafia, including Cressey's work "Theft of the Nation," or that Phil Charles, the short-term "boss" of a crime family in Philadelphia was reading DeMaris's book on Jimmy Fontana, "The Last Mafioso" (1981), and viewing "The Godfather" on his video (Abadinsky, 1985: 1). Most of the aged were illiterate, preferring eating, often in modest neighborhood ethnic restaurants. The one common feature of their retired life is social seclusion within their families, relatives or "business associates."

Many were able to move away from their past scene of operations, to the sunbelts; the Jews to Miami, and the Italians to other parts of Florida, to California or Arizona (e.g., Messik, 1972). Many still live, according to their means, in the appropriate ethnic enclaves. Some even stay in the same neighborhoods they inhabited in their middle life, when they were still active in Organized Crime.

Another common feature is that of being in a dilemma of "living," or giving the impression of ostentatiousness, of a lavish life which conflicts with the tradition of modesty of the economic and the family system, especially if it is a criminal business. The very fact of avoiding the IRS compels them to live modestly, to run efficient well-ordered businesses, while they want at last to enjoy the life of the comfortable, those rich Americans, who like them could not create or enter nobility status.

VII. FEARS OF THE AGED

From the literature it is observed that the aged in Organized Crime are subject to various fears because of their past and present affiliation with Organized Crime. They are constantly afraid of the government, the IRS, the District Attorney who may dig things up from the past, or will harass them in his zeal to prove he is earnestly fighting crime (DeMaris, 1981; Talese, 1971: 33).

If they are still members in a social family system and/or criminal economic enterprise they are under pressures of the life in crime, of the intergenerational struggle or from the ongoing inter-group competition, often actual war—over the constant drive for monopolization.

They know that the life in Organized Crime is that of survival, back-biting and double-crossing, so inherent to Organized Crime (Chandler, 1985; Nelli, 1976; San, 1971). Publicity is another source of fear. The media, the government and inter-group struggle often bring their name into the public arena. It endangers their quest for anonymity, and for rest. Publicity often brings the commission's reaction of demotion and even execution (Gage, 1971: 97).

All Organized Crime members, but especially the leaders in advanced age, harbor a constant anxiety from being jailed and imprisoned (DeMaris, 1981; McPhaul, 1970; Teresa, 1963). It is not only the "pain" of imprisonment (Sykes, 1958: 63-84) that they shiver from, but also the danger of revolt in their organization, of being demoted, of losing the race with their peer-competitors and the young who aspire to their position, or want to start a new economic venture, but are checked by the cautiousness of their elders. And like all aged, they have the worries of ill health, often exacerbated because of past and present lives of crime (so many of them suffer from ulcers and heart failures [Messik, 1972]). Or due to the constant struggle not to be compelled to retire, they have to prove their irreplaceability.

Those who build an economic business but without a social base for support must show continued acumen in handling the business. Those who run small businesses or hold jobs in legitimate or illegitimate ones fear for their standard of life; their fortune being eaten by the IRS, greedy lawyers and financing their past and present personal organizational fights.

VIII. EXCUSES AND JUSTIFICATION

Like everyone in middle and old age, the aged in Organized Crime must give accounts and valuations of their way of life and achievements. And like everyone who violates rules, he too must give to himself, and to others, accounts to excuse, justify or rationalize his past behavior and present way of life—if he still continues his life in crime. Biographies reveal that often the person uses both excuses and rationalization (Scott and Lyman, 1970), giving accounts like those of corporate white collar criminals, that is, theirs was only an economic activity in the framework of the American and capitalist value system (Geis, 1982: 7-103; Ermann and Lundman, 1982). As Al Capone said: "I followed the U.S. Constitution in my right to pursue happiness" (Kobler, 1971: 224). By this rationalization and other kinds of accounts they negotiate with society and themselves their identity, trying to rehabilitate their self-image, to diminish the negative implications of their past, trying to feel they are members of legitimate society.

Therefore, I could find some remarks of personal apologetica, but not of statements of regret, or a sense of moral failure. At most they admit that they made mistakes of misplaced confidence or wrong choice of friends, or foolish decisions. If otherwise, they could be more successful. On the contrary, they have professional pride in their economic achievements (Landesco, 1968).

A theme runs through their personal accounts—that they almost embody the Horatio Alger experience. Indeed, they came up from the slum, from the breeding grounds of delinquency and crime. In this sense, the biographies are excuse-making tools, using retrospective and retroactive excuses. The justification of re-biography is employed to reorganize their life stories, which will explain their past and present way of life. Snyder and his colleagues (1983) call it an attempt of "masquerading in search of grace" so that they can maintain positive self-images for themselves and for others.

More specifically, they use the known techniques of neutralization (see Matza and Sykes, 1957) such as:

– the sad story – they were raised in and from poverty. Thus they were compelled to grow up into a way of life they did not choose (Haller, 1971-2; Lupsha, 1981);
– condemnation of the condemners: they will argue that all people are hypocrites. Everyone has his own racket. This includes the police, the criminal justice system and the politicians. Those who prosecute them actually profit from this politically and as an economic business in the guise of moral righteousness;
– diminishing the injury to the victim. The victims are but customers who assiduously search for their services of supplying their merchandise – vice (Landesco, 1968: 213-215);
– appealing to higher morality, for example, they protected and helped their own people.

Their operations, so they say, emerge from the need to survive in a corrupt and hostile world where only by manipulation and bribery can one survive. Moreover, in a pose of moral righteousness they claim that they did a lot of favors and charity to individuals, to their peoples, to the church and even to the government. Al Capone boasted that he helped search for the Lindbergh kidnapped infant (Kobler, 1971). In short, they were dispensing "distributive justice" (Merton, 1957).

Besides the individual justification, they also employ social political accounts. They see themselves as an economic organization that supplies goods and services and not a conspirative social system. Only the police and the media confer to them the double status of an ethnic social system and a criminal organization.

Moreover, they see themselves as the paragons of the capitalistic system, part of free enterprise, the symbol of business—shrewdness. They are the true democrats and anti-communists (Caputo, 1974) and complain that they are portrayed as villains (Talese, 1971: 216, 357, 361; Kobler, 1971: 331). They wonder why the government wages war on them—old and tired Dons (Homer, 1974: 357; Talese, 1971: 357; Teresa, 1963). Ironically, they do not or may not know that some of the scholars confer upon them legitimacy—as providers of services to deprived communities (e.g., Merton, 1957). Or they are viewed not only as almost public servicemen but as an inherent part of the American economy, playing a structural role as brokers and mediators (Smith, 1979).

IX. THE GOVERNMENT AND THE AGED IN ORGANIZED CRIME

In terms of organizational perspectives there are three approaches to the war against Organized Crime. The first is the membership attrition tactic, the attempt to arrest and convict any identifiable member of Organized Crime, even those who seem retired from Organized Crime. The second approach is the leadership attrition tactic. Known leaders of Organized Crime groups are harassed, prosecuted in the belief that this will disorganize the group because of the struggle for assuming the vacated leadership position. Certain groups are believed to be more vulnerable to the elimination of its leadership: when the leadership is still of the charismatic type, or when the organization is in its crystallizing phase or in the beginning of its economic and social expansion. The third tactic is to hurt Organized Crime both by former tactics and with the additional efforts to disorganize and destroy its economic base and operations (Homer, 1974).

For the individual member, the fear of the government is a constant existential fact. Even the aged are continuously harassed for their criminal and seemingly legitimate business, usually through income tax investigation, subpoenas and summons issued on almost any pretext, especially when new laws are enacted by which a restaurant lunch of two or more aging and retired dons is considered a "criminal conspiracy." Here, again, the aged cannot, are not allowed to retire, even when they thought that they are immune from contact with the criminal justice system. However, it seems that the aged who are still active in the economic enterprise of Organized Crime, or are members of boards of criminal-social or economic organizations—"the commission"—are the targets of law enforcement.

X. THEORETICAL CONSIDERATIONS

The sociological and psychological literature on the aged and on aging often laments the distorted images of the aged in our society. They are viewed as passive, conservative, helpless and dependent. This stereotype leads to policies that often validate the stereotype. Thus, they become a self-fulfilling prophecy (Foner, 1975).

A small but selective sample of the aged in Organized Crime are still active and continue to execute roles of management and leadership. By this they resemble those in legitimate corporations or viable social communities, like in rural villages. These aged are still scheming to amass wealth and power, or use wisely the fortune they already harvested. They still show great acumen in reorganization of their roles and in manipulating their social environment, even when they were eased out of functioning in the economic sphere. They are very active, striving not to be idle, dependent, helpless or alone. However, they mingle mainly with their own kind, which is most often not the conformist society from which they were segregated most of their lives.

The social reaction and policy outcome to the images of the aged can be grouped on two continua: the *first* is that of integration vs. segregation; the *second* but different continuum of reaction to aging is that of humanism vs. dehumanism. Crossing the two continua we obtain the following four outcomes.

1. The combination of integration and humanism, i.e., the aged is integrated in a multi-age organization with the tendency to view the aged as a *whole* person with a definite identity and with clear-cut roles. We can see this alternative in simple, agricultural societies, in villages in the Mediterranean (e.g., Blok, 1974; Davis, 1977; Foner, 1984; Hess, 1973). The aged has important resources of knowledge and experience that his

surrounding needs. He begets respect and honor. A more modern example would be the aged politician, the old executive in corporations, mainly in family business, and also the boss, the don, in organized families or syndicates (Anderson, 1979; Ianni, 1972).

2. The second alternative is that of *integration* and *de-humanization*. Here the aged is still within the community but he is deprived of important roles. In some family businesses (legitimate or criminal) he may remain the patriarch of the family, may be holding a titular symbolic role also as the director of the business, but actually he has no definite power nor any role (Ianni, 1972). Withdrawing from the main role comes often after a coup is staged by the young. It is a crisis that may lead to finding substitute secondary roles, if not complete abdication from roles.
3. The third alternative is that of *segregation* and *humanism*. It seems paradoxical, but the aged is segregated from the multiage surrounding, from his native milieu, but functions as a whole person in a separate community for aged persons, e.g., the sunbelt communities of aged citizens who can live comfortably and actively on the wealth they have amassed (e.g., Talese, 1971).
4. The fourth, extreme alternative to accommodate the aged is that of segregation and dehumanization. The sad example of such arrangements is old-age homes, they are not and cannot be subjects for our study.

The literature places the aged in Organized Crime in the *first*, *second* and *third* classifications, but mainly in the *first* and *second* ones. When the boss is both the head of the family and is the active director of the business, he belongs to the first alternative of integration and humanism. Others remain only the patriarch of the family. They are accorded respect and deference; they have authority but mainly in the social affairs of the family.

Two seemingly conflicting theories of general sociological theories are often debated, which attempt to answer the question of why the aged, or groups of people in various sectors of society, behave the way we observe them. Empirically, what is actually tested are theories of adjustment, life-satisfaction or morale.

The *first* theory in its appearance is the disengagement theory; the other is the activity theory (Grandale, 1980: 97-124).

The gist of the disengagement theory is that social aging is a gradual process of withdrawal from society and of surrendering of social roles, or change in the quality of their exercise. The process is accelerated when it is combined with severe changes in health and motility of the aging person (Loetmer, 1975; Cummings, 1963; Cummings and Henry, 1961; Hochchild, 1975).

The disengagement process, which is inevitable, is also a mutual one. Disengagement theory assumes that society is interested in the withdrawal and disavowal so that the young can replace the relinquished roles of the aged. This is the social level of this functionalist theory. On the personal-functional level, the gradual process of role-exist prepares the aged for his final departure—death.

It is therefore also both a volitional and enforced process (e.g., enforced or compelled retirement). The one who is not ready for this will either sink into passivity or depression or will seek substitute roles—depending on his level of education and health, but mainly on his self-image or status-rigidity (Maddox, 1964, 1970).

Some of the aged we describe defy disengagement theory. This may be the reason we know so much about them. We found that they may reduce or halt their illegal economic activity but still be active in the legitimate sector of their economic affairs. Some take more active roles in social affairs, including being judges and referees in criminal disputes. They do not let themselves be dependent and helpless, cut out from involvement in society, at least their subculture.

It seems that our subjects deserve the attention of the second sociological theory of aging—the activity theory (Grandale, 1980: 111-113).

According to this theory the adjusted and satisfied older person is the one who persists and continues to be active in his original social roles, which he acted upon during his middle years of life (Maddox, 1964, 1970). Moreover, his high morale will persist if the aged will apply the principles of change and substitution, that is, finding new roles and involvement for the ones he has to relinquish.

There are variations in the actual adjustment of the aged to the principles of change and substitution. It depends on what roles one was exercising in terms of their centrality and significance, on his role-flexibility, and again on his status image, i.e., open or closed, rigid or flexible (Havinghurst, 1959: ch. 3, 6, 8; 1954) or on having a support system (Lemon et al., 1972).

Activity theory fits aged organized criminals, because it is basically an "American" theory, i.e., utilitarian, emphasizing efforts, achievements and the importance of being active. Yes, some of our aged are very "rigid" in materializing these ideals; they are almost compulsively active, refusing to be out of action. Thus while some roles are reduced, others discontinued, others are assumed for the first time and others are intensified.

If more cases were available to study and different types of Organized Crime (e.g., the Japanese Yakuza or the French kind), we would find that activity theory describes only one kind of adaptation to aging while disengagement theory is another kind. And it may be that aging in the framework of economic organization which is also criminal lends to special kinds of adaptation to old age (see e.g., Shanas, 1968: 332; Foner, 1984). also let us remember that some prefer voluntarily to disengage, to become just a "rocking-chair" gentleman (Havinghurst, 1969).

We shall have to add some other variables to the theory, such as those of subcultures which define the appropriate style of life for the aged, types of segregation, as well as variables such as social class, minority status, education, etc. (Rose, 1965; Philips, 1957).

Another theory may be partly applicable: role theory. It was suggested (Rosow, 1976) that all social roles have two major dimensions: First, the clarity of role behavior and role expectation associated with the role. The second is the clarity of the status of the role. Institutional roles are those in which behavior and expectations are quite clear to all actors involved. They include most occupational and family roles. The elders are most likely to adapt informal or tenuous roles, which also have not clearly defined status, i.e., associated behavior and expectations may be extremely unclear. Other examples of tenuous roles are nominative offices and deviant roles in which status (although low), behavior and expectations are vague, if at all defined. For the elderly Italian in Organized Crime, because of the tradition to accord them respect and honor, there is a partial solution of this dissonance between status and behavior. Their status includes and is partly based on attribution of power and stereotypes about their past of wielding power in family affairs and in the outside (mainly the ethnic milieu) world. It is also based on stereotypes of their past behavior and achievements (as a general statement see Solomon, 1979). Thus, although in their informal role their status is tenuous, tradition confers to their role an institutional nature. But tension still exists between the aged and the young, because although no longer the director, the Boss of the business, he is still the ruler of the family. Tenuousness creates between the status and the role and the ensuing expectations, and especially in regard to the continuity of the role.

If the elder fails to create and adopt a tenuous role he has the choice to leave the scene as many Jewish "bosses" did, or some Italian aging Mafiosi (e.g., Bonnano or Jimmy Fontana). That they often succeed, and thus remain on the scene, is due to being able to establish a secure economic base for themselves, so they won't be helpless, vulnerable. It allows them to keep in touch with people, to be connected with some Organized Crime affairs. Thus they avoid apathy and alienation.

We can also study the effect of labelling on the aged in Organized Crime, especially the effect of government agencies' harassment on the level and nature of activities of the aged, which reinforce a certain style of life (Bengston, 1973).

And it could be that only individual variations on the basis of personal characteristics and life experiences will explain the variability of adjustment to aging in Organized Crime (Havinghurst et al., 1969; Lowenthal and Haven, 1968; Rosow, 1967). Patterns and regularities persist even in what seems to be extreme variability. What can be drawn on the social level from the accounts reviewed is the responsibility of the social structure in creating such types of retired chiefs of organized crime. What can be drawn from the individual level approach is the phenomenological tradition, i.e., the world view of the aged in Organized Crime, its origin and how it influences, and when in his cycle of life, his behavior as an aged person, who was and still is, in a varied capacity, a member of organized crime.

REFERENCES

Abadinsky, H. (1981) *Organized Crime*, Boston: Allyn and Bacon, Inc.
Abadinsky, H. (1983) *The Criminal Elite*: Professional and Organized Crime. Westpost, CT: Greenwood.
Abadinsky, H. (1985) *Update*, 1 (2): 1
Albini, J. (1971) *American Mafia: Genesis of a Legend*, New York: Appleton-Crofts.
Amir, M. (1985) "The Role of Georgian Jews in Organized Crime in Israel," *Crossroad* 14: 57-59.
Anderson, A. (1979) *The Business of Organized Crime*, Stanford University Press: The Hoover Institute.
Barzini, L. (1964) *The Italians*, New York: Atheneum.
Bengton, V. (1973) *The Social Psychology of Aging*, New York: Bobbs-Merrill.
Block, A. (1980) *East-Side West-Side: Organizing Crime in New York, 1930-1950*, University College Cardiff Press.
Blok, A. (1975) *The Mafia of a Sicilian Village, 1860-1960*, New York: Harper.
Boissevain, J. (1974) *Friends of Friends: Network, Manipulations and Coalitions*, Oxford: Basil Blackwell.
Cage, N. (1971) *The Mafia is Not an Equal Opportunity Employer*, New York: McGraw Hill.
Caputo, D. (1974) *Organized Crime and American Politics*, New Jersey: General Learning Process.
Chandler, D. (1975) *Brothers in Blood: The Rise of the Criminal Brotherhood*, New York: E. P. Dutton and Co.
Clinard, M. B. (1983) *Corporate Ethics and Crime: The Role of the Middle Management*, Beverly Hills, CA: Sage.
Cressey, D. R. (1969) *Theft of a Nation*, New York: Harper.
Cressey, D. R. (1973) "Advance Notice and Government by Law Within Criminal Confederation," *International Journal of Criminology and Penology* 1 (1): 55-67.
Cummings, E. (1963) "Further Thoughts on the Theory of Disengagement," *International Social Science Journal* 15: 377-393.
Cummings, E. and W. Henry (1961) *Growing Old*, New York: Basic Books.
Davis, J. (1977) *People of the Mediterranean*, London: Routledge and Kegan Paul.
De Maris, O. (1981) *The Last Mafioso*, New York: Bantam.
Downs, A. (1966) *Inside Bureaucracy*, Boston: Little, Brown.
Enrich, R. (1967) "Cultural Anthropological Analysis of Organized Crime," in S. A. Yefsky (ed.), *Law Enforcement, Science and Technology*, p. 41-46.
Ermann, D. and R. Lundman (1982) *Corporate and Governmental Deviance*, New York: Oxford University Press.
Evan, W. M. (1976) *Organization Theory: Structure, System and Environment*, New York: John Wiley.
Finney, H. C. and H. R. Lesieur (1982) "A Contingency Theory of Organiza-

tional Crime," in S. B. Bacharach (ed.), *Research in the Sociology of Organizations*, Greenwich, CT: JAI Press.

Foner, A. (1975) "Age in Society: Structure and Change," *American Behavioral Scientist*, 19 (2): 144-165.

Foner, N. (1984) *Age in Conflict: A Cross-Cultural Perspective on Inequality between Old and Young*, New York: Columbia University Press.

Fried, A. (1980) *The Rise and Fall of the Jewish Gangster in America*, New York: Holt, Rinehart and Winston.

Fustenburg, N. (1969) "Violence and Organized Crime," in *Crime of Violence: A Staff Report to the National Commission of the Causes and Prevention of Violence*, Vol. 13: Appendix 18: 911-930.

Gambino, R. (1974) *Blood of My Blood: The Dilemma of the Italian-American*, New York: Anchor Books.

Geis, G. (1982) *On White-Collar Crime*, Lexington, MA: Lexington Books.

Grandale, R. C. (1980) *Gerontology: A Behavioral Science Approach*, Reading, MA: Addison-Wesley, ch. 5: 97-124.

Gross, E. (1980) "Organization Structure and Organized Crime," in G. Geis and E. Statland (eds.) *White Collar Crime: Theory and Research*, Beverly Hills, CA: Sage.

Havinghurst, R. (1954) "Flexibility and the Social Role of the Retired," *American Journal of Sociology* 39: 309-311.

Havinghurst, R. G. et al. (1969) *Adjustment to Retirement: A Cross-National Study*, New York: Humanities Press.

Heller, M. (1971-2) "Organized Crime in Urban Society: Chicago in the 20th Century," *Journal of Social History*, Winter: 210-234.

Hess, H. (1973) *Mafia and Mafiosi: The Structure of Power*, Lexington: D. C. Heath.

Hochchild, A. (1975) "Disengagement Theory: A Critique and Proposal," *American Sociological Review*, 40: 553-569.

Homer, F. (1974) *Guns and 'Garlic': Myth and Realities of Organized Crime*, Purdue University Press.

Ianni, F. (1972) *A Family Business*, New York: Russell Sage Foundation.

Ianni, F. (1974) *Black Mafia*, New York: Simon and Schuster.

Kobler, J. (1971) *Capone*, New York: Putnam.

Landesco, J. (1968) *Organized Crime in Chicago*, Chicago University Press.

Lemon, B., V. Bengston and I. Peterson (1972) "Exploration of the Activity of Aging," *Journal of Gerontology*, 27:511-23.

Loether, H. (1975) *Problems of Aging* (2nd edition), Encino, CA: Dickenson Publishing.

Lowenthal, M. and C. Haven (1968) "Interaction and Adaptation: Intimacy as a Critical Variable," in B. C. Newgarten (ed.), *Middle Age and Aging*, Chicago: Chicago University Press.

Lupsha, P. (1981) "Individual Choice, Material Culture and Organized Crime," *Criminology* 19 (1): 3-24.

Maas, P. (1968) *The Valachi Papers*, New York: Bantam.

Maddox, G. (1964) "Disengagement Theories: A Critical Evaluation," *The Gerontologist* 4: 80-82.

Maddox, G. (1970) "Themes and Issues in Sociological Theories of Human Aging," *Human Development* 13: 17-27.

Matza, D. and G. Sykes (1957) "Techniques of Neutralization," *American Sociological Review* 22:667-669.

McPhaul, J. (1970) *Johnny Torrio*, New Rochelle, NY: Arlington House.

Merton, R. (1957) "Social Structure and Anomie," in *Social Theory Structure* (2nd edition), New York: The Free Press.

Messik, H. (1972) *Lansky*, New York: Putnam.

Messik, H. (1973) *The Silent Syndicate*, New York: Macmillan.

Nelli, H. (1976) *The Business of Crime: The History of Italian Syndicates in the United States*, Oxford University Press.

Philips, B. (1957) "Role Theory Approach to Adjustment in Old Age," *American Sociological Review* 22: 212-217.

Rose, A. (1965) "The Subculture of Aging: A Framework for Research in Social Gerontology," in A. Rose and W. Peterson (eds.), *Older People and Their Social World*, Philadelphia: Davis, pp. 3-16.

Rosow, I. (1967) *Social Integration of the Aged*, New York: The Free Press.

Rosow, I. (1976) "Status and Role Change Through the Life Span," in R. Binstock and E. Shamus (eds.), *Handbook of Aging and the Social Sciences*, New York: Van Nostrand, p. 457-482.

Rubin, P. (1968) "The Economic Theory of the Criminal Firm," in S. Rothenberg (ed.), *The Economics of Crime and Punishment*, Washington, D.C.: The American Enterprise Institute, p. 155-166.

Salerno, R. and J. Tompkins (1969) *The Crime Confederation*, New York: Doubleday.

San, B. (1971) *Kill the Dutchman*, New York: Popular Library.

Scott, M. and S. Lyman (1970) "Accounts, Deviance and Social Order," in J. D. Douglas (ed.), *Deviance and Respectability*, New York: The Free Press, p. 89-120.

Servadio, G. (1976) *Mafioso: The History of the Mafia*, New York: Delta Books.

Shanas, E. et al. (1968) *Old People in Three Industrial Societies*, New York: Atherton.

Smith, D. C., Jr. (1978) "Organized Crime and Entrepreneurship," *International Journal of Criminology and Penology* 6:161-177.

Snyder, C. R., R. C. Higgins and R. J. Stucky (1983) *Excuse: Masquerades in Search of Grace*, New York: John Wiley.

Sykes, G. (1958) *The Society of Captives*, Princeton: Princeton University Press.

Solomon, K. (1979) "The Development of Stereotypes of the Elderly," in E. P. Lewis et al. (eds.) *Sociological Research Symposium Proceedings* IX, Richmond, VA: Commonwealth University, p. 180-197.

Talese, G. (1971) *Honor Thy Father*, New York: Fawcett.

Talese, G. (1963) *My Life in the Mafia*, New York: Fawcett.

Toby, J. (1958) "Hoodlum or Business: An American Dilemma," In M. Sklar (ed.) *The Jews: Social Patterns of an American Group*, Glencoe, IL: The Free Press.

Vaugham, E. (1982) "Toward Understanding Unlawful Organizational Behavior," *Michigan Law Review* 80:1377-1402.

Zeiger, H. A. (1971) *Sam the Plumber*, New York: Mentor.

PART II: SENTENCING: BLIND JUSTICE?

Defendant's Advanced Age as a Prepotent Status in Criminal Case Disposition and Sanction

Gary Feinberg
M. David McGriff

INTRODUCTION AND REVIEW OF THE LITERATURE

Allegations of discriminatory practices have long been hurled in the direction of America's criminal courts. Gender, race, ethnicity,

---

Gary Feinberg is Assistant Professor of Sociology at St. Thomas University. He has an MA (1966) from Brooklyn College. He is formerly Assistant Director, Criminal Justice Programs, Nova University and has taught at the University of South Florida-Tampa.

M. David McGriff is the Executive Director of the Advocate Program, Inc. and a Visiting Professor at Florida International University. He has a PhD in criminal justice from the University of Miami (1985). He is a former Criminal Justice Coordinator for the Dade County Courts.

This paper was presented at The Conference on Elderly Offenders, April 23, 24, 1987, San Bernardino, CA.

and social class have each been targeted by researchers as possible sources of decision-making bias among prosecutors, judges, juries, probation officers, and other court officials (e.g., Willick et al., 1975; Frazier, Bock et al., 1983; Chesney-Lind, 1977; Hagan, 1974; Alder, 1984; Lichtenstein, 1982; Steffensmeier and Kramer, 1982; Walsh, 1984; Holmes and Daudister, 1984; Kelly, 1976; Welsh et al., 1984). Moreover, no major stage in the court processing of defendants has been exempt from criminological sleuthing for empirical evidence to either support such allegations or lay them to rest (e.g., Perry, 1977; Greenwood et al., 1976; Willison, 1984; Farrington and Morris, 1983; Welsh et al., 1984; Pope and Feyerherm, 1981; Myers and Tolarico, 1985; Wheeler, 1983; Friday et al., 1981).

Less well researched as a possible source of discriminatory practice in the criminal justice system is the variable of defendant's age. However, recent growing interest in elderly criminality, and especially shoplifting by the elderly, has spawned a number of studies about the basis, operation, and consequences of elderly justice. A recurring question addressed by several of these studies is: "Does a defendant's advanced age shield him from the more punitive reactions of the courts?" A considerable body of empirical data exists which supports the position that elderly offenders are indeed given sentencing breaks by criminal justice decision makers. An early example is a study by Dickens (1969) which found that both elderly and youthful offenders tend to be prosecuted less frequently in general than other age groups. A Canadian study of decision making by store security investigators echoes this finding, while at the same time noting that the defendant's age was second only to the value of the merchandise stolen in predicting whether or not a shoplifting case was referred for prosecution (Feuerverger and Shearing, 1983). In addition, Shichor (1985) infers from arrest patterns that elderly females might be handled more leniently than younger females where minor offenses are concerned. Cutshall and Adams (1983) look at senior shoplifters and the effect that the defendant's advanced age may have upon the prosecutor's decision to either prosecute or dismiss these cases relative to those involving younger shoplifting defendants. They too found support for the belief that elderly defendants are treated less severely than younger adult shoplifters. Advanced age, they contend, may be a mitigating factor in the enforcement of legal norms, at least with respect to nominal criminal offenses such as misdemeanant shoplifting. There is also Amir and Berman's (1976) study of elderly criminality and its prosecution in Israel. In addition to their observation that the majority of Israel's elderly offenders commit their first crime after age fifty—an important indication that aging itself may generate criminality—they found that case dispositions and sanctions for the elderly were not only different from those of younger defendants, but that they were especially less likely to be imprisoned and more likely to be fined. Lastly, we note here Jensen's (1977) finding that elderly prison inmates are only half as likely as their younger counterparts to commit additional offenses while in prison, and only one-third as likely to be punished for it.

Equally, a considerable body of empirical literature may be cited to support the position that elderly offenders are more severely sanctioned than similarly accused younger defendants. Primary among these is Bachand's 1983 study of official statistics regarding elderly defendants accused of either drunkenness or driving while intoxicated. His data led him to conclude that these aged defendants are more severely sanctioned for their misdemeanant behavior than similarly accused juvenile and younger adult defendants. Using a "mock jury experimental approach," Smith and Hed (1979) observed that "older defendants accused of either burglary or racketeering were judged more harshly than young defendants." The desire to protect the future of young persons, a minimal concern when sanctioning elderly persons, is their explanation for these findings. Feinberg and Khosla (1985), exploring judicial beliefs and attitudes about the kind of sanctions appropriate for misdemeanant elderly defendants, demonstrate that most judges are not especially sympathetic towards these defendants, tend to reject any effort to accord them special treatment solely because of their advanced age, and impose fines and court costs upon them despite beliefs that economic need motivates these offenses. Although the study does not go so far as to conclude that the elderly are more severely treated than similarly accused younger defendants, its findings are not inconsistent with such a position. In a major study of shoplifters by Lundman (1978), it is observed that elderly persons were more likely referred for further police action by lay persons, i.e., private security personnel, than similarly accused younger defendants. Lastly, we note Greenwood et al.'s (1980) study of variances in sanctions by age among three different jurisdictions which reports that younger adults received more lenient sentences than older (although not necessarily elderly) offenders. Further confounding our understanding of the relationship between the defendant's age and decision-making by the court is a cadre of research which suggests that any such relationship is really spurious. For example, Sordo and Fishman's (1981) analysis of the treatment of elderly defendants in the Israeli criminal justice system found that "none of the elderly differ significantly from those imposed on other age groups, and the proportion sent to prison was similar to that in other age groups." Similarly, Karpes and Farrington (1981), in an experimental study of sentencing by magistrates, observed that while severity of sanctions varied according to both legal variables (e.g., seriousness of the offense and previous record) and extra-legal variables (e.g., sex and socioeconomic status of the defendant), age did not have significant effects. Hagan (1974), in turn, studying both capital and noncapital cases, concludes that in either instance age is irrelevant to the judicial disposition when legal factors are controlled.

OBJECTIVES

As a case transits the criminal justice system it encounters a series of decision-making junctions where it is reviewed, evaluated, and disposed. Each disposition, in turn, typically involves a decision-making process in which a number of alternative courses of action are considered. These courses of action may be understood as ranging from more to less severe in their punitive aspect. This study explores the possibility that their advanced age may shield elderly misdemeanant theft defendants—a common type of elderly defendant from the more retributive reactions of the courts, resulting in age-based preferential treatment at these major decision-making junctions. The dispositional treatment accorded these defendants at seven major decision-making junctions is examined. Included are: (1) the likelihood of an arrest escalating into a prosecution; (2) the likelihood of a defendant receiving pretrial intervention; (3) the likelihood that a prosecution results in an acquittal; (4) the likelihood that a defendant is found guilty, but the judge withholds the conviction (adjudication) from the record; (5) the likelihood that a defendant is convicted; (6) the type of sanction imposed; and (7) the severity of the sanction imposed.

Although no formally derived hypotheses are tested in this exploratory study, three major questions give direction and meaning to our efforts: (1) Are elderly misdemeanant theft defendants securing comparable dispositions and sanctions as similarly accused younger defendants?; (2) Does any observed variance in the dispositions or sanctions accorded elderly misdemeanant theft defendants, relative to similarly accused younger defendants, suggest that advanced age results in the former receiving more lenient or more severe treatment by the court?; (3) Does a more adversarial defense posture taken by elderly misdemeanant theft defendants override any special treatment they would otherwise receive due to their advanced age?

METHOD

Using records of the Dade County Court, Eleventh Judicial Circuit of Florida, for the year end 1985, all defendants charged with misdemeanant theft were computer accessed. If defendants had multiple misdemeanant charges, they were included only when the most serious charge was theft. The sample unit is the defendant, not the case. Consequently, each defendant appears only once in the sample. Defendants are separated into three age groups; (1) 60+, "The Elderly" (N = 682); (2) 25-59, "Mainstream Adults" (N = 5,203); and (3) 18-24, "Young Adults" (N = 1,995). Each age group is further subdivided to control for sex (male/female) and race (black/white). The total sample contains 7,880 defendants, including 392 elderly females, 290 elderly males, 36 elderly blacks and 646 elderly whites. Similar elaboration procedures are used to control for three legal variables believed to affect case disposition and sanction: (1) Plea (Guilty, including Nolo Contendere/Not Guilty); (2) Attorney (Represented/Unrepresented); (3) Type of Attorney (Public Defender/Private Counsel).

Those who plead not guilty and who employ a private attorney are designated "More Adversarial." Those who plead guilty but who abstain from representation by a private attorney are designated "Non Adversarial." The remainder are intermediaries: those pleading guilty but having a private attorney are labelled more adversarial than those pleading guilty without a private attorney, and those pleading not guilty but engaging a pro se defense are determined to be less adversarial than those pleading not guilty but who enjoy the benefits of a private legal representation. All efforts to interpret the presence or absence of an attorney as indicative of a defendant's adversarial propensity are limited solely to instances where attorneys are privately secured by the defendant. Those represented by public defendants are excluded. This is necessary because judges in this jurisdiction have a confounding influence upon the likelihood that public defenders are present in misdemeanant theft cases. Specifically, judges will provide public defenders to misdemeanant theft defendants only when the prosecutor seeks a jail sentence. Correlatively, in such instances, judges will reject a pro se defense, and will appoint a public defender to any defendant who refuses the services of, or cannot afford, a private attorney. For all other descriptive and analytic purposes in this research study, however, any reference to attorney presence or absence includes public defenders and private attorneys alike.

Two sets of dependent variables are distinguished and operationalized: (1) Case Dispositions and (2) Sanctions. Case dispositions are subdivided into five categories: (1) Dismissed; (2) Pretrial Intervention; (3) Acquittal; (4) Withheld Adjudication; and (5) Conviction. Sanctions are divided into three categories and several subcategories: (1) Economic Penalties (including: [a] fines—rate and amount—plus court costs and [b] bond estreatures); (2) Probation (including: [a] reporting probation and [b] non-reporting probation); and (3) Total Incarceration Liability (including: [a] time served and [b] jail sentence). Where multiple sanctions are imposed, each is included as a separate entry when calculating sanction frequencies.

Analyses are simple and direct. Essentially a series of 2 × 2 and 2 × 3 tables are constructed systematically interfacing the dependent and independent variables. Chi-Square tests of significance complemented by Phi-Square tests of association are implemented.

In addition, difference in proportions tests (Z-scores and T-tests depending upon subsample size) are employed as we systematically compared and rotated the various case disposition alternatives and interfaced them with alternative combinations of age, sex, race, and defense styles. The .05 level of significance is used throughout. However, given the study's exploratory nature, occasionally probes are done to see if observed statistically significant relationships endure at more conservative levels of significance.

Limitations

Four problems especially concerned us in making our analyses. We did not control for previous arrest record. While others who have studied elderly offenders and their treatment in the arms of the criminal justice system have been plagued by a similar dilemma, there are at least three mitigating circumstances in the research at hand. (1) Known third time offenders are processed as felons and are thus removed from our data bank. (2) While previous arrests may influence judicial and prosecutorial decision-making regarding case disposition and related sanctions, it does so only where the court is aware of such a record. This court typically retrieves only two years when searching a misdemeanant defendant's previous arrest history and current warrants. Such searches are further restricted in that crimes committed in other states or countries within this period may not be called up at all due to the cost and time involved. Add to this the problems of alias use and lost identities, and any notion that the court itself consistently and validly distinguishes between previous offenders and first timers is highly questionable. (3) We do not control for offense seriousness. While this is somewhat mitigated by the fact that we are working solely with misdemeanant theft and the overall seriousness of the offense thereby has a limited range, still we must realize that the court likely distinguishes between the amateur theft of a two dollar can of tuna fish for personal consumption and the professional theft of a ninety dollar camera for resale when considering alternative dispositions and possible sanctions. To the extent that this is not controlled, our findings are limited and must be viewed with caution. (4) Dade County is not a typical American county and very possibly the elderly living here differ in significant ways from the elderly nationwide. To the extent that they do indeed differ, any effort at generalizing our findings must be suitably checked. At the same time, it must be recognized that Dade County, Florida and its elderly population are not totally unique. Indeed, we posit that in many ways relevant to this research they are typical of the elderly living in other sunbelt states, and thus profile a significant minority of the elderly. In addition, we project that if the elderly in Dade County are somewhat wealthier than the elderly nationally, and if they are also somewhat more mobile, better educated, and of higher occupational status than the rest of the nation's elderly, they probably constitute an anticipatory sample of what this greater population will look like five years hence.

FINDINGS

Does a Defendant's Advanced Age Effect Case Disposition?

The majority (57/3%) of elderly misdemeanant theft defendants are convicted, generally after entering a guilty plea (65.4%). However, this is a significantly lower conviction rate than the 66.8% observed for their counterparts 25-59 (Z = 4.91) or the 66.1% noted for those 18-24 (Z = 4.13). At the same time, these elderly misdemeanant theft defendants are significantly more likely to enjoy the grace of a withheld adjudication, a special disposition equivalent to a conviction but which mitigates its negative consequences by preventing the existence of a criminal record. Specifically, 47.4% of all dispositions involving elderly misdemeanant theft defendants consummate in withheld adjudications compared to only 22.4% of those involving defendants ages 25-59 (Z = 13.87) or 29.3% of those 18-24 (Z = 8.43). Approximately one-fourth (24.1%) of all elderly misdemeanant theft defendants terminate in some form of pretrial intervention. A disposition often considered more lenient, pretrial intervention is used only infrequently for younger misdemeanant theft defendants 25-59 (12.5%) or 18-24 (11.7%). However, comparisons with both younger groups reveal that pretrial intervention is significantly more likely to be given to those ages 60+ (Table 1).

Misdemeanant theft defendants regardless of age rarely have

TABLE 1. Correlating Age, Plea, and Disposition of Misdemeanant Theft Defendants, Dade County, Florida, 1985, Both Races and Sexes Combined

Disposition	Plea	Percent of Each Age Group Receiving Stated Dispositions — AGES 60+	25-59	18-24	Variance between those 60+ and 25-59 (z-score)	Variance between those 60+ and 18-24 (z-score)
Conviction	Guilty	65.4	81.9	83.2	9.23*	8.81*
	Not Guilty	17.8	8.5	9.2	2.91*	2.28
	TOTAL	57.3	66.8	66.1	4.91*	4.13*
Dismissed	Guilty	-	-	-	-	-
	Not Guilty	34.4	28.5	32.1	1.17	0.41
	TOTAL	6.7	8.4	10.3	1.52	2.78
Pretrial Intervention	Guilty	31.1	15.8	15.2	8.99*	8.26*
	Not Guilty	-	-	-	-	-
	TOTAL	24.1	12.5	11.7	8.24*	7.85*
Withheld Adjudication	Guilty	52.7	26.1	34.7	13.08*	7.51*
	Not Guilty	13.3	3.9	3.2	3.94*	3.73*
	TOTAL	47.4	22.4	29.3	13.87*	8.43*
Acquitted	Guilty	-	-	-	-	-
	Not Guilty	42.0	59.5	55.6	2.95*	1.89*
	TOTAL	5.7	9.3	8.6	3.11*	2.43*

NOTE: *Indicates statistical significance at the .05 level.

their case dismissed. Interestingly, elderly misdemeanant theft defendants are actually significantly less likely to have their case dismissed than their counterparts 18-24, 6.7% versus 10.3% (Z = 2.78), but they are no more prone to dismissal than those 25-59 (Z = 1.52). Since failure of a witness to appear is a major reason underlying these case dismissals, and further, since such failures may be related to fears of retaliation, it is perhaps understandable that youthful misdemeanant theft defendants are more likely to have their cases dismissed than older, less threatening types. However, this interpretation is somewhat marred by the fact that those 25-59 are about equally likely to be dismissed as thosc 60+ (Table 1).

Lastly, it appears that if elderly misdemeanant theft defendants fail to have their case dismissed or diverted from the courts through pretrial intervention, then it is highly unlikely they will be acquitted. Only 5.7% of all dispositions of elderly misdemeanant theft defendants result in an acquittal, a figure significantly lower than the 9.3% (Z = 3.11) or the 8.6% (Z = 2.43) manifest by their counterparts 25-59 or 18-24 respectively. Focusing solely upon those eligible for acquittal, i.e., those pleading not guilty, shows that elderly misdemeanant theft defendants are still significantly less likely to enjoy an acquittal (42.0%) than either those 25-59 (59.5%) or 18-24 (55.6%).

In sum, elderly misdemeanant theft defendants are in certain ways more leniently processed than younger misdemeanant theft defendants, i.e., they are more likely to receive pretrial interventions, withheld adjudications, and generally speaking, they are less likely to be convicted. However, their acquittal rates are also much lower than those enjoyed by younger misdemeanant theft defendants.

Do More Adversarially Oriented Elderly Defendants Suffer Similar Case Dispositions as Their Less Adversarial Cohort? Correlatively, Does Their Disposition Profile More Closely Resemble that of Similarly Oriented Younger Defendants or Their Less Adversarial Cohort?

Plea

Four informative observations emerge with respect to the influence of plea and age upon case disposition:

1. Elderly misdemeanant theft defendants who plead guilty are significantly less likely to be convicted than their younger counterparts 25-59 (65.4% versus 81.9%, Z = 9.23) or 18-24 (65.4% versus 83.2%, Z = 8.81). However, where these older defendants plead not guilty and thereby evidence a more adversarial posture, their conviction rates significantly *exceed* conviction rates of corresponding defendants 25-59 (17.8% versus 8.5%, Z = 2.91) or 18-24 (17.8% versus 9.2%, Z = 2.28).

2. Irrespective of age, a not guilty plea by misdemeanant theft defendants significantly reduces the likelihood that the court will offer leniency in the form of a withheld adjudication. Such beneficence appears reserved more for those who demonstrate the contrition of a guilty plea.

3. The relevance of plea in predicting the likelihood of either withheld adjudications or convictions decreases as defendants reach advanced age. This suggests that advanced age supersedes the significance of the defendant's plea in determining case disposition when charged with misdemeanant theft. Correlatively, plea is very relevant in determining conviction or withheld adjudication rates for younger misdemeanant theft defendants. Even the ratio of acquittals to convictions demonstrates that while plea is relevant for younger misdemeanant theft defendants in determining case disposition, its significance pales with advancing age. To illustrate: 59.5% of those 25-59 who plead not guilty are acquitted and 81.5% are convicted, a ratio of about 7 to 1. By comparison, for those 60+ who plead not guilty, the respective acquittal and conviction rates are 42.0% and 17.8%, constituting a ratio of only about 2.5 to 1.

4. Elderly male and female misdemeanant theft defendants who plead guilty are about equally likely to be convicted, 65.9% versus 65.0% respectively. However, where they plead not guilty, elderly females are significantly more likely than elderly males to have their cases so disposed, 24.6% versus 6.1%. Thus, it appears that entering an adversarial defense is more costly to elderly females than elderly males, at least when measured in terms of conviction rates. Alternatively, plea proves irrelevant in predicting the likelihood of conviction when comparing males to females ages 25-59 or those 18-24.

Attorney Presence or Absence

Attorney presence or absence is not especially determinative of whether or not elderly misdemeanant theft defendants will have their case dismissed. Correlatively, their failure to secure an attorney does not jeopardize this form of leniency. Nor does it effect their chance of receiving a withheld adjudication. In this the elderly differ from defendants 18-24 who are significantly more likely to enjoy the grace of a withheld adjudication if they assume a less adversarial posture, i.e., offer a pro se defense, than if they challenge their accusers through legal representation. On the other hand, having an attorney reduces the likelihood that the elderly misdemeanant theft defendant will receive pretrial intervention. This holds relative to younger defendants who have attorneys, but also relative to their age cohorts who enter a pro se defense. Concomitantly, having an attorney improves the probability that elderly defendants will be acquitted by almost 100%: 65.0% of those 60+ who have attorneys are acquitted as compared to only 37.1% of those who do not (Z = 4.91). In this they recapitulate the pattern evidenced for younger defendants. Alternatively, and somewhat unexpectedly, elderly defendants without attorneys prove significantly less likely to be acquitted than their younger counterparts. For example, 37.1% of those 60+ who lack attorney representation as compared to 53.5% of those 25-59 who lack attorney representation are acquitted. Lastly, in general attorney presence or absence is irrelevant to the likelihood of conviction among elderly misdemeanant theft defendants: 55.2% of those having an attorney are convicted as compared to 62.6% of those entering a pro se defense. Younger defendants demonstrate a similar nominal variance in conviction rates by attorney presence and absence.

Does the Elderly Defendant's Sex Effect the Disposition?

Elderly male and elderly female misdemeanant theft defendants are about equally likely to have their case dismissed. Furthermore, elderly females are not favored with a higher case dismissal rate than younger females. Nor are elderly males more likely to have their case dismissed than younger males 25-59. In addition, males 25-59 and 18-24 prove about equally likely as their female counterparts to enjoy any leniency associated with a given dismissal rate.

Taken together, there is not support here for the so-called "Chivalry Thesis" (e.g., Adler, 1975; Armstrong, 1977).

Essentially equal proportions of elderly female and elderly male misdemeanant theft defendants have their cases disposed of through pretrial intervention, 25.8% and 26.9% respectively (Z = 0.323). By contrast, females 25-59 are three times more likely to receive pretrial intervention than their male counterparts, 22.1% versus 6.8% respectively. A similar, if less dramatic, variance occurs between females and males 18-24, who manifest pretrial intervention rates of 17.0% and 8.5% respectively. These rates suggest that advanced age may be a prepotent status, eliminating sex-based differential treatment in case disposition by changing disposition reactions to males and bringing them into line with those used for females. Indeed, if anything, chivalry towards females in the form of higher pretrial intervention rates continues into advanced years, with males 60+ at last being accorded such special treatment too.

Younger females are significantly more likely to receive a withheld adjudication than their male counterparts. For example, females 25-59 have about twice the withheld adjudication rate as males 25-59, 24.9% versus 14.8% (Z = 3.79). However, elderly males and elderly females have approximately equal rates of withheld adjudication, 41.0% and 50.3% respectively (Z = 1.78). This suggests that while chivalry may be at work protecting younger females against the pains of a full conviction, such advantage of females relative to males disappears with advanced age. Moreover, this variance is eliminated because male rates of withheld adjudication become more like those of females as they achieve advanced age. In this manner, again advanced age is seen as a source of leniency in case disposition. It also appears to benefit males more than females, at least as measured by withheld adjudications. Taken together, these findings suggests that advanced age as a prepotent status surpasses sex as a determinant of leniency in the form of a withheld adjudication.

Generally speaking males at any age are more frequently acquitted for misdemeanant theft than their female counterparts (Tables 2 and 3). Focusing solely upon those pleading not guilty shows elderly males have somewhat, but not significantly, higher acquittal rates than elderly females, 54.5% versus 36.8% (χ^2 = 2.67). If anything, advanced age renders females significantly less likely

TABLE 2. Correlating Age, Plea, and Disposition of Male Misdemeanant Theft Defendants, Dade County, Florida, 1985

Disposition	Plea	Percent of Each Age Group Receiving Stated Dispositions, AGES: 60+	25-59	18-24	Variance between those 60+ and 25-59 (z-score)	Variance between those 60+ and 18-24 (z-score)
Conviction	Guilty	65.9	89.8	87.1	10.89*	7.79*
	Not Guilty	6.1	7.7	8.0	0.34	0.38
	TOTAL	56.9	70.4	66.1	4.77*	2.94*
Dismissed	Guilty	-	-	-	-	-
	Not Guilty	33.3+	29.5	35.1	0.45+	0.20+
	TOTAL	6.9	10.1	12.3	1.753	2.63
Pretrial Intervention	Guilty	32.2	8.9	11.6	11.08*	7.80*
	Not Guilty	-	-	-	-	-
	TOTAL	26.9	6.8	8.5	11.82*	8.69*
Withheld Adjudication	Guilty	48.0	18.5	27.4	10.81*	6.16*
	Not Guilty	3.0	3.4	1.3	0.12	0.75
	TOTAL	41.0	14.8	22.2	11.40*	6.52*
Acquittal	Guilty	-	-	-	-	-
	Not Guilty	54.5	59.5	54.2	X^2=0.31*	X^2=0.00
	TOTAL	6.2	10.2	9.8	Z=2.27	Z=1.91

NOTE: *Indicates statistical significance at the .05 level.
+N = 33, insufficient to be statistically stable.

TABLE 3. Correlating Age, Plea, and Disposition of Female Misdemeanant Theft Defendants, Dade County, Florida, 1985

Disposition	Plea	Percent of Each Age Group Receiving Stated Dispositions AGES 60+	25-59	18-24	Variance between those 60+ and 25-59 (z-score)	Variance between those 60+ and 18-24 (z-score)
Conviction	Guilty	65.0	67.9	77.5	1.02	4.14*
	Not guilty	24.6	10.4	12.2	2.87*	1.95
	TOTAL	57.7	60.7	66.0	1.11	2.76
Dismissed	Guilty	-	-	-	-	-
	Not Guilty	35.1	26.4	24.4	1.32	1.40
	TOTAL	6.6	5.6	7.0	0.77	0.25
Pretrial Intervention	Guilty	31.0	26.4	20.5	1.70	3.60*
	Not Guilty	-	-	-	-	-
	TOTAL	25.8	22.1	17.0	1.59	3.53*
Withheld Adjudication	Guilty	57.1	36.2	44.4	7.03*	3.72*
	Not Guilty	19.3	4.8	7.8	3.75*	2.07
	TOTAL	50.3	24.9	39.8	10.09*	3.37*
Acquitted	Guilty	-	-	-	-	-
	Not Guilty	36.8	59.6	55.6	X^2 =9.72*	X^2 4.89*
	TOTAL	5.4	7.7	6.6	Z= 1.59	Z=0.80

NOTE: *Indicates statistical significance at the .05 level.

than elderly males to so terminate. At the same time, advanced age has no impact upon the likelihood that elderly males who plead not guilty will be acquitted relative to their younger counterparts. Moreover, elderly females pleading not guilty actually prove significantly less likely to be acquitted than their younger counterparts 25-59 (36.8% versus 59.6%, χ^2 = 9.72) or those 18-24 (36.8% versus 55.6%, χ^2 = 4.89). Finally, no support for the chivalry thesis is to be found with respect to acquittals for misdemeanant theft (Tables 2 and 3).

Sex is essentially irrelevant to predicting conviction likelihood: 57.7% of elderly female and 56.9% of elderly male misdemeanant theft defendants are convicted, Z = 0.261. Focusing upon the more adversarial types, i.e., those pleading not guilty, elderly females are four times more likely to be convicted than elderly males, 24.6% versus 6.1% respectively. However, the variance, though extensive, is not statistically significant, Z = 2.221 (Tables 2 and 3). In general, adult females ages 25-59 are significantly less likely than their male counterparts to be convicted, 60.7% versus 70.4% respectively, Z = 7.19. Meanwhile, females 18-24, including those who plead guilty and those who plead not guilty, and their male counterparts share almost equal conviction rates, 66.0 and 66.1% respectively. In sum, for those refusing to plead guilty, females at any age are slightly but not necessarily significantly more likely than their male counterparts to be convicted (Tables 2 and 3). For example, 10.4% of females 25-59 who plead not guilty as compared to 7.7% of males pleading not guilty are convicted, Z = 1.27. By sharp contrast, among adults 25-59 who plead guilty, and thereby demonstrate a more contrite stand, females are significantly less likely to be convicted than males 67.9% versus 89.8% respectively, Z = 16.48. Young adult females 18-24 who acknowledge their guilt are also significantly less likely to be convicted than their male counterparts, 77.5% versus 87.1% respectively, Z = 4.96.

In sum, the data brought to bear with respect to the question of whether or not elderly female misdemeanant theft defendants are preferentially treated in the form of reduced conviction rates is at best inconsistent. Where they plead guilty they are no less likely to be convicted than elderly males, although they are indeed less likely to be so sanctioned than their younger female counterparts. However, where they assert a more adversarial posture and plead not guilty, they actually seem to elevate their conviction rates, both relative to elderly male and even their younger female counterparts. Alternatively, elderly males who plead not guilty are no more likely to be convicted than younger males who so plead. Thus, the court not only does not necessarily treat elderly female misdemeanant theft defendants more preferentially by limiting convictions, but indeed, where they assert themselves and challenge their accusers by pleading not guilty, the court appears to react more severely than it does to similarly defensive elderly males.

Does the Elderly Defendant's Race Effect the Disposition?

With rare exception, neither elderly whites nor elderly blacks are determined to be significantly more or less likely than their younger counterparts to have their case dismissed. Although eligible elderly blacks have a higher dismissal rate than eligible whites, 57.1% versus 32.5%, the number of blacks in this subset is too small (N = 7) to permit stable comparisons (Tables 4 and 5).

Elderly black and elderly white misdemeanant theft defendants receive pretrial intervention with about equal frequency, 27.6% versus 26.0% (Z = 0.222). Alternatively, younger whites prove to be significantly more likely than younger blacks to receive leniency in this form. For example, 18.9% of whites 18-24 are so terminated as compared to a nominal 3.6% of blacks 18-24, Z = 10.62. In sum, while racially based discrimination may occur between younger black and white misdemeanant theft defendants such that the former are less likely to receive pretrial intervention, it disappears among elderly misdemeanant theft defendants, at least with respect to pretrial intervention. Advanced age becomes the master status, replacing race and contributing to greater equality in the distribution of pretrial intervention. Thus, pretrial intervention rates of blacks grow to resemble those of whites as they achieve their senior years.

Advanced age for whites and blacks appears to mitigate conviction through withheld adjudication. However, elderly whites are not significantly more likely than elderly blacks to have their case terminate in a withheld adjudication, 48.2% versus 32.4% (Z = 2.32). Conversely, whites 25-59 are indeed significantly more

TABLE 4. Correlating Age, Plea, and Disposition of White Misdemeanant Theft Defendants, Dade County, Florida, 1985

Disposition	Plea	Percent of Each Age Group Receiving Stated Dispositions — AGES: 60+	25-59	18-24	Variance between those 60+ and 25-59 (z-score)	Variance between those 60+ and 18-24 (z-score)
Conviction	Guilty	65.6	72.1	72.9	3.01*	2.87*
	Not Guilty	19.3	10.5	11.1	2.28	1.78
	TOTAL	58.0	59.6	57.8	0.75	0.08
Dismissed	Guilty	-	-	-	-	-
	Not Guilty	32.5	28.3	39.2	0.78	1.04
	TOTAL	6.2	7.6	12.0	1.29	3.96*
Pretrial Intervention	Guilty	30.8	24.8	24.7	2.87*	2.47
	Not Guilty	-	-	-	-	-
	TOTAL	26.0	19.8	18.9	3.51*	4.69*
Withheld Adjudication	Guilty	53.3	39.1	42.2	8.00*	4.01*
	Not Guilty	14.5	5.3	2.9	3.07*	3.47*
	TOTAL	48.2	30.1	35.3	3.69*	5.14*
Acquitted	Guilty	-	-	-	-	-
	Not Guilty	43.4	56.8	57.3	2.25*	2.08*
	TOTAL	5.6	8.7	7.4	2.61*	1.44

NOTE: *Indicates statistical significance at the .05 level.

TABLE 5. Correlating Age, Plea, and Disposition of Black Misdemeanant Theft Defendants, Dade County, Florida, 1985

Disposition	Plea	Percent of Each Age Group Receiving Stated Dispositions: AGES 60+	25-59	18-24	Variance between those 60+ and 25-59 (z-score)	Variance between those 60+ and 18-2 (z-score)
Conviction	Guilty	63.0	95.8	94.8	8.00*	6.66*
	Not guilty	19.3	6.4	6.9	+	+
	TOTAL	47.2	76.1	75.4	4.01*	3.80*
Dismissed	Guilty	-	-	-	-	-
	Not Guilty	57.1+	28.7	23.6	+	+
	TOTAL	16.71	9.2	8.5	1.54	1.70
Pretrial Intervention	Guilty	2.7	3.7	4.6	8.56*	7.10*
	Not Guilty	-	-	-	-	-
	TOTAL	27.6	2.9	3.6	8.37*	5.54*
Withheld Adjudication	Guilty	40.7	14.3	26.4	X^2 =14.82*	X^2 =2.71
	Not Guilty	00.0	2.2	3.5	+	+
	TOTAL	32.4	12.2	21.8	X^2 =12.32*	X^2 =2.13
Acquitted	Guilty	-	-	-	-	-
	Not Guilty	42.9	62.7	65.3	+	+
	TOTAL	8.3	10.1	10.0	X^2 = 0.12	X^2 =0.11

*Indicates statistical significance at the .05 level.
+N60+ N= 7 (too small a subsample to calculate stable comparisons).

likely to enjoy the grace of a withheld adjudication as compared to blacks 25-59, 30.1% versus 12.2% respectively, Z = 14.92. Similarly, whites 18-24 are over 50% more likely to receive withheld adjudication than their black counterparts, 35.3% versus 21.8%, Z = 6.14. This difference is also statistically significant. Thus, racial variance in withheld adjudications disappears with advanced age, further indication that advanced age is a master status, supplanting race as a predictor of disposition leniency in the form of a withheld adjudication. Correlatively, it is observed that such equalization accompanying advanced age largely impacts upon blacks, increasing their withheld adjudication rates, and bringing them to a par with whites. No variance by race is observed for any age group in the likelihood of a withheld adjudication where defendants are more contentious and plead not guilty. It is when they are more acquiescent and plead guilty that one observes whites at any age are significantly more likely to be granted a withheld adjudication than blacks. The variance, however, is least for the elderly defendants (Tables 4 and 5).

Focusing upon those eligible for acquittal, i.e., those pleading not guilty, reveals that elderly blacks and elderly whites are about equally likely to be acquitted, 42.9% and 43.4% respectively. Corresponding younger blacks are slightly, if not significantly, more likely to have their cases terminate in acquittals than younger whites. For example, 62.7% of blacks 25-59 who not plead guilty compared to 56.8% of their white counterparts receive acquittals, Z = 1.70. While younger blacks are significantly more likely to be convicted than their white counterparts, elderly blacks and elderly whites are about equally likely to be convicted, 47.2% and 58.0% respectively, X^2 = 1.62. Elderly whites who plead not guilty are slightly more likely than elderly blacks to be convicted, 19.3% versus 0%. Younger blacks who so plead are also less likely to be convicted than their white counterparts. To illustrate: 6.4% of blacks 25-59 are convicted on a not guilty plea as compared to 10.5% of their white counterparts, Z = 2.06. In neither instance is the difference statistically significant.

Does Attorney Presence or Absence Effect the Disposition?

Attorney presence does not improve the likelihood of elderly misdemeanant theft defendants having their cases dismissed. The variance with those elderly who enter a pro se defense is not statistically significant, Z = 0.554. In addition, while entering a pro se defense is as likely to result in case dismissal among elderly defendants as it is for those 25-59, abstaining from attorney representation renders these elderly defendants significantly less likely to know any special leniency in the form of dismissals compared to their counterparts 18-24, Z = 3.11. Conversely, those represented by private attorneys, regardless of age, are about equally likely to result in dismissals, i.e., between 6% and 7%.

Having attorney representation reduces the likelihood that elderly misdemeanant theft defendants will receive pretrial intervention relative to younger defendants. Conversely, entering a pro se defense increases their chances of being given pretrial intervention, and, correlatively, enjoy any leniency inherent in such a disposition.

Attorney presence, regardless of plea, does not significantly improve the chance that elderly defendants will receive a withheld adjudication. Alternatively stated, failure of elderly misdemeanant theft defendants to secure legal counsel does not negatively impact upon their chances of receiving leniency in the form of a withheld adjudication.

On the other hand, attorney presence is relevant to the likelihood that these elderly defendants will be acquitted. Moreover, this holds for both elderly males and females, blacks and whites. At the same time, presence or absence of an attorney is irrelevant to the likelihood that they will be convicted: 54.2% of those having an attorney are convicted compared to 57.6% of those entering a pro se defense, Z = 0.505.

In sum, those elderly misdemeanant theft defendants who make recourse to legal counsel to protect their interests thereby reduce the likelihood that they will receive pretrial intervention. Nor does having an attorney improve their chances for obtaining such potentially mitigating dispositions as dismissal or withheld adjudication. Lastly, while attorney presence or absence is irrelevant to the likelihood of conviction, having an attorney definitely improves the elderly defendant's chances for acquittal. It also follows that the improved likelihood of acquittal associated with attorney presence on the part of these elderly defendants is achieved not by reducing the conviction rate but at the expense of higher pretrial intervention rates.

Does the Defendant's Advanced Age Effect the Sanction Received?

Age appears to be one of the most significant determinants of sanctions for convicted misdemeanant theft defendants. The dominant sanction for youthful violators is clearly a period of incarceration, either "time served" or a jail term. Indeed, 56.0% of those 25-59 and 46.6% of those 18-24 had spent some time in jail in conjunction with being accused and convicted of misdemeanant theft. By contrast, only 11% of those ages 60+ had been so incarcerated. The differences in the incarceration rate for elderly defendants and each of the younger age groups are statistically significant, Z = 16.60 and Z = 12.71 respectively (Table 6). Simply stated, elderly misdemeanant theft defendants are not spending time in jail while comparably accused younger defendants are. Quite

TABLE 6. Common Sanctions Applied to All Misdemeanant Theft Defendants by Age and Plea (Stated in Percents)

	Age		
Sanction	60+	25-59	18-24
Fines	22.8	8.1	5.6
Guilty	22.5	7.6	5.3
Not Guilty	31.3	34.8	20.7
Probation	31.8	20.2	27.2
Guilty	31.8	18.8	27.0
Not Guilty	31.3	30.6	37.9
Jail Time*	11.0	56.0	46.6
Guilty	11.5	57.0	48.4
Not Guilty	6.2	15.3	31.0
Court Costs	30.7	12.1	16.3
Guilty	30.7	12.0	17.1
Not Guilty	31.3	17.8	3.4
Estreature	4.6	2.2	1.7
Guilty	4.8	2.2	1.8
Not Guilty	0.0	0.0	0.0

* Includes both "Time Served" and "Jail Term."

possibly arresting officers are more prone to offer a "promise to appear" option in lieu of standard arrest-booking processes to older than younger defendants. Restricting these analyses to jail terms stemming from a misdemeanant theft conviction and controlling out "time served" sentences reveals the elderly to be least likely of all three age groups to endure such a severe penalty. The rates for those 60+, 25-59 and 18-24 are 1.5%, 6.9%, and 3.0% respectively. Variance in the jail rate for those 60+ and those 25-59 is statistically significant, $\chi^2 = 4.19$. However, elderly misdemeanant theft defendants are equally likely to be jailed after a conviction as the youngest group 18-24, $\chi^2 = 1.62$.

If some time in jail is the primary sanction for convicted misdemeanant theft defendants under sixty years of age, what then is the dominant sanction for those sixty and older? Economic penalties, especially fines and/or court costs and secondarily estreated bonds, clearly constitute the main sanction suffered by convicted elderly misdemeanant theft defendants. Indeed, those 60+ are significantly more likely than younger defendants 25-59 or 18-24 to be fined and/or dunned court costs. The respective proportions are 53.5%, 20.2%, and 21.9%. The variances in the rates for the oldest group of defendants and either of the younger groups are statistically significant, $Z = 14.71$ and $Z = 13.96$ respectively. Similarly, bond estreatures, a tacit and voluntary agreement to accept a conviction and to suffer an economic sanction, i.e., the amount of the cash bond, though rare for both younger and older misdemeanant theft defendants, is somewhat more common among those 60+. For example, 4.6% of those 60+ estreat their bonds as compared to only 1.7% of those 18-24 or 2.2% of those 25-59. In sum, a total of 58.1% of all convicted misdemeanant theft defendants ages 60+ suffer some form of economic sanction, a significantly higher rate than comparably accused defendants 25-59 (22.4%, $Z = 15.24$) or 18-24 (23.6%, $Z = 12.89$). Apparently, the court translates the need to sanction elderly misdemeanant theft defendants into economic terms, while similarly convicted younger defendants are otherwise sanctioned.

Probation is also a common sanction for convicted misdemeanant theft defendants at any age. However, those 60+ are significantly more likely to receive probation than their younger counterparts 25-

59, 31.8% versus 20.2%. On the other hand, both elderly and youthful misdemeanant theft defendants 18-24 are about equally likely to be granted probation, 31.8% versus 27.2%. Correlatively, both are differentially treated relative to mainstream adults ages 25-59. It is also evident that for elderly misdemeanant theft offenders economic sanctions (fines plus court costs) are significantly more popular than probation. By contrast, for their younger counterparts probation and economic sanctions are used with about equal frepequency, and both are significantly less likely to be used than a period of incarceration, i.e., a combination of time served or a stated jail term.

Do Adversarial Elderly Defendants Suffer Sanctions Similar to Their Less Adversarial Cohort?

Plea

Elderly misdemeanant theft defendants who plead not guilty are not significantly more likely to be fined than those who plead guilty, 31.3% versus 22.5%, $\chi^2 = 0.675$. Nor does the average size of their fines significantly differ from one group to the other. An almost equal proportion of those who plead not guilty as those who plead guilty are granted some form of probation, 31.3% versus 31.8%, $\chi^2 = .004$. Even the overall likelihood of doing some jail time in conjunction with the accusation of a misdemeanant theft is not significantly more likely to occur among those who plead not guilty relative to those who plead guilty, 6.2% versus 11.5%, $\chi^2 = 0.358$. Correlatively, regardless of plea, economic sanctions (fines and/or court costs) outstrip the likelihood of probation for these elderly defendants, while total jail liability consistently ranks a distant third.

The significance of finding that plea is not relevant to making sanction predictions where convicted misdemeanant theft defendants are 60+ years of age becomes especially salient when compared to findings for convicted younger misdemeanant theft defendants. More specifically, those 25-59 who plead not guilty are significantly more likely to be fined than their counterparts who plead guilty, 34.8% versus 7.6%, Z = 7.82. The average size of their fines also tends to be significantly larger. Similarly, those 25-

59 pleading not guilty are almost twice as likely to be granted probation as those pleading guilty, 30.6% versus 18.8%, Z = 4.02. On the other hand, those who plead guilty are not more leniently treated. Indeed, they prove significantly more likely to suffer some jail time in conjunction with their misdemeanant theft accusation than those who plead not guilty, 57.0% versus 15.3%, Z = 7.39. Further comparative probing reveals that for mainstream adults 25-59 who plead guilty, a jail experience is significantly more common than probation or fine and/or court costs combined. Alternatively, for those pleading not guilty, fines and/or court costs significantly surpass either the corresponding probation or incarceration rate.

In sum, while plea plays a significant role in predicting sanction outcomes for misdemeanant theft defendants ages 25-59, its relevance disappears as defendants mature into their senior years. With advanced age it is the extra-legal variable of age and not the legal one of plea which seems the more determinative factor in the sanction decision.

The youngest group of convicted misdemeanant theft defendants provide an interesting contrast to those 60+ and those 25-59, a kind of middle group with respect to the significance of plea as a sanction determinant. As evidenced by those 60+, but unlike those 25-59, fines and/or court costs are equally likely to occur among convicted misdemeanant theft defendants 18-24 regardless of whether they plead guilty or not guilty, 22.4% versus 24.1% respectively, $\chi^2 = 0.161$. On the other hand, those 18-24 who plead guilty to accusations of misdemeanant theft are significantly more likely to be jailed at some stage in the criminal justice process than those who plead not guilty, 48.4% versus 31.0%, $\chi^2 = 3.42$. Here they parallel those 25-59, but contrast with those 60+. The probation rate is lower for those 18-24 who plead guilty than it is for those 18-24 who plead not guilty, 27.0% versus 37.9%. However, the difference is not statistically significant, $\chi^2 = 1.70$. Also noteworthy is the finding that those 18-24 who plead not guilty are more likely to receive probation than to experience jail time, 37.9% versus 31.0%. The reverse is true for their counterparts who plead guilty, 27.0 versus 48.4%, $\chi^2 = 3.11$. Thus, probation is more likely to result when cases involving convicted younger misdemeanant theft defendants, but only if they plead not guilty. If defendants assert a more adversarial posture and lose, a jail experience is much more likely to occur. Fines and/or court costs, in turn, regardless of plea, are less likely than either jail experience or even probation.

Essentially, then, our data tend to support the general belief that plea is relevant to sanction determination, but only for younger misdemeanant theft defendants. Its relevance disappears with advancing age. In addition, the evidence suggests that of age and plea, the former is more determinative of the type of sanction misdemeanant theft defendants receive. Lastly, elderly misdemeanant theft defendants are significantly more likely to receive probation than those 25-59, but only if they plead guilty. Those pleading not guilty are no more likely to receive probation than those 25-59. The most lenient sanctions, i.e., a fine and/or court costs, also seems more common among convicted elderly misdemeanant theft defendants than it is among those 25-59, but not if they refuse to plead guilty. The benefits of aging in securing the more lenient of the two sanctions, i.e., fines and/or court costs versus probation, is predicated upon the contrition of a guilty plea. The cost to the elderly defendant is the somewhat greater risk of a jail experience, 11.5% versus 6.2% (+100%). For those 25-59, this risk increases even more, from 15.3% to 57.0% (+ over 200%) (Table 6).

Attorney Presence or Absence

The presence of a private attorney in cases involving convicted elderly misdemeanant theft defendants results in a slightly greater likelihood of being fined and/or dunned court costs than is true for their counterparts who employ a pro se defense, 72.7% versus 51.1% respectively, $\chi^2 = 3.91$. Probation for these elderly defendants is equally likely regardless of whether private counsel represents their interests or they defend themselves. The respective probation rates are 27.3% and 30.1%, $\chi^2 = .077$. A jail experience, although rare for elderly misdemeanant theft defendants in general, is slightly more common where no attorney is present than when they enjoy such legal protection. None of the latter but 10.6% of the former are so sanctioned. The transcending impression emerges that presence of private legal counsel to support these elderly defendants and protect their interests is not especially relevant to predicting their sanctions much less mitigating them. It also follows that once convicted, more and less adversarial elderly misdemeanant theft defendants are equally liable to fines and/or court costs. The same egalitarian pose is true with respect to the likelihood of probation or even incarceration. On the other hand, presence or absence of private attorneys does play a significant role in predicting the type of sanction imposed upon defendants 25-59. For example, 68.8% of those having private attorneys compared to only 21.6% of those employing a pro se defense are fined and/or dunned court costs, Z = 12.04. While the latter are less likely to be fined and/or dunned court costs, their chances of being placed on probation significantly increases. Only 15.7% of those without private attorneys compared to 31.3% of those having attorneys are placed on probation, Z = 4.41. Lastly, those adults 25-59 represented by private attorneys are significantly less likely to experience a period of incarceration than their less protected, pro se defense employing counterparts, 3.6% versus 48.6%, Z = 9.34. In sum, with respect to mainstream adults ages 25-59 convicted of misdemeanant theft, the benefits of having private attorneys are readily evidenced. They are associated with: (1) reduced probabilities of incarceration, and (2) greater likelihood of less severe sanctions, including both probation and fines and/or court costs. This describes a substantially different role for the private attorney than the one portrayed in cases involving elderly misdemeanant theft defendants, where attorney presence or absence has little relevance to the sanction outcome.

For the youngest group, i.e., those convicted between the ages of 18-24, presence of an attorney drastically reduces the possibility of their experiencing either a jail term or probation. Instead, the likelihood of being fined and/or dunned court costs is maximized. Specifically, whereas 47.1% of those 18-24 employing a pro se defense spend some time incarcerated, none (0/31) of those represented by private attorneys are so severely sanctioned, $\chi^2 = 27.02$. Similarly, only 12.9% of those represented by private counsel as compared to 26.7% of their counterparts employing a pro se defense receive probation, $\chi^2 = 2.97$. Lower incarceration and probation rates are matched by significantly higher probabilities of being fined and/or dunned court costs. Specifically, for those 18-24, the fine and/or court cost rate increases from a low of 22.3% where no private attorney is present, to a high of 77.4% for those having retained private counsel. This difference is also statistically significant, $\chi^2 = 50.61$.

Does the Defendant's Sex Effect the Sanction?

Elderly males and elderly females are about equally likely to be fined, 21.9% versus 23.5% (Z = 0.396). Younger females, however, are significantly more likely to be fined than their male counterparts. For example, 11.8% of females as compared to only 6.1% of males ages 25-59 are so sanctioned, Z = 5.84 (Tables 7 and 8). Advanced age eliminates the impact of sex as a determinant of the likelihood of being fined. It does so especially by increasing their use among males by approximately 300% but by only 100% for females.

While no significant variance is observed in the use of fines between elderly males and females who plead guilty, quite a contrasting picture emerges for younger defendants. Younger females pleading guilty have significantly higher rates of being fined than younger males. For example, females ages 25-59 pleading guilty are twice as likely as their male counterparts to be fined, 11.2% versus 5.6% (Z = 5.85). Thus, once again advanced age is observed to function as a prepotent status, eliminating the influence of sex and race as a determinant of sanctions for misdemeanant theft. Correlatively, observing the direction of the changes that advanced age brings as an equalizing force in the sanction decision suggests that males are especially likely to experience its impact. The latter, in turn, come to resemble females in their likelihood of being fined if convicted of misdemeanant theft. Also, convicted elderly female misdemeanant theft defendants average slightly lower fines than elderly males, $113.96 versus $126.92, but the modal fine is the same, $105.00. In addition, elderly females are slightly more likely than elderly males to have their bond estreated, 5.8% versus 3.0%, a pattern replicated by younger females relative to younger males. The variances are not statistically significant at any age.

Elderly males are significantly less likely than elderly females to receive probation, 26.7% versus 35.8%, (Z = 3.65). This, too, replicates a pattern observed for younger male and female misdemeanant theft defendants (Tables 7 and 8). In addition, elderly females are significantly more likely than elderly males to be given probation if they assert a nonadversarial defense posture, and either is significantly more likely to be given probation than their younger counterparts, 25-59. However, any assertion of a more adversarial defense posture results in treatment equal to or less favorable than younger adversarials with respect to being given probation. Lastly, attorney presence or absence is irrelevant in predicting the probability of elderly males or elderly females receiving probation. This is also true of their younger counterparts.

Does the Defendant's Race Effect the Sanction?

Younger whites 25-59 are significantly more likely to be fined than blacks 25-59, 13.0% versus 2.9% (Z = 11.02) (Tables 9 and 10). Similarly, whites 18-24 are significantly more likely than blacks 18-24 to be so sanctioned, 9.5% versus 2.3% (Z = 6.36). However, by their senior years, elderly whites are no more likely than elderly blacks to be fined, 23.3% versus 11.8% (χ^2 = 1.18). Thus, advanced age appears to diminish the relevance of race in determining the likelihood of using fines to sanction misdemeanant theft. Correlatively, elderly whites are significantly more likely to be fined than those 25-59 (Z = 6.13) or those 18-24 (Z = 5.82). Elderly blacks are also more likely to be so sanctioned than either blacks 25-59 (χ^2 = 4.25) or 18-24 (χ^2 = 6.24). Thus, the equilibrating effect of advanced age upon the likelihood of convicted misdemeanant theft defendants being sanctioned with fines is achieved by blacks and whites alike. In addition, advanced age appears to encourage use of fines in lieu of probation or incarceration more so for blacks than for whites. Age also seems to neutralize the relevance of having or not having attorney representation, at least so far as these economic sanctions are concerned.

No significant variance is observed between elderly whites and elderly blacks who plead guilty in their likelihood of being fined, 22.9% versus 11.8%, Z = 1.07. This is in contrast to the picture emerging for younger defendants. To illustrate: 12.3% of whites 25-59 who plead guilty compared to a nominal 2.2% of their black

TABLE 7. Common Sanctions Applied to Male Misdemeanant Theft Defendants by Age and Plea (Stated in Percents)

	Age		
Sanction	60+	25-59	18-24
Fines	21.9	6.1	4.6
Guilty	21.0	5.6	4.2
Not Guilty	100.0	34.9	2.2
Probation	26.7	15.3	24.1
Guilty	26.9	15.1	24.1
Not Guilty	00.0	25.6	27.8
Jail Time*	17.7	66.7	55.4
Guilty	17.9	67.6	55.7
Not guilty	00.0	20.9	38.9
Court Costs	29.3	15.1	17.4
Guilty	29.6	14.4	17.2
Not Guilty	00.0	48.8	27.8
Estreature	3.0	1.3	1.3
Guilty	3.1	1.3	1.4
Not Guilty	0.0	0.0	0.0

*Includes Both "Time Served" and "Jail Term."

counterparts are fined (Z = 7.68). Thus, once again advanced age is observed to function as a prepotent status, eliminating the influence of race as a determinant of sanctions for misdemeanant theft. Correlatively, observing the direction of the changes that advanced age brings as an equilibrating force in the sanction decision suggests that males and blacks are especially likely to experience its impact. The latter, in turn, soon come to resemble females and whites in their likelihood of being fined and/or dunned court costs if convicted of misdemeanant theft. Lastly, although elderly whites are more likely to be fined than younger whites, the amount of these fines tends to be significantly lower. This is not the case, however, with respect to blacks. Only two elderly blacks are fined making it impossible to draw any generalizations. However, whites 25-59 average lower fines than blacks 25-59, $118.15 versus $168.12, but the reverse is true for those 18-24.

TABLE 8. Common Sanctions Applied to Female Misdemeanant Theft Defendants by Age and Plea (Stated in Percents)

	Age		
Sanction	60+	25-59	18-24
Fines	23.5	11.8	7.2
Guilty	23.6	11.2	7.0
Not Guilty	21.4	30.0	18.2
Probation	35.8	27.4	32.3
Guilty	35.8	27.2	31.8
Not Guilty	35.7	36.7	54.5
Jail Time*	6.6	36.2	1.6
Guilty	6.6	36.9	1.2
Not Guilty	7.1	6.7	18.2
Court Costs	28.8	22.8	23.1
Guilty	28.8	23.2	23.6
Not Guilty	28.6	10.0	0.0
Estreature	5.8	3.9	2.4
Guilty	6.1	4.0	2.5
Not Guilty	0.0	0.0	0.0

*Includes both "Time Served" and "Jail Term."

Whites suffer slightly higher rates of estreated bonds than blacks at each age level. To illustrate: 4.8% of whites 60+ estreat their bond, but none of the elderly blacks do. The variance at any age, however, is not statistically significant. Indeed, neither age, sex, nor race is relevant in determining the likelihood that misdemeanant theft defendants will endure estreated bonds.

Race is also relevant in predicting the likelihood that convicted misdemeanant theft defendants will receive probation. Indeed, probation is used to sanction convicted elderly white misdemeanant theft defendants twice as often as elderly blacks, 32.6% versus 17.7% (Z = 5.09). Alternatively, intergenerational variance in the use of probation among whites is inconsistent. It is used about equally for older white offenders and for whites 18-24 (32.6% versus 28.7%), but significantly more so in the case of the older group than it is for those 25-59 (23.5%). Elderly blacks are no more likely

TABLE 9. Common Sanctions Applied to White Misdemeanant Theft Defendants by Age and Plea (Stated in Percents)

Sanction	Age 60+	Age 25-59	Age 18-24
Fines	23.3	13.0	9.5
Guilty	22.9	12.3	9.0
Not Guilty	31.3	42.6	26.3
Probation	32.6	23.5	28.7
Guilty	32.7	23.5	28.6
Not Guilty	31.3	25.5	31.6
Jail Time*	10.7	34.6	30.1
Guilty	10.9	39.9	34.1
Not Guilty	6.3	8.5	28.6
Court Costs	30.5	21.1	25.1
Guilty	30.7	21.1	25.8
Not Guilty	25.0	19.1	5.3
Estreature	4.8	3.9	3.3
Guilty	5.0	4.0	3.4
Not Guilty	0.0	0.0	0.0

*Includes both "Time Served" and "Jail Term."

to receive probation than blacks 25-59 or 18-24. Generally elderly blacks as well as elderly whites are equally likely to receive probation regardless of whether or not that they are represented by private attorneys. Thus, for neither race is attorney presence relevant in predicting probation likelihood.

Elderly blacks like elderly whites are less likely than their younger counterparts to do jail time as a result of their misdemeanant theft accusation. Specifically, 23.5% of elderly blacks do jail time compared to 63.6% of those 25-59 (Z = 3.39) and 55.3% of those 18-24 (Z = 2.60). These differences are statistically significant. Similarly, only 10.7% of elderly whites do jail time compared to 34.6% of their counterparts 25-59 (Z = 9.89) and 30.1% of those 18-24 (Z = 7.83). Correlatively, elderly blacks are not significantly more likely to be so sanctioned than elderly whites (23.5% versus 10.7%, Z = 2.09). Jail sentences, as distinct from time

TABLE 10. Common Sanctions Applied to Black Misdemeanant Theft Defendants by Age and Plea (Stated in Percents)

Sanction	Age 60+	Age 25-59	Age 18-24
Fines	11.8	2.9	2.3
Guilty	11.8	2.2	2.1
Not Guilty	00.0	13.0	10.0
Probation	17.7	15.1	26.0
Guilty	17.6	14.7	25.6
Not Guilty	00.0	43.5	50.0
Jail Time*	23.5	63.6	55.3
Guilty	23.5	64.0	60.1
Not Guilty	00.0	30.4	30.0
Court Costs	35.3	5.8	8.7
Guilty	35.3	5.8	8.9
Not Guilty	00.0	4.3	0.0
Estreature	0.0	0.3	0.4
Guilty	0.0	0.4	0.4
Not Guilty	0.0	0.0	0.0

*Includes both "Time Served" and "Jail Term."

served sanctions, for convicted misdemeanant theft defendants are rare at any age, for blacks and whites alike. Elderly blacks, in turn, are about equally likely as elderly whites to endure a jail sentence, zero percent versus 1.6% respectively.

IN CONCLUSION

The majority (58.1%) of elderly misdemeanant theft defendants receive some form of economic penalty if convicted. Indeed, they are more likely to be fined, dunned court costs, or estreat their bond than similarly accused younger defendants. That the courts respond to these elderly offenders with economic sanctions twice as often as probation is especially important given their fixed income, the high proportion living in poverty, and judicial belief that they generally suffer more economically than younger populations (Feinberg and Khosla, 1985). Correlatively, recourse to fines relative to probation greatly increases with the defendant's advancing age. Younger misdemeanant theft defendants are rarely fined (the rate for those ages 18-59 is about 7%), but they are frequently given probation (over 23% are so sanctioned). This variance is also statistically significant.

Generally whether or not elderly misdemeanant theft defendants plead guilty or not guilty is irrelevant to predicting their sanction. This is especially interesting since the reverse is true for younger defendants. Even the amount of any fine is unrelated to plea for the elderly, a stark contrast to the fact that higher fines are directly correlated with not guilty pleas among younger defendants.

Attorney presence or absence does not help predict the specific sanctions given convicted elderly misdemeanant theft defendants. The latter are equally likely to receive probation regardless of whether or not they had attorneys. The same is true for being fined and/or dunned court costs. Again, the reverse is true for younger defendants. Among the latter, those asserting an adversarial posture are significantly more likely to suffer economic penalties if convicted than their acquiescent counterparts.

In their senior years the likelihood of being fined and dunned court costs increases significantly for black misdemeanant theft defendants while the probability of jail terms declines and that of probation remains relatively constant. White misdemeanant theft defendants also experience a positive linear relationship between increasing age and the likelihood of being fined, however, the increment is less dramatic than it is for blacks. Also, unlike blacks, whites evidence no significant increases by age in the imposition of court costs. Most importantly, one gains the impression that with advanced age differences by race in fines and other economic sanctions disappear. Correlatively, for whites and blacks alike, use of fines and court costs greatly increases in frequency by their senior years, with a concomitant decrease in the use of jail time. Probation is only occasionally used for convicted black misdemeanant theft defendants of any age, including the elderly. Alternatively, it is a fairly commonly used sanction for convicted white misdemeanant theft defendants. Another variance by race in the sanction used for these offenders is that youthful and mainstream adult blacks are rarely asked to pay court costs whereas such fees are often imposed upon white misdemeanant theft defendants, and with little variance by age. Elderly black misdemeanant theft defendants, on the other hand, like their white counterparts are frequently dunned court costs. Lastly, whites at any age are generally only half as likely to do jail time in conjunction with a misdemeanant theft accusation as blacks, and both races experience major decreases in the use of this severe response with increasing age. Nevertheless, even into advanced years, some period of incarceration is the most commonly used sanction for black misdemeanant theft offenders (exceeded only by court costs) whereas probation is the most commonly used sanction for their elderly white counterparts and a period of incarceration is the least commonly used sanction (with the exception of a few instances of estreatures). The overall generalization emerging here is that advanced age for the most part eliminates the relevance of race in predicting the sanction used for elderly misdemeanant theft defendants. The major exception concerns probation, which even in advanced age seems to be favored for whites over blacks.

Among the elderly, sex endures as a relevant determinant of sanction. Elderly males are significantly less likely to receive probation than elderly females, and they are significantly more likely to receive time served or endure jail sanctions. A variant of the "Chivalry Thesis" may be at work here. In addition, while elderly males and elderly females are about equally liked to be fined, elderly males typically pay higher fines.

REFERENCES

Alder, Christine (1984). "Gender Bias in Juvenile Diversion." *Crime and Delinquency*. 30:400-414.

Amir, Menachem and S. Bergman (1976). "Patterns of Crime Among Aged in Israel: A Second Phase Report." *The Israel Annals of Psychiatry and Related Disciplines*. 14:280-288.

Bachand, Donald (1983). "The Elderly Offender: A Question of Leniency in Criminal Processing." Paper presented at the 78th Annual Meeting of the American Sociological Association, August 31-September 4, Detroit, Michigan.

Chesney-Lind, Meda (1977). "Judicial Paternalism and the Female Status Offender: Training Women to Know Their Place." *Crime and Delinquency*. 23:121-130.

Cutshall, Charles and Kenneth Adams (1983). "Responding to Older Shoplifters: Age Selectivity in the Processing of Shoplifters." *Criminal Justice Review*. 8:1-8.

Dickens, Bernard M. (1969). "Shops, Shoplifting, and the Law," *The Criminal Law Review*. 464-472.

Farrington, D.P. and A.M. Morris (1983). "Sex, Sentencing, and Reconviction." *British Journal of Criminology*. 23:229-248.

Feinberg, Gary and Dinesh Khosla (1985). "Sanctioning Elderly Delinquents: Judicial Responses to Misdemeanors Committed By Senior Citizens." *Trial* 21:46-50.

Feuerverger, Audrey and Clifford D. Shearing (1982). "An Analysis of the Prosecution of Shoplifters." *Criminology* 20:273-289.

Frazier, Charles E., Wilbur E. Bock, and John C. Henretta (1983). "The Role of Probation Officers in Determining Gender Difference in Sentencing Severity." *The Sociological Quarterly*. 24:304-318.

Friday, Paul C., Katherine R. Malzahn-Bass, and Donna K. Harrington (1981). "Referral and Selection Criteria in Deferred Prosecution: The Impact on the Criminal Justice System." *British Journal of Criminology*. 21:166-172.

Greenwood, Peter W., Sorrell Wildhorn, Eugene C. Poggio, et al. (1976). *Prosecution of Felony Defendants*. Lexington, Mass.: D.C. Heath.

______, Joan Petersilia, and Franklin E. Zimring (1980). *Age, Crime, and Sanctions: The Transition from Juvenile to Adult Court*. Santa Monica, California: Rand Corporation.

Hagan, John L. (1974). "Extra-Legal Attributes and Criminal Sentencing: An Assessment of a Sociological Viewpoint." *Law and Society Review*. 8:357-383.

Holmes, Malcolm and Howard C. Daudistel (1984). "Ethnicity and Justice in the Southwest: The Sentencing of Anglo, Black, and Mexican Origin Defendants." *Social Science Quarterly*. 65:265-277.

Jensen, Gary F. (1977). "Age and Rule-Breaking in Prison: A Test of Sociocultural Interpretations." *Criminology*. 14:555-568.

Karpardis, Andreas and Daniel P. Farrington (1981). "An Experimental Study of Sentencing by Magistrates." *Law and Human Behavior*. 5:107-121.

Kelly, Henry E. (1976). "A Comparison of Defense Strategy and Race as Influences in Differential Sentencing." *Criminology* 14:241-249.

Lichtenstein, Karen R. (1982). "Extra-Legal Variables Affecting Sentencing Decisions." *Psychological Reports*. 50:611-619.

Lundman, Richard J. (1978). "Shoplifting and Police Referral: A Reexamination." *Journal of Criminal Law and Criminology*. 69:395-401.

Myers, Martha A. and Susette M. Talarico (1985). *Disparity and Discrimination in Sentencing: The Case of Georgia*. Athens, Georgia: U.S. National Institute of Justice.

Perry, Ronald W. (1977). "The Justice System and Sentencing." *Criminology*. 15:225-234.

Pope, Carl E. and William H. Feyerherm (1981). "Race and Juvenile Court Dispositions: An Examination of Initial Screening Decisions." *Criminal Justice and Behavior*. 8:287-301.

Smith, Edward D. and Anita Hed (1979). "Effects of Offenders' Age and Attractiveness on Sentencing By Mock Juries." *Psychological Reports*. 44:691-694.

Sordo, I. and G. Fishman (1981). "The Elderly Offender in the Israeli Criminal Justice System." *Society and Welfare*. 4:27-41.

Steffensmeier, Darrell and John H. Kramer (1982). "Sex-Based Differences in the Sentencing of Adult Criminal Defendants: An Empirical Test and Theoretical Overview." *Sociology and Social Research*. 66:289-304.

Walsh, Anthony (1984). "Gender Based Differences: A Study of Probation Officers' Attitudes About, and Recommendations for, Felony Sexual Assault Cases." *Criminology*. 22:371-387.

Walsh, D. P. (1978). *Shoplifting: Controlling a Major Crime*. London: Macmillan Press, Ltd.

Welch, Susan, John Gruhl, and Cassia Spohn (1984). "Dismissal, Conviction, and Incarceration of Hispanic Defendants: A Comparison with Anglos and Blacks." *Social Science Quarterly*. 65:257-264.

Wheeler, G.R. (1983). "The Benefits of Legal Representation in Misdemeanor Court." *Criminal Law Bulletin*. 19:221-233.

Willick, Daniel H., Gretchen Gehlker, and Anita Mc Farland Watts (1975). "Social Class As A Factor Affecting Judicial Disposition: Defendants Charged with Criminal Homosexual Acts." *Criminology*. 13:57-77.

Willison, David (1984). "The Effects of Counsel on the Severity of Criminal Sentences: A Statistical Assessment." *The Justice System Journal*. 9:87-99.

The Elderly Offender and Sentencing Leniency

Gerri S. Turner
Dean J. Champion

INTRODUCTION

The U.S. Census Bureau reported in 1980 that there were nearly 26 million persons age 65 and over in the United States, or about 11% of the U.S. population. Within the next two decades, this figure will probably rise to over 32 million persons (Harris and Cole, 1980).

As the numbers of elderly increase, a corresponding increase in the amount of elderly crime has been observed by various researchers (Newman, Newman and Gewirtz, 1985; Wilbanks and Kim, 1985). Because crime committed by the elderly is often unreported or is handled differently compared with offenses committed by younger persons, estimates of the actual amount of elderly crime have varied considerably from one year to the next. Estimates of elderly crime range from 300,000 to 500,000 per year. Currently, no one really knows how much elderly crime is committed annually. But experts agree that crime committed by elderly is on the increase. In fact, there is evidence to suggest that elderly crime is increasing at a rate more rapid than for that associated with other age categories (Wilbanks and Kim, 1984).

Gerri S. Turner is an educational evaluator with the Tennessee Department of Education. She has an MA from Tusculum College and is presently attending Nashville School of Law.

Dean J. Champion is Professor of Sociology at University of Tennessee-Knoxville. He received his BS and MA degrees from Brigham Young University in 1962 and 1963; he received his PhD from Purdue University in 1965.

Elderly offenders pose particularly difficult problems for police, prosecutors, judges, and corrections officials. First, much of the crime committed by the elderly is nonviolent crime, although violent crimes by the elderly are increasing rather dramatically. While elderly offenders currently account for less than 5% of all crimes committed annually, their growing numbers suggest that dealing with elderly criminals will become increasingly problematic for all organizations within the criminal justice system.

In the corrections sector of the criminal justice system, current conditions of jail and prison overcrowding are forcing judges to be more lenient in their sentencing of most convicted defendants, shying away from incarcerating convicted felons whenever possible. Felony probation is rapidly becoming the rule rather than the exception (Petersilia, 1985). And the elderly offender is one of the most frequent recipients of felony probation.

In addition to prison overcrowding, our prison and jail systems are simply not equipped to deal with the special needs of the elderly class of offender. Special diets, special housing, and special medical treatments are often beyond the normal capabilities of most jail and prison facilities. Confining an elderly offender for any prolonged period taxes most jail and prison systems. In short, jails and prisons are designed for more youthful offenders. Recreational and educational programs are aimed at younger offenders, as well as vocational rehabilitation programs and counseling services. There is not much point to a rehabilitation program where a 90-year-old felon is involved (Newman, Newman, and Gewirtz, 1984; Shichor, 1985).

Much of the research on sentencing severity has focused on the influence of variables such as gender, race or ethnic affiliation, and socioeconomic status. Studies have shown that judges are more lenient with female offenders, more harsh with younger male offenders, and more harsh with blacks and other nonwhites as well as those from lower socioeconomic status categories (Gibson, 1978; Gertz and Price, 1985; Hagan, 1974; Hopkins, 1977; Kleck, 1981). Few studies have systematically investigated the impact of age on sentencing severity, however. Especially lacking have been investigations focused specifically upon the elderly offender. To what extent do judges extend leniency through lessening sentencing severity toward elderly offenders?

The present study examines sentencing severity of elderly offenders in a random sample of counties in Kentucky, Virginia, and Tennessee. Specifically examined are sentencing differentials between older and younger offenders in selected counties, and sentencing trends for offenders in diverse age categories.

METHODOLOGY

A survey was conducted of 166 city and county prosecutors randomly selected in a number of rural counties in Kentucky, Tennessee, and Virginia in 1985-1986. Bar association representatives in various counties hand-delivered questionnaires to local prosecutors. Questionnaires contained information pertaining to prosecutorial priorities, types of cases handled, and a host of other relevant variables.

Records of participating prosecutors were examined to determine types of defendants prosecuted, types of offenses, convictions, age, gender, and race/ethnic identity of defendants, and socioeconomic levels of convicted persons. Additional data examined pertained to the severity of sentence imposed by judges upon conviction. Sentencing severity was measured by taking the actual sentence imposed by a judge (in numbers of months) and calculating a ratio against the maximum possible sentence[1] a judge could impose by statute, considering the offense(s) committed. This yielded an AS/MS ratio (Actual Sentence/Maximum Sentence). Thus, an actual sentence of two years (24 months) where the maximum penalty might be ten years (120 months) would be 24/120 or .20. In situations where probation was imposed, this yielded a ratio of .00. Separate calculations were made for sentences involving some degree of incarceration as opposed to sentences involving probation as the alternative.

The period examined by the present research extends from 1970 to 1984. Only felony convictions were examined in these jurisdictions for this fifteen-year period. The category 65 and over resulted in so few cases, that it was decided to reduce the age of elderly offenders to "60 and over." This resulted in substantially more cases for comparative purposes.

Sentencing severity ratios were determined for all elderly felons in the participating jurisdictions for the 1970-1984 period. Ratios were also calculated for violent offenders compared with property offenders during the same time frame. Ratios were also compiled for a random sample of younger offenders for the same period, taking into account the similarity of offenses in both violent and property categories to make comparisons more meaningful. Thus, it was possible to compare overall sentencing severity ratios for elderly offenders with those ratios for younger offenders, controlling for type of crime committed and prior record of offender. Table 1 shows the number of convicted elderly offenders for the years 1970-1984, together with AS/MS ratios, for all participating jurisdictions.

There were 3,264 elderly offenders convicted in the participating jurisdictions for the 1970-1984 period. Table 1 shows that based on the AS/MS measure of sentencing severity, overall sentencing severity of these offenders appeared to decrease fairly steadily during the 15-year period from averages of .13 in 1970 to .06 in 1984. A significant reduction in sentencing severity occurred during the 1975-1976 time period, and lower sentencing severity ratios were observed in the succeeding years. Proportions of property and violent crimes among these elderly offenders for all years surveyed remained fairly similar.

Figure 1 shows AS/MS ratios for the 1970-1984 period. Clearly there is a downward trend during this fifteen year period when portrayed graphically. Again the drop in AS/MS ratios is particularly noticeable for the 1975-1976 period. Next, these offenders were divided according to whether or not they had prior records involving previous felony convictions, and whether these offenses involved violent or property crimes. Table 2 shows a distribution of 3,264 elderly offenders for the 1970-1984 time period according to prior convictions and AS/MS ratios.

Of the 3,264 elderly felons, 1,274 or 39% were prior offenders compared with 1,990 or 61% first offenders. First offenders were elderly felons with no previous criminal conviction. The proportion of elderly prior offenders is somewhat higher in these jurisdictions than is otherwise reported in national figures annually.

Table 2 shows that AS/MS ratios for elderly offenders with prior records are about twice as large for property offenders for each of the years examined. Also, there appears to be a systematic decline in sentencing severity for elderly persons with prior records compared with first offenders during this time interval. Elderly offenders with prior records had AS/MS ratios of .15 in 1970. These decline to .06 in 1984, compared with an initial first offender AS/MS ratio of .08 in 1970 dropping to .03 in 1984.

Figure 2 shows separate plots for AS/MS ratios for persons with prior records as well as first-offenders. Again, a similar decline in sentencing severity is noted, as measured by the AS/MS ratio.

In a subsequent comparison of AS/MS ratios for elderly persons who were convicted of violent offenses compared with property offenses, similar sentencing severity differentials were observed. Table 3 shows a comparison of violent offenders with property offenders for the 1970-1984 period. Table 3 shows that violent offenders account for about 35% of all elderly convictions. Property offenses account for about 65% of all convictions. The most frequent violent offense among these 1,143 offenders was robbery, accounting for about 45% of the total. Aggravated assault accounted for another 30%. Homicides accounted for about 8%, and rapes for about 4%.

In this instance, there are significant differences in AS/MS ratios for elderly offenders convicted of violent offenses compared with property offenses. Again, these violent offense AS/MS ratios are on the average about double the ratios for property crimes. Between 1970 and 1984, the sentencing severity declined for both sets of offenders, and dramatically so. For example, in 1970, violent offense AS/MS ratios were .19, decreasing ultimately in 1984 to .10, almost half. For the same period, property offenders had AS/MS ratios in 1970 of .09, and these systematically decreased to .03 in 1984.

Figure 3 shows graphically the difference in AS/MS ratios for violent and property offenses for the 1970-1984 period. Again, there are significant discrepancies in sentencing severity, and these discrepancies become more pronounced from one year to the next during the 1970-1984 period.

A key question is whether sentencing severity differs significantly for elderly offenders compared with young offenders when controlling for crime similarity. Because robbery represented the most frequent violent crime committed by elderly offenders, robbery convictions for younger offenders were selected and a sample of robbery convictions for younger offenders was compared with robbery convictions for elderly offenders. There were 516 elderly cases between 1970-1984 involving robbery convictions. For the same period, a random sample of 550 robbery convictions was selected from all younger offender convictions. These convictions were divided into those convicted felons (both older and younger) with prior records and those first offenders. Table 4 shows the results of this comparison.

Table 4 shows that when we control for whether the convicted felon has a prior record, younger robbers receive sentences which have AS/MS ratios over twice as large as the sentences received by older offenders. By the same token, first offenders who are younger receive sentences that are less than half the severity compared with the sentences they receive if they have prior records. This holds true for older offenders as well. But when we contrast younger and older offenders, older first offenders again receive a sentence having an AS/MS ratio which is about half that of younger first offenders.

A fairly large number of offenders, both old and young, received probation in lieu of incarceration. Since a sentence involving probation tended to skew AS/MS ratios downward, further analysis was required. For example, of the 550 younger offenders in Table 4, 48% (264) received probation, whereas 78% (402) of the elderly offenders were placed on probation. When the remaining younger and older offenders were compared according to their sentencing severity on the basis of actual incarceration, younger offenders (N = 286) had an AS/MS ratio = .55, whereas older offenders (N = 114) had an AS/MS ratio = .28.

The conclusion drawn from this table is that younger offenders are penalized much more severely compared with their older counterparts, when committing the same offense under similar circumstances. Controlling for prior records, older offenders with prior records who commit robbery stand a good chance of being penalized about half as severely as those offenders who are convicted robbers with prior records. There is a systematic leniency practiced by judges in their sentencing of older offenders compared with younger offenders convicted of the same offense.

Of course, it is impossible to control for all aggravating or mitigating circumstances surrounding the commission of any crime. Perhaps the youthful offenders are more violent in committing their particular robberies, or perhaps there is personal injury involved to a greater degree compared with robberies committed by elderly offenders. These are variables that are virtually impossible to control. However, considering a fifteen-year period in selected jurisdictions in three different states, reported figures suggest greater leniency accruing to a convicted felon because of age.

CONCLUSIONS AND DISCUSSION

Morally and ethically, it is difficult to accept judicial sentencing decisions pertaining to similar offenses which vary markedly from one case to the next. Normally, a first offender would tend to receive less severe treatment compared with someone who has a rather extensive criminal record. While it is difficult, if not impossible, to control for all aggravating and mitigating circumstances surrounding the commission of any particular offense, a general comparison of sentencing severity for particular offense categories should yield some rather consistent similarities.

If significant differences in sentencing severity were observed between persons of different races, for instance, the system would be attacked as racist and serious challenges to higher appellate courts could be made on the basis of discriminatory sentencing practices. If similar differences in sentencing severity were observed to occur for persons on the basis of gender or socioeconomic status, similar allegations of discrimination would be forthcoming.

These types of discrimination are difficult to detect, unless, of course, a researcher engages in painstaking content analysis of sentencing data, unravels the contents of pre-sentence investigative reports, does a background check of defendants, their employment record and other socioeconomic information, and performs extensive comparisons of sentencing patterns for persons of different statuses or racial/ethnic affiliations. Even after performing these various methodological manuevers, the result is often an indirect indicator of discrimination rather than a direct one. The presence or absence of either aggravating or mitigating circumstances can make all the difference in the world between a short sentence imposed and a long one. Who is to question the soundness of a judge's decision when a sentence is passed?

Age is an important variable in the sentencing process. In this research, age was seen as a determining factor in influencing sentencing severity. Older persons receive lighter sentences for committing the same or similar offense compared with younger persons. Logically, there should be little or no distinction on the basis of one's age, except, of course, when age is used as a mitigating factor. Age generally functions to excuse a person's offense in the case of a child or an extremely old adult. But should persons in their sixties be given lighter treatment compared with someone in their fifties or forties, particularly when similar offenses are committed and where all persons considered either have prior records or are first offenders?

In this research, AS/MS ratios were used to chart sentencing severity for elderly offenders during the 1970-1984 period. During this fifteen-year period, AS/MS ratios systematically declined. AS/MS ratios for elderly offenders, considering all convictions across all jurisdictions investigated, were less than half as large in 1984 compared with AS/MS ratios observed in 1970. The actual numbers of elderly offenders fluctuated considerably during the same time period. Therefore, no systematic increase or decrease in actual numbers of offenders was observed.

Considering one's prior record compared with elderly first offenders, first offenders typically received less severe sentences. This differentiation persisted over the fifteen-year period examined, and it was significant ($p < .001$, Z test for differences between proportions applied to all yearly comparisons). Persons with prior records received sentences, on the average, that were 15% of the maximum sentence in 1970, and by 1984, they received sentences that were about 6% of the maximum sentence. The use of probation was particularly prominent for a large majority of elderly offenders, regardless of whether they were offenders with prior records or first offenders. By the same token, first offenders in 1970 received sentences averaging about of their maximum sentences, while in 1984, these percentages decreased to 3% of the maximum sentences which could be imposed.

Elderly violent offenders compared with elderly property offenders fared less well in terms of their sentence severity. However, these sentences were much lighter for both categories of offenses when compared with younger persons in both crime categories. Elderly violent offenders in 1970 received sentences which were about 19% of the maximum sentences that could be imposed. For elderly property offenders, however, the sentences averaged about 9% of the maximum. By 1984, these differences had dropped to 10% and 3% of the maximum sentence respectively for violent and property offenders.

One of the most glaring differences likely attributable to age was observed to occur for robbery offenses, when controlling for first offender status and prior record status. Elderly first offenders and elderly with prior records who were convicted of robbery were compared with a random sample of younger first offenders and younger persons (age 25 or lower) with prior records who had also obtained robbery convictions.

Young robbers with prior records received sentences which were about 36% of the maximum sentence compared with elderly robbers with prior records who received sentences which were about 17% of the maximum sentence. When all offenders receiving probation were excluded (probation was counted as .00 in AS/MS ratios and thus skewed these ratios downward), sentencing severity climbed to 55% of the maximum sentence for those younger offenders who were incarcerated. This compared with 28% of the maximum sentence involving incarceration for older offenders. For first offenders, similar differences were observed. For instance, younger first offenders convicted of robbery received sentences which were 16% of the maximum sentence they could receive, whereas elderly first offenders convicted of robbery received sentences which were only 8% of their maximum sentences. Does it pay to commit serious crimes when you are particularly old? These findings would suggest that this is the case. Older robbers with and without prior records do much better in court compared with their younger counterparts, at least in the jurisdictions examined in the present research.

Obviously, there are associations between prison and jail overcrowding and the sentences convicted felons receive which involve incarceration. At present, our prison systems are designed for younger offenders and are not particularly suitable for older offenders. Older offenders presently pose special problems for corrections personnel, and no doubt these are considerations taken into account by judges when imposing sentences on convicted felons.

Age functions as a mitigating circumstance, but it appears to account for greater discrepancies in sentencing severity that it should, at least from the "just deserts" perspective. If we pay attention only to the crimes committed and ignore the qualities of the person committing the crime, then we must conclude that at least in these jurisdictions examined, the older offenders do not "get what they deserve." And, by the same token, younger offenders are discriminated against on the basis of their age.

But as various writers have noted, the numbers of elderly offenders, though not presently significant, are growing annually. It may very well be that by the year 2000, the system will be forced to make modifications in corrections and change drastically currently sentencing policies relating to elderly offenders. Perhaps prisons resembling retirement villages will need to be created, staffed with geriatric specialists who can cater to the needs of growing numbers of elderly offenders. The saying that "crime does not pay" apparently is not true presently for some age categories. Eventually, it will have to apply to all felons, regardless of their ages. This seems to be an inevitable consequence of present crime trends.

NOTE

1. It is important to note that the researchers disagree about calculating measures of severity or leniency in sentencing. Some researchers argue, for instance, that if two offenders are both incarcerated for one year for different kinds of offenses, this is identical severity (or leniency). However, one offender may have faced a possible maximum ten-year sentence, whereas the other offender may have faced a two-year term. For the person facing the ten-year sentence which could have been imposed by the judge, the one-year term is proportionately less severe than the sentence meted out to the person who could have served two years

in prison. Obviously, there is some relativism about how severity and leniency are interpreted. Use of "minimum possible sentence provided by statute" would not address the harshness of judicial decisions.

REFERENCES

Cavender, Gray, 1984. "Justice, Sanctioning, and the Justice Model." *Criminology* 22:203-213.

Champion, Dean J. 1987. "Felony Offenders, Plea Bargaining, and Probation." *The Justice Professional* (forthcoming Fall, 1987).

Cramer, James A. 1981. *Courts and Judges*. Beverly Hills, CA: Sage.

Eisenstein, J. and H. Jacob. 1977. *Felony Justice: An Organizational Analysis of Criminal Courts*. Boston, MA: Little, Brown.

Farnworth, M. and P.M. Horan. 1980. "Separate Justice: An Analysis of Race Differences in Court Processes." *Social Science Research* 9:381-399.

Frazier, C. E. and E. W. Bock. 1982. "Effects of Court Officials on Sentence Severity: Do Judges Make a Difference?" *Criminology* 20:257-272.

Gertz, Marc G. and Albert C. Price. 1985. "Variables Influencing Sentencing Severity: Intercourt Differences in Connecticut." *Journal of Criminal Justice* 13:131-139.

Gibson, J. L. 1978. "Race as a Determinant of Criminal Sentences: A Methodological Critique and a Case Study." *Law and Society Review* 12:455-477.

Goldsmith, Jack and Sharon S. Goldsmith. 1976. *Crime and the Elderly*. Lexington, MA: Lexington Books.

Green, E. 1961. *Judicial Attitudes in Sentencing*. New York, NY: St. Martin's Press.

Greenberg, David F. 1985. "Age, Crime, and Social Explanation." *American Journal of Sociology* 91:1-21.

Hagan, J. 1974. "Extra-Legal Attributes and Criminal Sentencing: An Assessment of a Sociological Viewpoint." *Law and Society Review* 8:357-383.

Hagan, J. and C. Albonetti. 1980. "The Differential Sentencing of White Collar Offenders in Ten Federal District Courts." *American Sociological Review* 45:802-820.

Harris, Diana K. and William E. Cole. 1980. *Sociology of Aging*. Boston, MA: Houghton Mifflin.

Hopkins, A. 1977. "Is There a Class Bias in Criminal Sentencing?" *American Sociological Review* 42:176-177.

Kelly, H. E. 1976. "Comparison of Defense Strategy and Race as Influences in Differential Sentencing." *Criminology* 14:241-249.

Kleck, G. 1981. "Additional Evidence on the Death Penalty." A Critical Evaluation of Evidence with *American Sociological Review* 46: 783-805.

LaFave, W. L. 1970. The Prosecutor's Discretion in the United States." *American Journal of Comparative Law* 18:532-548.

Newman, Donald J. and Evelyn S. Newman. 1982. "Senior Citizen Crime." *Justice Reporter* 2:5-10.

Newman, Evelyn S., Donald J. Newman, and Mindy L. Gewirtz 1984. *Elderly Criminals*. Cambridge, MA: Oelgeschlager, Gunn, and Hain.

Peterson, R. D. and J. Hagan. 1984. "Changing Conceptions of Race: Toward an Account of Anomalous Findings in Sentencing Research." *American Sociological Review* 49:56-70.

Rhodes, W. M. 1979. "Plea Bargaining: Its Effect on Sentencing and Convictions in the District of Columbia." *Journal of Criminal Law and Criminology* 70:350-375.

Shichor, David. 1985. "Male-Female Differences in Elderly Arrests: An exploratory Analysis." *Justice Quarterly* 2:399-414.

Spohn, C., J. Gruhl, and S. Welch. 1981. "The Effect of Race on Sentencing: A Re-Examination of an Unsettled Question." *Law and Society Review* 16: 71-88.

Sutton, L. P. 1978a. *Variations in Federal Criminal Sentences: A Statistical Analysis at the National Level*. Albany, NY: Criminal Justice Research Center.

Thomson, R. and M. Zingraff. 1981. "Detecting Sentence Disparity." *American Journal of Sociology* 86:869-880.

Unnever, J. D., C. E. Frazier, and J. C. Henretta. 1980. "Race Differences in Criminal Sentencing." *Social Quarterly* 21:197-206.

Welch, Susan, John Gruhl, and Cassia Spohn. 1984. "Sentencing." *Criminology* 22:215-227.

Wheeler, S., D. Weisburd, and N. Bode. 1982. "Sentencing the White Collar Offender: Rhetoric and Reality." *American Sociological Review* 47:641-659.

Wilbanks, William and Paul K. H. Kim. 1984. *Elderly Criminals*. Lanham, MD: University Press of America.

Zatz, M. S. 1984. "Race, Ethnicity, and Determinate Sentencing." *Criminology* 22:147-171.

TABLE 1. Number of Convicted Elderly Offenders in Participating Jurisdictions in Kentucky, Tennessee, and Virginia, 1970-1984, Together with AS/MS Ratios

YEAR	NUMBER OF CONVICTIONS	AS/MS RATIOS*
1970	184	.13
1971	254	.12
1972	171	.11
1973	190	.10
1974	221	.13
1975	336	.11
1976	185	.08
1977	172	.09
1978	163	.09
1979	232	.07
1980	294	.08
1981	193	.06
1982	187	.06
1983	244	.07
1984	238	.06
TOTAL	3,264	

*AS/MS Ratio = Actual Sentence/Maximum Sentence in numbers of months.

TABLE 2. Elderly Offenders and Sentencing Severity for the 1970-1984 Period According to Prior Record/First Offender Status

YEAR	PRIOR RECORD		FIRST OFFENDER	
	N	AS/MS RATIO	N	AS/MS RATIO
1970	85	.15	99	.08
1971	91	.16	163	.06
1972	88	.14	83	.07
1973	90	.14	100	.06
1974	89	.15	132	.07
1975	121	.14	215	.05
1976	74	.11	111	.04
1977	71	.11	101	.05
1978	61	.09	102	.03
1979	75	.08	157	.03
1980	98	.07	196	.03
1981	87	.07	106	.03
1982	68	.06	119	.02
1983	106	.06	138	.03
1984	70	.06	168	.03
TOTALS	1,274 (39%)		1,990 (61%)	

TABLE 3. Elderly Offenders Compared According to Property vs. Violent Offenses on Sentencing Severity 1970-1984

YEAR	VIOLENT OFFENSES		PROPERTY OFFENSES	
	N	AS/MS RATIO	N	AS/MS RATIO
1970	51	.19	133	.09
1971	72	.18	182	.09
1972	70	.17	101	.08
1973	89	.17	101	.07
1974	74	.16	147	.06
1975	92	.13	244	.04
1976	75	.15	100	.05
1977	79	.14	93	.04
1978	53	.13	110	.04
1979	71	.14	161	.03
1980	95	.12	199	.02
1981	59	.11	134	.03
1982	74	.10	181	.03
1983	92	.11	152	.02
1984	97	.10	141	.03
TOTALS	1,143	(35%)	2,121	(65%)

TABLE 4. Younger and Older Offenders Compared According to Sentencing Severity for Robbery Convictions, Controlling for Prior Records

	AS/MS RATIO	
RECORD	YOUNGER OFFENDER N = 550	OLDER OFFENDER N = 516
PRIOR RECORD	.36	.17
FIRST OFFENDER	.16	.08

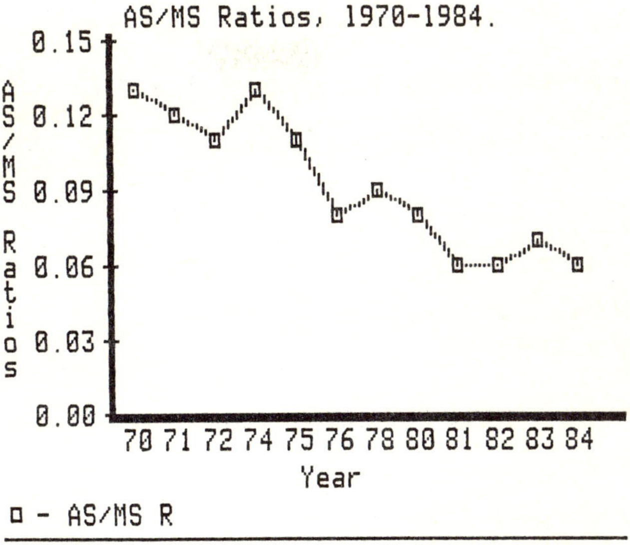

FIGURE 1. AS/MS Ratios for Elderly Offenders, 1970-1984

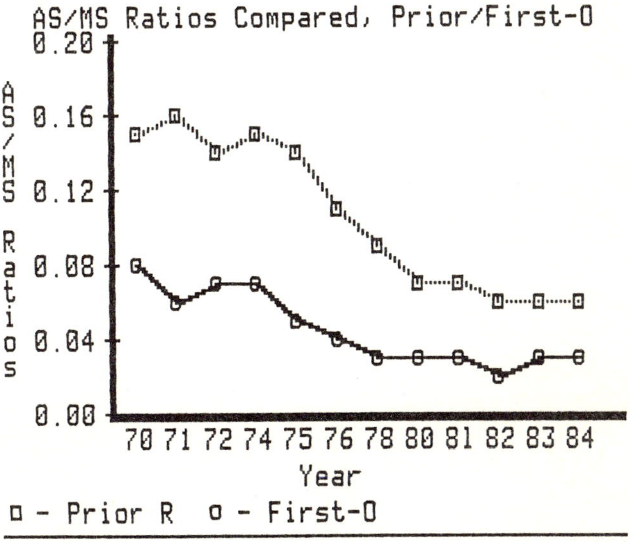

FIGURE 2. AS/MS Rations for Elderly Offenders, Prior Record/First Offender Status, 1970-1984

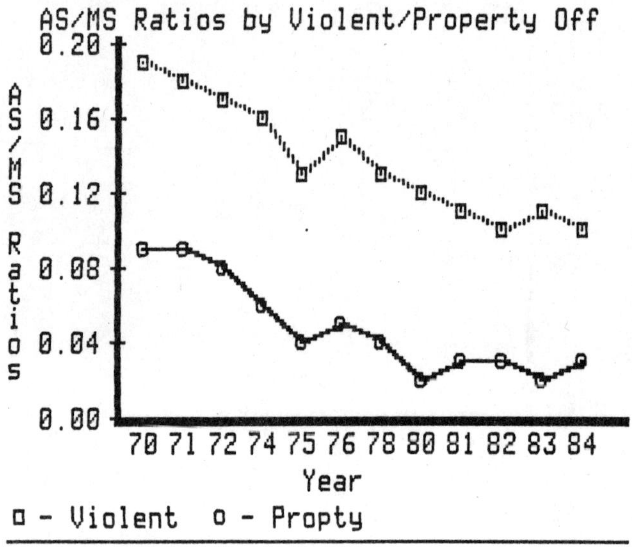

FIGURE 3. AS/MS Ratios for Elderly Offenders, Property vs. Violent Offenses, 1970-1984

Legal and Social Alternatives in Treating Older Child Sexual Offenders

J. Mark Watson

INTRODUCTION

The "Dirty Old Man" image of the child molester is fairly described as a popular stereotype. Actually, the arrest rate for sex offenses for males over 65 is dramatically less than that for males 25 to 29 (Atchley, 1985:293). Males over 65 are by no means grossly overrepresented, nor are they anywhere near a majority of molesters. The older offender represents some special problems to both the social services and the criminal justice system, however. The theme of this paper is to emphasize the complex nature of discussions involving situations in which the accused is an older person.

This paper is based on the author's experiences over five years on a professional review panel which advised social service agencies and the courts in the disposition of child abuse cases. The majority of the cases dealt with sexual abuse as at least one aspect of the situation. Older obusers, while not uncommon, were not the majority of the cases but did present some of the more complex situations. The author also teaches in the field of social gerontology and has worked in community mental health in areas such as mental illness, alcoholism, and related problems. In that capacity he has been involved as either caseworker or consultant in a range of deci-

J. Mark Watson is Professor of Sociology at Tennessee Technological University. He has an MA (1970) and PhD (1974) in Sociology from University of Tennessee and MBA (1984) from Tennessee Technological University. He has taught at University of North Carolina-Charlotte.

sions regarding the disposition of cases involving deviant geriatric clients.

The paper is not presented as original research, but as an attempt to organize personal professional experience into a format from which others might benefit in their attempts to either deal with similar clinical situations or as a basis for developing empirical research designs.

THE PRINCIPLE OF DIMINISHED RESPONSIBILITY

The legal literature on the principles of sanity and culpability indicate that guilt depends on either one's ability to control one's behavior or one's awareness of the difference between right and wrong (Sykes, 1967). We have briefly mentioned the stereotype of the "dirty old man" child molester which may lead to an exceptional sensitivity to suspicious behavior among older males in child-contact situations. Regardless of the validity of the stereotype, its existence does lead to a number of accusations directed toward older males. A parallel stereotype, variously defined but generally referred to as senility, may offer a legal defense against accusations (Hall, 1966). Senility, arteriosclerosis of the brain, organic brain syndrome (O.B.S.), senile dementia, Alzheimer's Disease, and similar age related diagnoses can offer a legally and socially legitimate excuse for inappropriate sexual behavior between the older person and a child. Most older people have a history which, when "reconstructed" in the light of an accusation, can be used as a defense against culpability (Wand, 1969).

The public generally wants to disassociate itself from sexual deviants, and generally believes that normal older people are sexless or have a significant reduction in interest in sexual issues (Harris and Associates, 1975). Without credible sexual motive due to advanced age, it is not difficult to invoke a diminished capacity or similar defense.

A diminished capacity defense is particularly beneficial in an emotionally charged area such as child molestation because it defuses the revenge motive for prosecution. Older people, if properly portrayed, present a reasonably pitiable self, so the public is generally ready to accept an excuse such as one based on age-related diminished responsibility. Prosecutors probably are relieved as well, faced with competing problems in deciding what to do with an older offender. These issues are not trivial questions. Failure to prosecute often severely limits other, nonlegal, alternatives for treatment, however.

REHABILITATION VERSUS REVENGE

The classical dilemma of rehabilitation versus revenge is particularly easily resolved with the older accused. The issue usually comes down squarely on the side of rehabilitation, if possible. If not possible, restricting access to children is the preferred sanction, a relatively mild alternative and yet the sanction closest to a revenge or punishment approach. The problem for the case manager is not making a choice for action, but implementing it. There is no evidence that child molesters of any age can be rehabilitated (Prentky and Knight, 1986). This is an issue with younger offenders, as society is generally more interested in revenge or punishment. For the older offender, however, the desire to find appropriate rehabilitation services is common.

TREATMENT ALTERNATIVES

Prisons

Courts are reluctant to resort to long-term incarceration for both humanitarian and legal reasons. Few prisons are capable of caring for elderly, especially frail elderly persons. To the frail elderly, a prison sentence can be a death sentence. The usual expense of prison can also be exacerbated by the very high cost of medical care for older people, averaging about three times that of younger people (Brady and Persily, 1984). Studies of forced relocation of older people indicate an exceptionally high death rate, so a cruel-and-unusual-punishment defense would easily be mounted in many cases (Lieberman, 1961; Lawton and Yaffe, 1970).

Psychiatry

The psychiatric bias against older people leads back to Sigmund Freud, who believed that psychoanalysis was for younger people (Kastenbaum, 1969). Added to this bias is the medical bias against geriatric patients, and the tendency to use untreatable diagnoses for older patients (e.g., O.B.S., arteriosclerosis, etc. [see Riley, Johnson and Fauer, 1972]). Consequently, psychiatric treatment is generally useless for older sexual offenders.

Vocational Rehabilitation

State rehabilitation service policies also are a problem. Many forms of mental or behavioral problems (drugs, alcohol, etc.) are the basis for qualification as a funded rehabilitation client. Such programs are usually titled Vocational Rehabilitation Programs. Older people are not generally eligible, because they are not seen as a valid vocational subject—too old to work or to return the taxpayer's investment before retirement or the development of another disability. A pattern of discrimination in a whole range of social services against older clients has been documented by the U.S. Commission on Civil Rights (U.S. Commission on Civil Rights, 1977).

Institutionalization

Environmental manipulations involving total institutions such as nursing homes, mental hospitals, or restructuring family living situations are more frequent than actual personal rehabilitation. Some problems exist with this option, also. I have never seen a nursing home that would knowingly admit a sexual deviant (or most other forms of behavioral deviance). Many consider *any* sexually active resident a problem. However, many deviant older people are placed in nursing homes based on some medical diagnosis, with no mention made of the "precipitating event" (Baer et al., 1970).

Mental Health

Court commitment to a mental hospital remains a distinct alternative, but the recent trend is toward emptying these institutions. Commitment is a lengthy and expensive process, so it is generally reserved as a last resort by prosecutors. A criminal conviction could result in the criminally insane ward becoming a possibility, but in the absence of a conviction, this may not be viable.

Family Placement

Though not necessarily a formal process, families may intervene and persuade authorities that they can prevent a recurrence by exercising control over the older member. This can work if the offender is not being placed in a family unit in which the victim also resides. Inappropriate placement is rare, but in cases where Grandpa lives with the uncle and aunt of the victim, there are frequent occasions for repeat offenses. In the isolated extended family found in some areas, the repeat offense of incestuous molestation is common. Unfortunately, family traditions may be difficult stop, and family defenses may be raised in some cases of outside intervention.

Family placement is the most unfortunate in terms of lack of alternatives. Frankly, when no one wants to treat, rehabilitate, or even warehouse the older molester, much less the younger offender, the family is the last resort. With the isolated family, the offender represents an untenable extra burden. Family denial of the problem is common. Custody of the offending parent may be accepted, though rarely is supervision exercised. Generally, little is done by the family to restrict access to children and case workers may become overworked and actively resented in their roles as watchdogs. It is not uncommon to enlist neighbors or in-laws in this "watchdog" process. There are some obvious risks of civil action in recruiting neighbors or others as watchdogs as this may involve public discussions of the character of an unconvicted accused. In the absence of effective prosecution, civil risk of slander is especially real.

CONCLUSION

The elderly child molester is a problem with which no one wants to deal. The public is not readily convinced that the accused is culpable. Motive and accountability are hard to demonstrate.

Personal rehabilitation services generally prefer younger clients either by design or due to age-related prejudice.

Penal facilities are expensive and not suitable for older persons, especially frail older persons. Private care facilities such as nursing homes do not want problem clients.

The net result is that the family, as an institution of last resort, is burdened with caring for the accused. This is especially unfortunate if the original offense is incestuous as it puts an overwhelming burden on families with children present.

The most promising programs at present include family casework counseling supplemented by community awareness and support for the caseworker. This approach, while effective, may not be tenable in the face of slander or liable threats against the caseworkers which can result if there is no conviction of the accused subject.

A final alternative is commitment to a state mental hospital for mere warehousing. This alternative is expensive and difficult to implement as the trend is in the direction of community treatment.

Finally, the importance of prosecution and conviction should be emphasized because they:

1. reduce the liability threat to protectors of victim (i.e., caseworkers);
2. open institutionalization alternatives;
3. increase the caseworker's ability to force offender and family to accept outside supervision of the offenders.

REFERENCES

Atchley, Robert C. (1985). *Social Forces and Aging*. Belmont, CA: Wadsworth Publishing.

Baer, P.E., et al. (1970). "Familial Resources of Elderly Psychiatric Patients." *Archives of General Psychiatry* 22: 343-350.

Bennett, A. (1984). "The Guilt of the Fathers" *New Statesman* 108: 8-9 D7.

Brady, Stanley, J. and Persily, Nancy A. (1984). *Hospitals and the Aged*. Rockville, Maryland: Aspen, p. 17.

Capel, William C. et. al. (1972). "The Aging Narcotics Addict: An Increasing Problem for the Next Decade." *Journal of Gerontology* 27 (1): 102-106.

Dowmen, Gregg W. (1974). "Must a Transfer Order Be a Death Sentence for SNF Patients?" *Modern Health Care* 3 (October): 44-47.

Garet F. K. (1975). "The Psychiatrist's Involvement with Aged Patients." *American Journal of Psychiatry* 132 (1): 63-65.

Garfinkle, Renee (1975). "The Reluctant Therapist." *The Gerontologist* 15 (2): 136-137.

Ginsburg, Arlene B. and Steven G. Goldstein (1975). "Age Bias in Referral for Psychological Consultation." *Journal of Gerontology* 29 (4): 410-415.

Hall, Gertrude H. (1966). *The Law and the Imperial Older Person*. New York: National Council on Aging.

Harris, Louis and Associates (1975). *The Myth and Reality of Aging in America*. Washington, D.C.: National Council on Aging.

Kastenbaum, Robert (1964). "The Reluctant Therapist" in Robert Kastenbaum (ed.) *New Thoughts on Old Age*. New York: Springer, pp. 139-145.

Kucharsi, L. Thomas et al. (1979). "Age Bias, Referral for Psychological Assistance, and The Private Physician." *Journal of Gerontology* 34 (3): 423-428.

Lawton, M. Powell and Yaffe, S. (1970). "Mortality, Morbidity, and Voluntary Change of Residence by Older People." *Journal of the American Geriatrics Society* 18: 823-831.

Lawton, M. Powell and Leonard Gottlesman (1974). "Psychological Services to the Elderly." *American Psychologist* 29 (4): 689-693.

Lieberman, Morton A. (1961). "Relationship of Mortality Rates to Entrance to a Home for the Aged." *Geriatrics* 16:515-519.

Prentky, R. A. and Knight, R. A. (1986). "Impulsivity in the Lifestyle and Criminal Behavior of Sexual Offenders." *Criminal Justice and Behavior* 13: 141-146 June.

Riley, M. W., Johnson, Marlyn and Fauer, Anne (1972). *Aging and Society*, Vol. 3, *A Sociology of Age Stratification*. New York: Russell Sage Foundation.

Rubenstein, Daniel (1982). "The Older Person in Prison." *Archives of Gerontology and Geriatrics* 1:287-96.

Starr, Bernard D. and Weiner, Marcella B. (1982). *The Starr-Weiner Report on Sex and Sexuality in the Mature Years*. New York: McGraw-Hill.

Sykes, Gresham (1967). *Crime and Society*. New York: Random House. pp. 38-43.

United States Commission Civil Rights (1977). *Age Discrimination Study*. Washington, D.C.

Wand, H. Shan (1969). "Organic Brain Syndromes" in *Behavior and Adaption in Late Life*, E. W. Busse & E. Pfeiffer, (eds.). Boston: Little, Brown and Co., pp. 263-288.

Wersham, Harold J. (1977). "Reality Orientation for Gerontologists: Some Thoughts about Senility." *The Gerontologist* 17:297-302.

More Than a Case Number: Older Offenders on Probation

Cathleen Burnett
Alice Kitchen

INTRODUCTION

Elderly Offenders have been largely ignored in research and policy arenas alike. Nationally, offenders who are over 55 years of age represent only about 3% of all offenders – a small proportion of the larger crime problem. But the older offender poses disproportionate problems for a criminal justice system that attempts to deal with issues of equity and punishment. Dilemmas range from the police decision to arrest (Wilbanks, 1986) to the management of incarcerated felons (Goetting, 1983; Newman et al., 1984).

One option available for handling the older offender is probation. Feinberg (1984) reports that judges prefer probation to other sentencing options 56% of the time; McCarthy and Langworthy (1986) state that the single largest group of adjudicated older offenders are those under community supervision. Despite this strong representation, very little is known about the older offender on probation. Most research has remained descriptive, using arrest statistics of age, race and sex to speculate about the social processes involved in

---

Cathleen Burnett is Associate Professor of Sociology and Administration of Justice at University of Missouri-Kansas City. She has an MA (1975) and a PhD (1980) in Sociology from Vanderbilt University. She is founder and President of the Society of Interdisciplinary Research on Elderly Offenders (1985-present). Her scholarly articles have appeared in *Legal Studies Forum, Criminal Law Bulletin*, and the *Journal of Crime and Justice*.

Alice Kitchen is the former Chief Probation Officer for Kansas City, MO. She has a MSW from University of California-Los Angeles (1972).

offending (Burnett and Ortega, 1984; Sapp, 1985; and Shichor, 1984). Alston (1986) indicates that lack of information about the older offender pervades the justice system. The one study conducted of state level probation and parole populations over 50 years of age (McCarthy and Langworthy, 1986) indicates twice as much information missing for older offenders as for younger offenders. Thus, qualitative information of background characteristics concerning older offenders is virtually unknown.

Clearly, decision makers in all aspects of the criminal justice system are faced with new challenges . . . preparing for an ever-increasing older population in a system designed for the young offender. Information regarding special needs and motivations of the older offender are important elements to insuring successful completion of the probation plan. From the agency's point of view, a profile of the typical older offender would assist in providing supervision that is appropriate and effective. Staff education and sensitivity can be developed when the probationer is recognized as belonging to this group, and sharing the common characteristics associated with those older probationers.

The objective of the project reported here was to develop such a social profile of older offenders on probation and to recommend services tailored to their special needs. This research, conducted during the fall of 1986, focused on those persons over the age of 55 years being supervised by the Kansas City Office of Probation. Those in diversion programs or on unsupervised computer probation administered by the Municipal Court were not included. Indepth interviews probed four areas of interest: (1) demographic identifiers, (2) social and financial support, (3) legal histories, and (4) attitudes and opinions of life adjustment.

This study offers a rare opportunity to gain insight into an increasingly significant area of research, combining academic interests of criminology and gerontology with the applied interests of social service and corrections. Therefore, research findings are presented along with policy recommendations. As with any research, the study has generated additional questions in the process of addressing the initial research objectives. Implications for program evaluation are also discussed.

METHODOLOGY AND SAMPLE

The Kansas City Office of Probation supervises persons placed on probation by the Municipal Division of the Sixteenth Judicial Court and those persons referred by the appeals court, The Associate Circuit Division of the 16th Circuit. Eight Judges preside five days a week, typically hearing more than 1,000 cases per day. Persons convicted at both levels may be placed under supervision for a maximum of two years.

The Office of Probation is a division of the Urban Community Services Department, one of 20 city departments. The staff consists of 17 probation officers and five clerical support staff. The level of probation supervision varies according to the conditions ordered by each Judge. Supervision may include checking police records for repeat contact with law enforcement, regular meetings with a probation officer, group meetings, or specialized services dealing with alcohol/drug abuse, shoplifting, and sex offenses. Persons who comply with the conditions required by the Court successfully complete their probation. Those who do not fulfill those obligations are scheduled to go before the Judge to explain their non-compliance.

A first offender pretrial diversion program, Project Redirection, is administered by the Office of Probation. This program receives referrals primarily from the Prosecutor's Office. Although the program is generally thought to be designed for youthful first offenders, many judges have referred persons over 50 who appear to have no previous police record. Since Project Redirection is totally separate in structure from probation, their participants were not included in the study. Excluding this group may distort the characteristics of older offenders under community supervision, especially in the area of the shoplifting offense.

STATEMENT OF PROBLEM

At the time this project was begun, persons over the age of 55 years comprised 8.5% of the caseload of the Kansas City Probation office. This is a somewhat larger proportion of elderly than has been reported in other jurisdictions, typically 1-3%. We knew only that the breakdown of charges for this group was 48% alcohol related offenses, 35.5% traffic violations, 4.5% shoplifting, 4% disorderly conduct, and 4% destruction of property. The other 7.5% were miscellaneous city ordinance violations. It was our goal to identify a sample of these probationers for interviews, and thereby get to know their needs and resources so as to better serve both those on probation and the community that wants these persons to be supervised for a certain length of time.

The study made use of random, stratified sampling. Four strata were identified within the population of probationers (N = 324)—those with charges involving crimes against persons, property offenses, alcohol-related charges, and other moving traffic violations. A randomly sorted list of persons in each stratum was prepared, and selections were made in order from the start of each list. The study sample included a higher proportion of persons in the smaller categories of crimes against persons and property offenses in order to reduce the sampling error within these subpopulations. Letters were sent to 124 selected probationers telling them about the study. Interviews began in mid-August and ended October 1, 1986. Out of 164 attempts, 62 interviews were completed, a 38% success rate.

The characteristics of the subjects are presented in Tables 1 and 2. The sample is primarily traffic offenders (N = 25; 40%), with property offenders overrepresented in the sample group (N = 16; 26%). Male offenders predominate (N = 48; 77%) and the racial composition is almost evenly divided between whites and blacks, with slightly more blacks included (N = 32; 52%). Of those in the sample, median age tends to be older than the population over 55 years (64 versus 61 years). It does not appear that the sample obtained is unusually different from the population group.

Our sample achieves the proportion of offenses that we wanted to attain. It represents an over-sampling of person and property offenses and underrepresentation of alcohol and traffic offenses. Other demographic identifiers demonstrate that the sample has proportionally more females and more blacks than the population from which it is derived (see Table 2). It is possible that these persons are more likely to be reached due to conditions of unemployment or some other factor. However, our interviewers were extremely persistent in making attempts to reach their people. We held two train-

TABLE 1

FREQUENCY OF OFFENSE TYPE

	Traffic	Property	Alcohol	Persons	Total
Sample	25 (40%)	16 (26%)	13 (21%)	8 (13%)	62 (100%)
Population	144 (44%)	52 (16%)	104 (32%)	24 (7%)	324 (100%)

TABLE 2

DEMOGRAPHIC COMPARISONS

Variable	Sample	Population
Sex - Male	48 (77%)	285 (88%)
Female	14 (23%)	29 (12%)
Race - White	30 (48%)	180 (56%
Black	32 (52%)	144 (44%)
Median Age	64 years	61 years

ing sessions and a mid-study meeting with interviewers to encourage their efforts and catch any problems they might be facing. Despite these efforts, 58 persons were not interviewed. Typical reasons were that the person had moved and left no forwarding address, had no telephone, was deceased, was in the hospital, an appointment time could not be coordinated, or the person refused to be interviewed. Nonetheless, with the randomization of names and the repeated efforts to locate individuals, sampling bias has been minimized.

GENERAL CHARACTERISTICS

The entire survey sample of elderly probations is 62 respondents. As a group, these people gave us quite a bit of information about their background. (See Table 3.)

Home Life. There seems to be a significant degree of stability in this group. Seventy-six percent (76%) live in a house, while 66% own their residence. Ninety percent (90%) have lived many years at the same location.

However, social supports or networks for this group could be described as weak. Forty-two percent (42%) live alone, 34% live with just one other person, and 22% live with more than one other. Thirty-nine percent (39%) are currently married, and 61% are currently single. Fourteen percent (14%) report that they have no family living in the Kansas City area. Sixty-three percent (63%) say they never see their own siblings during the course of the year. Interestingly, 28% do not have any children, and 40% have no grandchildren. Perhaps reflecting a sense of isolation, 77% of the sample (N = 48) responded "No" when asked, "Are any of these family members dependent on you now?" Apart from these human connections, 42% of the sample indicate that they have at least one pet.

Friendship Networks. While it does appear that these people have friends, the extent of organized participation in group activities is fairly limited. Forty-eight percent (48%) say they have a lot of friends (although 11% state they do not have any close friends). Eleven percent (11%) do not have a telephone in their home. Sixty percent (60%) do not belong to any group, although 92% claimed they had some religious affiliation. Baptists and Catholics predomi-

TABLE 3

GENERAL CHARACTERISTICS

(percentages may vary depending on missing cases)

		N	%
HOME LIFE			
1.	Live in a house	47	76
	Live in an apartment	10	16
	Other, room, group home	5	8
2.	Own residence	41	66
	Rent	16	26
3.	Live alone	25	42
	Live with others	35	56
4.	Married	24	39
	Widow(er)	17	27
	Divorced	11	18
	Separated	3	5
	Never Married	7	11
5.	No family living in Kansas City	9	14.5
	Don't ever see siblings in a year	24	63
	No children	17	28
	No grandchildren	24	40

		N	%
FRIENDSHIP NETWORKS			
1.	Have lot of friends	30	48
	Have a few friends	28	45
	No close friends	7	11
2.	No telephone	7	11
3.	Don't belong to any groups	37	60

TABLE 3 (continued)

	N	%
4. What is your church affiliation		
Baptist	24	39
Catholic	12	19
Never attend church	24	39
5. Do not know how to drive	13	21
Do not have valid drivers license	27	44
Do not own car	20	32
SKILLS AND RESOURCES		
1. Did not complete high school	37	59
2. Have a job	29	48
Full time	20	67
Part time	10	33
3. Retired	32	53
Received social security	31	52
Received wage or salary last year	30	50
4. Earned less than $5,000 last year	20	33
Earned less than $7,500 last year	37	62

	N	%
HEALTH		
1. No health problems reported	7	11
Five or more conditions bothering them	20	33
2. Problems		
Bone-Joint arthritis	25	40
Blood pressure	19	31
Dental	17	27
Back ailments	15	24
Nervousness	15	24
Sinus	14	23

TABLE 3 (continued)

	N	%
Glaucoma or vision	14	23
Foot, leg	12	19
Hearing or eye problems	12	19
Pain	12	19
3. Do not smoke at all	26	43
Rarely drinks	18	28
4. No days of activity lost due to sickness in the last year	33	56
LEGAL EXPERIENCE		
1. Reported having prior arrests	40	66
2. Type of lawyer		
private attorney	37	60
public attorney	10	16
no attorney	15	24
3. Reported satisfaction with		
police treatment	40	67
court treatment	40	68

nate (making up 58% of the sample). However, 39% say they hardly ever attend church services or functions. Mobility was an issue for a relatively large group. Twenty-one percent (21%) did not know how to drive, 44% did not have a valid driver's license and 32% did not own a car.

When asked, "What do you consider your biggest problems or worries?" the most frequent response (48%) was "Money." "Health" was mentioned next most often (19%), and another 3% mentioned "Health and money." Overall, more than 70% of the sample were concerned about money or health.

Skills and Resources. With the mean level of education for the sampling being tenth grade, 59% had less than a high school degree. Yet when asked whether my "education was sufficient for my needs," 73% believed that statement was true.

Because the study included persons over 55 years of age, it is not surprising that 48% of the sample had jobs, and most of those (N = 20 or 67%) were full time. Fifty-three percent (53%) said they were retired and fully 52% said they received social security payments, while 50% said they received a wage or salary in the last year. Unfortunately this somewhat comfortable statement of financial resources does not portray the limited degree of income of most of these persons. Thirty-three percent (33%) of the entire sample made less than $5,000 last year, and almost two-thirds (62%) of the sample made less than $7,500, representing a marginal standard of living.

Health. The other main concern expressed by the sample probationers was health. Only seven people (or 11% of the respondents) had no health problems whatsoever. Half of the sample claimed between one and four conditions as problems. Despite these percentages, 56% (33 people) said they lost no days of activity due to sickness. The most frequent health problems were bone-joint arthritis (40%), high blood pressure or hypertension (31%), dental problems 27%, back ailments 24%, were nervous or unable to sleep; sinus problems, glaucoma or vision problems bothered 23%, and 19% had foot or leg problems, hearing or eye problems, or other pain. On the surface, these types of complaints seem to be mostly gross physical problems generally associated with growing older.

Twenty-eight percent (28%) classified themselves as rare or infrequent drinkers and 43% said they do not smoke.

Legal Experience. Table 3 presents the legal experience of these persons on probation. Sixty-six percent (66%) admitted prior arrests. By report, 24% had no attorney, whereas 60% said they had a private attorney, and 16% had a court-appointed attorney. Most people were relatively satisfied by their treatment in the criminal justice system. Sixty-seven percent (67%) felt positive about their treatment by the police, and 68% said they were satisfied with their treatment by the court.

CONCLUSIONS

We have completed a comprehensive examination of a sample of older offenders served by the Kansas City Office of Probation. This seems to be a fairly respectable group, that is, they are not the persistent trouble-makers that we are so familiar with in the younger age categories. They seem to have physical and financial problems that have aggravated their ability to maintain a law abiding lifestyle. The persons we interviewed tended to be in need of services and supervision rather than rehabilitation. Social networks (friends and family) are spotty.

We continue to speak of this as a group, suggesting that it has identifiable characteristics which become more pronounced as the clients age. Because of the tremendous volume of cases handled in the Municipal Court, older persons tend to be processed together with all the other violators. The harm encountered by the older offender is clear in this sample of probationers. Many respondents stated that they were most angry about their treatment by the police and frightened by the courtroom experience. All personnel need to be aware of potential hearing difficulties which would impede responses by the older person to ordinary routine questioning. Alcohol offenders placed in AA meetings with younger people reported not being able to understand the language of the younger generation. Lack of ability to communicate can interfere with every goal of the justice system. Older persons (and their attorneys) do not recognize many practical implications of procedures – for example, dismissing a driving charge will not automatically erase the record and the driver may find his insurance raised, despite a dismissed charge. The problems faced by this particular group demand that each agency and agent in the justice system take notice of the special needs of the older person without reverting to the routine activity of processing cases. Some (Cohen, 1984) have suggested that a separate court for older offenders needs to be established, just as we have a juvenile division. Or perhaps a Special Advocate needs to be assigned to the Court. Such policy questions need to be aired in public forum. The purpose of this study is to provide tangible information that can assist in the discussion.

REFERENCES

Alston, L. (1968). *Crime and Older Americans*. Springfield, Charles C. Thomas.

Booth, D. (1985). "Health Status of the Incarcerated Elderly: Issues and Concerns," paper presented at the Third National Conference on Elderly Offenders, Kansas City.

Burnett, C. and Ortega, S. (1984). "Elderly Offenders: A Descriptive Analysis" in Wilbanks and Kim (eds.): *Elderly Criminals*. Lanham, University Press of America, pp. 17-40.

Cohen, F. (1984). "Old Age As A Criminal Defense" in Newman, et al. (eds): *Elderly Criminals*. Cambridge, Mass., Oelgeschlager, Gunn and Hain, pp. 113-142.

Goetting, A. (1983). "The Elderly in Prison: Issues and Perspectives." *Journal of Research in Crime and Delinquency*. 20:291-309.

McCarthy, M. And Langworthy, R. (1986). "Older Offenders on Probation and Parole," forthcoming.

Newman, E., Newman, D. and Gerwirtz, M. (eds.) (1984). *Elderly Criminals*. Cambridge, Mass., Oelgeschlager, Gunn and Hain.

Sapp, A. (1985). "Arrests For Major Crimes: Trends and Patterns for Elderly Offenders," presented at the Third National Conference on Elderly Offenders, in Kansas City.

Shichor, D. (1984). "Patterns of Elderly Lawbreaking in Urban, Suburban and Rural Areas: What Do Arrest Statistics Tell Us?" in Wilbanks and Kim (eds.) *Elderly Criminals*. Lanham, University Press of America, pp. 53-69.

Wilbanks, W. (1986). "Are Elderly Felons Treated More Leniently by the Criminal Justice System?" *Journal of Aging and Human Development*, forthcoming.

PART III: INSTITUTIONS: CUSTODY, CARE, OR THERAPY?

Mature Mentally Ill Offenders in California Jails

Patricia A. Washington

INTRODUCTION

Information pertaining to mature or elderly men incarcerated in county jails is limited (Golden, 1984; Bureau of Justice Statistics, 1980; and U.S. Department of Justice, 1980). There is even less information on mature offenders who are mentally ill. This is a descriptive study of mature mentally ill male offenders incarcerated in five California county jails. The demographics, prior contacts with the criminal justice system, type of offense and prior contact with the mental health system will be explored. Interaction between

---

Patricia A. Washington is Assistant Professor and Chairperson of Minority Studies at Wichita State University. She has an MA in Counseling from University of Northern Iowa, an MSW and a PhD in Social Work from University of Pittsburgh. She has taught at the University of Wisconsin-Madison.

This study was sponsored by the National Institute of Mental Health Research Service Award #14641.

alcohol dependency and mental illness will also be explored. These data are part of a larger project initiated by the California legislature in 1975 to determine the mental health needs in the county jail system. These data are unique in that this is the only available study of mental illness among mature men incarcerated in jails based upon a random sample of the entire jail population. Included in the study are those incarcerated men with a psychiatric diagnosis according to criteria from the American Psychiatric Association, *Diagnostic and Statistical Manual of Mental Disorders*, Second Edition, 1968 (DSM-II). Individuals diverted from the criminal justice system to a mental health facility during arraignment or pretrial hearing have not been included in this sample.

LITERATURE REVIEW

Although there are a number of studies on mature offenders, 50 years of age and older, these studies have examined arrest rates, types of offenses, and provided descriptions of mature offenders (Jensen, 1977; Shichor and Kobrin, 1978; Reed and Glamper, 1979; Malinchak, 1980; Newman et al., 1984; and Wilbanks and Kim, 1984). Studies focusing on mental disorder in local jails have noted the true prevalence rate of severe mental disorder (i.e., psychoses) ranges from 1% to 7% with rates of less severe forms of mental illness (i.e., neuroses and personality disorders) ranges from 15% to 20% (Morrissey, Steadman and Kilborn, 1983; Schuckit et al., 1977; Petrich, 1976; Swank and Winer, 1976; Matlick and Sweet, 1970). Unfortunately, the preceding studies did not assess the incidence of mental illness among mature offenders.

Although mature offenders presently represent a small proportion of the incarcerated population their numbers are increasing. Mature offenders may evince disruptive or self-destructive behaviors assumed to be associated with mental illness. In reality, these behaviors may be a combination of many factors: stress of aging in an environment created for youthful offenders, undetected strokes, drugs in conflict, or chronic alcoholism (Abrams, 1984). For an aging incarcerated man whose declining or inability to exhibit the typical behaviors required of males in prison—"toughness, confidence, lack of vulnerability, self reliance, etc.," (David and Brammon, 1976) – mental illness may be the only protection available. Incidences of mental illness among mature offenders must be investigated in order to adequately serve those who are mentally ill as well as those persons who may be forced to use mental illness as a survival mechanism.

METHODS

These data were obtained from a study conducted by Arthur Bolton and Associates as part of a 1976 contract with the California Department of Health to conduct a mental health needs assessment for jail inmates. Five California jails believed to be representative of the state of California in geography, size, and urbanization were included (Los Angeles, Fresno, Santa Clara, Sonoma, and Humboldt).

Data Collection

A total of 940 men were included in the study sample. Of these, 64 men were identified as 50 years of age or older. There were 25 from Los Angeles county, 15 from Fresno, 12 from Humboldt, 6 from Santa Clara, and 5 from Sonoma. A standardized questionnaire was used to record demographic information. Interviews were used to arrive at a DSM-II diagnosis. The DSM-II is the American Psychiatric Association's classification system for mental disorders. This system is comprehensive, respected and widely used among mental health professionals. Furthermore, the DSM-II includes organic as well as pathologies excluded from other classification systems such as mental retardation, drug addiction, and functional disorders (Hollis and Donn, 1980). This was the most current version of the diagnostic manual available at the time the original data were gathered. Data deemed unreliable or incomplete has not been included in this analysis. This author was not involved in the original research design or data collection. For a more detailed description of sampling techniques and data collection refer to Arthur Bolton and Associates (1978) or Washington and Diamond (1985).

Analysis

This is a descriptive study of mature mentally ill offenders. The odds ratio has been used where data are nominal to determine the strength and the direction of relationships between variables as well as to assist in the creation of a profile of mature male mentally disordered offenders (MDO). The odds ratio is a symmetric index. The author cautions the reader in the interpretation of these data because of the small sample size (n = 14).

RESULTS

Profile of Mature Offenders

The term mature offender rather than elderly offender is used in this study because the author finds no consensus in the definition of elderly offender in either national crime statistics (FBI, Uniform Crime Reports, 1980) or criminal justice studies (Burnett and Ortega, 1984; Goetting, 1983; and Malinchak, 1980). The cutoff point may be 65, 45, 60 or 55 years of age. Due to the small number of men 60 years of age or older in the sample, the age designating mature offenders in this sample is 50 years or older.

Creating a profile of mature mentally ill offenders is a difficult task since one must consider: variable age cut off and differences in demographics among jail and prison populations. The profile of elderly prison inmates obtained from a national prison sample (Goetting, 1983) is similar in some respects to the profile of mature offenders in this study. That sample is 55 years of age and older and includes women as well as men, although the majority (96.4%) are men.

The mature offenders in the California jails were single (73.4%), with a mean educational level of 10.22 years, the majority were white (57.8%), nearly a quarter had been arrested for drunk driving (24.2%), most were employed (65.5%) at the time of arrest and an overwhelming majority (89.1%) were recidivists. When comparisons were made between the California sample and the national prison sample on demographics and type of offense, the men were similar in several categories. Mature persons in the national sample had a mean educational level of 7.62 years, they were single (65.52%) and slightly less than half (48.05%) were white, most were employed at the time of arrest (61.82%), a significant proportion of their offenses involved violence (70.3%) and half (50.19%) were recidivists (Goetting, 1983).

The differences in these two samples may be the result of different populations of offenders served by jails and by prisons. Jails serve a much more diverse population than prisons. Prisons are likely to have large numbers of persons incarcerated for violent acts. Despite the differences, both samples have mature men offenders who are primarily single, with less than 12 years of formal education, employed at the time of arrest, with high rates of recidivism. (See Table 1.)

M-II Diagnoses and Alcohol Dependence

One fifth (20.3%) of the 64 mature offenders received a DSM-II diagnosis. Those men given diagnoses will be referred to hereafter as mentally disordered offenders (MDO). Those who did not receive a diagnosis will be referred to as non-mentally disordered offenders (non-MDO). The percentage of MDO men varied considerably from a high of 46.2% in Fresno to a low of 7.7% in Humboldt and Santa Clara. The majority of the MDO men had personality disorders (76.9%), 15.4% were schizophrenic, 15.4% received a diagnosis of neurotic depression, and one person had a combined diagnosis of neurotic depression and adjustment reaction (7.7%). (See Table 2.) Since more than three fourths of the men received a diagnosis of personality disorder, a discussion of this disorder is warranted. Personality disorder refers to,

> A large group of mental disorders (that) involve long term, relatively fixed and stable, maladapted patterns of social behavior and emotional responsiveness. Most become manifest during childhood or adolescence, are identifiable as character traits, lead to poor social adjustment, and sometimes result in considerable personal distress. Persons suffering from personality disorders usually continue to function in society. (Lafrancois, 1980, p. 505)

Table 1

Comparison of Jailed California Men 50 Years or Older to a National Jail Sample

	Inmates	
	California n=64	National n=248
Demographics		
Married	26.6	34.4
White	57.8	48.0
Fulltime employment	22.4	62.0
Type of Offense		
Violence	11.3	70.0
Property	6.5	16.7
Drugs	.03	4.8
Drunk Driving	nd	24.2
Recidivists	50.19	89.1

nd No data available

Alcohol Dependence and Mental Illness

The appearance of personality disorders is not unusual in persons who are dependent upon alcohol. A significant proportion of the MDO men were alcohol dependent (61.5%). The high rates of alcohol dependence may be confounding the diagnosis given by the interviewers. These rates suggest the possibility of a connection

Table 2

DSM II Diagnosis of Mature Men in Five California County Jails

Diagnosis	% of Entire Population n=64	% of MDO Men n=13
Schizophrenia	3.2	15.4
Personality		
Disorder	15.9	76.9
Neurotic Depression	3.2	15.4
Adjustment Reaction	1.6a	7.7
Alcohol Dependent	33.3	12.7

[a]Please note that there is one subject with two diagnoses, adjustment reaction and neurotic depression.

between behaviors believed to be manifestations of mental illness and dependence on alcohol.

Prior Contact with the Criminal Justice System and the Mental Health System

An examination of prior contact with the criminal justice system indicates that many of the MDO men were recidivists. All have had prior incarcerations as adults (100.0%). Their previous convictions were for felonies (84.6%) and misdemeanors (76.9%). Considering the high rates of alcohol dependence the fact that nearly one third (30.8%) had prior convictions for driving under the influence is not unusual. (See Table 3.)

Data on prior use of mental health facilities by these men provides evidence of use of a variety of facilities. The MDO men had been voluntary patients in state hospitals (38.5%), county mental health inpatients (30.8%), and patients in the psychiatric wards of

Table 3

Mature Men in Five California Jails:

Contact with the Criminal Justice System

	% of All Men n=64	%MDO men n=13
Prior incarceration as adult	20.3	100.00
Prior misdemeanor conviction	15.6	76.9
Prior felony convictions	17.2	
Prior Driving under the influence conviction	6.3	30.8
Current charge of driving under the influence	8.1	38.5

veterans hospitals (30.8%). Although these men had prior contact with mental health facilities, those contacts were not as numerous as their contact with the criminal justice system. (See Table 4.)

Odds ratios are used in the final table to pull together key demographic variables to create a profile of MDO men. The key variables are: ethnicity, marital status and education. Mentally ill offenders in this study are likely to be mature, white, single men with less than 12 years of formal education. Formerly married white men with less than 12 years of formal education are also likely to be mentally ill offenders. Black men, Hispanic men and men from other minority groups are less likely to appear in this mentally ill population of mature offenders. (See Table 5.)

DISCUSSION

These data present a profile of mentally ill men who are predominantly white, mature, unmarried with less than twelve years of for-

Table 4

Mature Men in California Jails:

Contact with Mental Health System

	% of All Men n=65	% MDO Men n=14
Voluntary patient state hospital	7.8	38.5
Involuntary patient state hospital	4.7	23.1
County mental health outpatient	7.4	30.8
County mental health inpatient	7.4	30.8
Veterans hospital patient psychiatric unit	7.0	30.8

mal education, alcohol dependent, and live alone. Although most were employed at the time of their arrest, only a few held full time jobs (22.4%). In addition, many of the MDO men had high rates of alcohol dependency and a history of recidivism with the criminal justice system as well as the mental health system. Collectively, the preceding factors suggest that these men experience difficulty functioning in society.

The large number of men who reported dependence on alcohol is not unusual if one considers two factors, the profile of the mature alcoholic and the substantial number with a primary diagnosis of personality disorder. A study by Harrington and Price (1962) on institutionalized alcoholics provided evidence of a connection between personality disorders and chronic brain syndrome. Later studies by Simon (1968) and Hyman (1973) generated additional evidence of alcoholism among elderly mentally ill patients. Klatsky (1977) noted that the peak drinking age for white males was

Table 5

Odds Ratio

Race	Observed Frequency	Expected Frequency	Odds Ratio
Single MDO Men with Less than High School Education			
White	4.0	2.21	1.81
Blacks	1.0	3.80	.26
Hispanics & Others	3.0	1.81	1.65
Separated, Divorced Widowed MDO Men with less than High School Education			
White	6.00	4.21	1.42
Blacks	3.00	2.45	1.22
Hispanics & Others	4.00	3.00	1.33

50-59. Each of the preceding studies suggest the possibility of a connection between behaviors identified as manifestations of mental illness and dependence on alcohol.

According to Schuckit and Pastor (1978:218), "Depression is almost uniformly present in actively drinking alcoholics. Resulting in pharmacologic effects of alcohol generated by an active drinking lifestyle similar to an affective disorder. But most will snap back into a normal mood after a few days abstinence." Therefore, any attempt to understand these men is based upon an understanding of the linkages between their past offenses, present offenses, alcohol abuse, and mental illness. The significant number of driving while intoxicated offenses causes one to conclude that the problems of many of these MDO offenders may be related to alcohol dependency.

Jails are designed to incarcerate dangerous youthful offenders who present a threat to the community. Therefore, it is not surprising that most existing jails are primarily places of confinement with limited (if any) facilities for mature offenders who are mentally ill or alcohol dependent (Newman, 1984). Furthermore, institutional overcrowding has reached epidemic proportions resulting in severe strains on meager resources (Kiel, 1979). Often, community mental health facilities have neither the personnel nor the resources to provide services to mature MDO men upon their release from jail.

Finally, there is concern that the jails have become dumping grounds for those individuals society chooses not to provide with services (Lamb, 1984; Bassuk and Gerson, 1978; and Teplin, 1984). A similar response has been accorded to mentally ill women offenders who are substance dependent (Washington and Diamond, 1985). Additional research is needed in order to better understand the intersystem processing of these mature MDO men. Also, the possible relationship between the three variables (mental illness, criminal behavior, and alcohol abuse) should be thoroughly examined. These activities are without substance if fiscal commitments to reduce overcrowding are not forthcoming immediately along with improved mental health programs that include a special component for those who are substance dependent. Those programs should be based upon need, gender and age of the various individuals for whom they have been created.

REFERENCES

Abrams, A. (1984). Incidence and types of crimes committed by elderly. In E. S. Newman, D. J. Newman, and M. L. Gewirtz and Associates (Eds.) *Elderly Criminals* Cambridge: Oelgeschlager, Gunn & Hain Publishing.

Arthur Bolton Associates. (1976). *A study for the need for mentally disordered jail inmates and juveniles in detention facilities*. California: Department of Health.

Bassuk, E. L., and Gerson, S. (1978). Deinstitutionalization and Mental Health Services. *Scientific American*, 238: 46-53.

Burnett, C. and Ortega, S. T. (1984). Elderly Offenders: A Descriptive Analysis. In W. Wilbanks and P. K. Kim (Eds.) *Elderly Criminals* (pp. 17-31). Lanham: University Press of America.

Calahan, D. (1970). *Problem Drinkers*. San Francisco: Jossey-Bass.

Calahan, D. and Room, R. (1974). *Problem Drinking Among American Men*. New Brunswick, NJ: Rutgers Center for Alcohol Studies.

Epstein, L. J., Mills, C., and Simon, A. (1970). Antisocial Behavior of the Elderly. *Comprehensive Psychiatry* 11: 36-42.

Goetting, A. (1984). The Elderly in Prison: A Profile. *Criminal Justice Review*, 9 (2): 14-24.

Golden, D. (1984). Elderly Offenders in Jail. In E. S. Newman, D. J. Newman & M. L. Gewirtz and Associates (Eds.) *Elderly Criminals*. Cambridge, MA: Oelgeschlager, Gunn and Hain Publishing.

Harre, R., and Lamb, R. (Eds.) (1986). *The Dictionary of Physiological and Clinical Psychology*. Cambridge: MIT Press.

Harrington, J. G. and Price, A. C. (1962). Alcoholism in a Geriatric Setting. *Journal of the American Geriatric Society* 10: 197-211.

Hyman, M. M. (1973). Alcoholics 15 Years Later. In E. P. Williams, B. Carruth and M. M. Hyman (Eds.) *Alcoholism and Problem Drinking Among Older Persons*. New Brunswick: Rutgers University Press.

Keller, O. J. and Vedder, C. B. (1968). The crimes that old persons commit. *Gerontologist* 8: 43-50.

Kiel, R. (1979). Health Care is a Major Issue of Courts and Civil Rights. *Corrections Today* 41: 6-28.

Lamb, H. (1982). The Mentally Ill in an Urban County Jail. *Archives of General Psychiatry* 39: 17-22.

Mattick, H. and Sweet, R. (1970). *Illinois Jails: Challenge and Opportunity for the 1970's*. Chicago: Illinois Law Enforcement Commission.

Morrissey, J. P., Steadman, H. J., and Kilburn Jr., H. C. (1983). Organizational Issues in the Delivery of Jail Mental Health Services. In *Research in Community and Mental Health*, Volume 3 JAI Press.

Newman, D. J. (1984). Elderly Criminals and American Crime Patterns. In E. S. Newman, D. J. Newman, M. L. Gewirtz and Associates (Eds.) *Elderly Criminals*. Cambridge: Oelgeschlager, Gunn & Hain Publishing.

Petrich, J. (1976). Rate of Psychiatric Morbidity in a Metropolitan County Jail Population. *American Journal of Psychiatry* 133 (12): 1439-1444.

Russell, M., Welte, J. W., Hottwick, M. A. and Hadden, W. (1978). *Estimation of Alcohol Consumption from Hanes Questions*. Presented at the Society for Epidemiology Research 11th annual meeting Iowa City, Iowa, June 14-16.

Schuckit, M. A., Herman, G., and Schuckit, J. A. (1977). The Importance of Psychiatric Illness in Newly Arrested Prisoners. *Journal of Nervous and Mental Diseases* 165: 118-125.

Swank, G. E., and Winer, D. (1976). Occurrence of Psychiatric Disorders in a County Jail Population. *American Journal of Psychiatry* 33: 1331-1333.

Teplin, L. A. (1984). Criminalizing Mental Disorder. *American Psychologists* 39 (7): 794-803.

United States Department of Justice. Bureau of Justice Statistics. (1978). *Profile of Jail Inmates*. Washington, DC: USGPO.

United States Department of Justice. Bureau of Justice Statistics. (1983). *Sourcebook of Criminal Justice Statistics*. Washington, DC: USGPO.

Washington, P. and Diamond, R. J. (1985) Prevalence of Mental Illness among Women Incarcerated in five California County Jails. In *Research in Community and Mental Health*, Vol. 5 JAI Press.

Prison Environments and Their Impact on Older Citizens

Ernest O. Moore

The needs of the elderly in terms of health care, life cycle roles, friendships, and security are similar regardless of where these older people may find themselves. In prison environments, many of these needs are left inadequately fulfilled as the elderly prisoner finds himself a member of the forgotten minority.

The study to be discussed had its beginning in a major research project conducted at the State Prison of Southern Michigan (S.P.S.M.) in Jackson, Michigan (Moore, 1981-82). Approximately 6,000 men were housed in what is considered one of the largest walled prisons in the United States. The study was investigating the influence of environmental factors on the frequency of health service demands or attendance at sick call, an indirect measure of stress (Twaddle, 1976). Prior research has established abnormally high demands for health-care as common in total institutions (Gunderson, Rahe, and Arthur, 1974). The issue of stress as a causal factor for attendance at sick call has roots in the research of Hans Selye (1976). Many of the responses of the older subjects were related to their experiences while at S.P.S.M. Background for the present study of older inmates describes the prison environment and some of the findings of the major study before going on to the issues directly related to the elderly.

Ernest O. Moore is Professor of Architecture at the University of Nebraska-Lincoln. He has a BS in Architecture Engineering (1951) from the University of Illinois-Champaign and a PhD in Architecture (1980) from the University of Michigan-Ann Arbor. He has taught at the University of Michigan.

S.P.S.M. ENVIRONMENTS

The physical plant and site layout is shown in Figure 1. The 55-acre site was utilized with cell blocks arranged in a U shape at one end of the prison compound. Half of the cell blocks (1, 2, 3, 4, 5) were of a *spine* design and half (6, 8, 11, 12) were of an *open* design as shown in Figure 2. This provided a very direct compari-

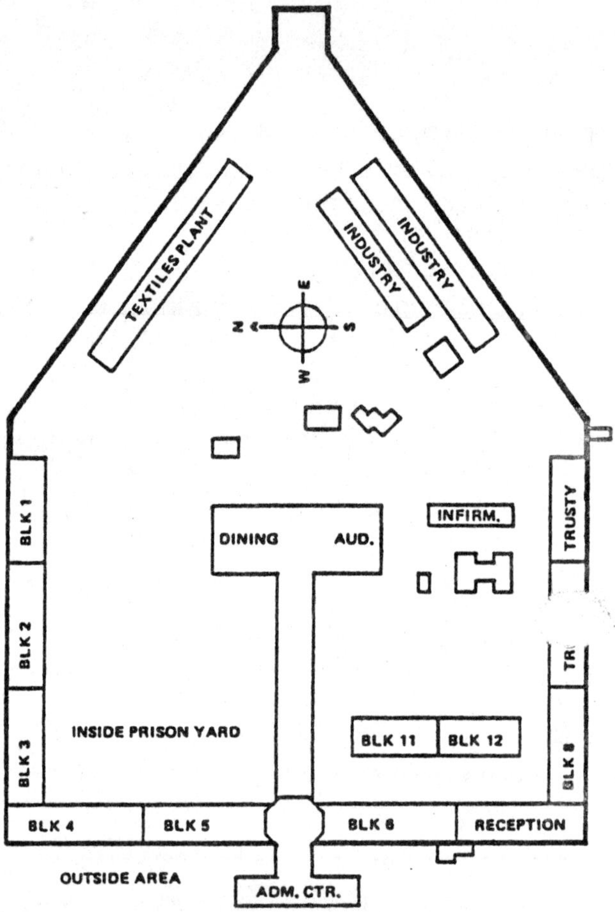

FIGURE 1. Prison Site Plan

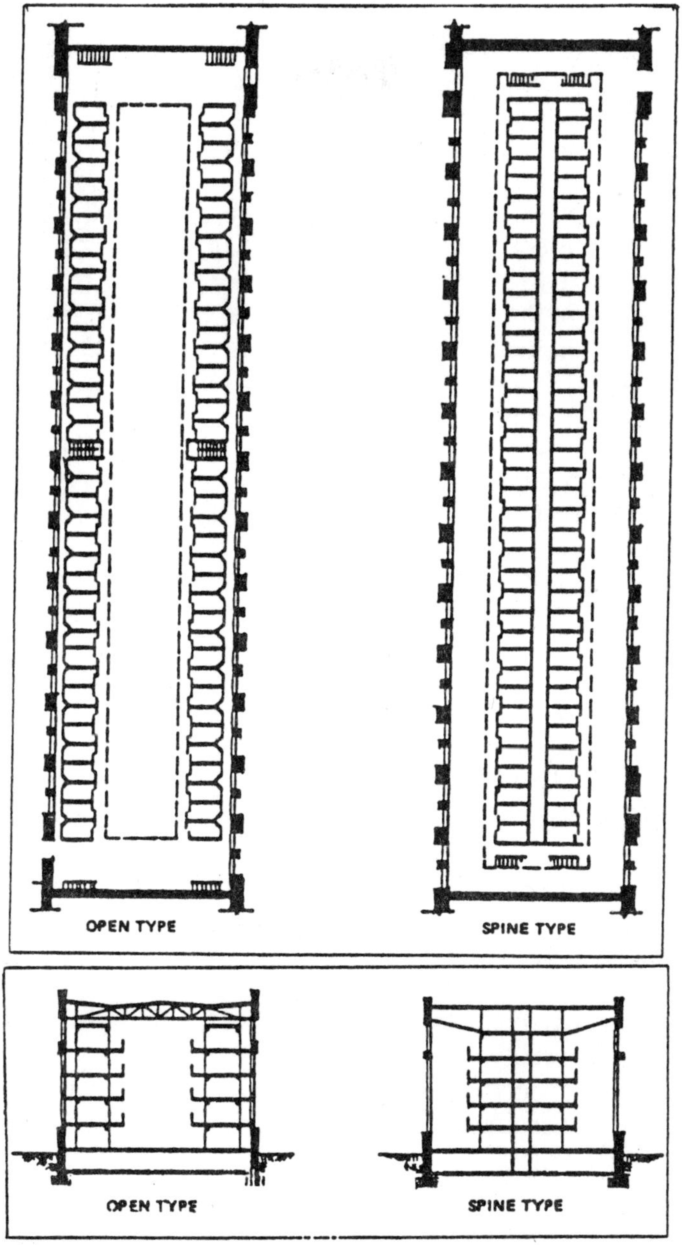

FIGURE 2. Typical Gallery Floor Plan of Cell Blocks

son of two types of environments. In the spine design, prisoners' cells backed up against a utility corridor and the prisoner's view was out toward the exterior walls of the cell blocks. Approximately 400 men were housed in each cell block and there were 5 galleries or stories in each cell block. The open cell blocks were arranged with cells along the exterior walls facing across an open space toward each other. In this manner, prisoners in the open cell blocks were never afforded the possibility of visual privacy. In addition, there were two types of segregation cell blocks in each of the wings of the prison. In the spine cell block design a punitive segregation cell block 5 was established for those prisoners who had violated various rules of the prison. In the open cell block wing, cell block (6) was devoted to protective custody for those prisoners who were threatened with bodily harm for whatever reason. In addition, there was one open cell block (12) dedicated as an honor block. This unit housed only prisoners that requested that housing unit. To qualify, prisoners had to have a prison job and no record of trouble for at least one year. Prisoners had to request this unit.

Over the course of this study, noise levels were recorded in each cell block for a 24 hour period of time and all who came to sick call during a one month period were counted. Information collected from those coming to sick call included data on race, age, time in prison, cell block location, reason for coming to sick call, and services rendered during the sick call.

Charts 1 and 2 show the distribution of complaints registered at sick call and the services rendered. This information reveals a rather interesting profile of the types of illnesses that prisoners seemed to have in greatest frequency and also it illustrates an unusual pattern of services required. Note that most of the services centered around medication and many of the requests were for pharmaceuticals that free people would typically purchase at a local drug store or grocery store.

Patterns of sick call attendance within each cell block and gallery level are shown in Chart 3. It is quite obvious that the two blocks where segregation was established generated high levels of sick call. Cell block 5 in the spine type cell block and cell block 6 in the open type cell block represent the two segregation units. You will note that the honor block, number 12, has an extremely low fre-

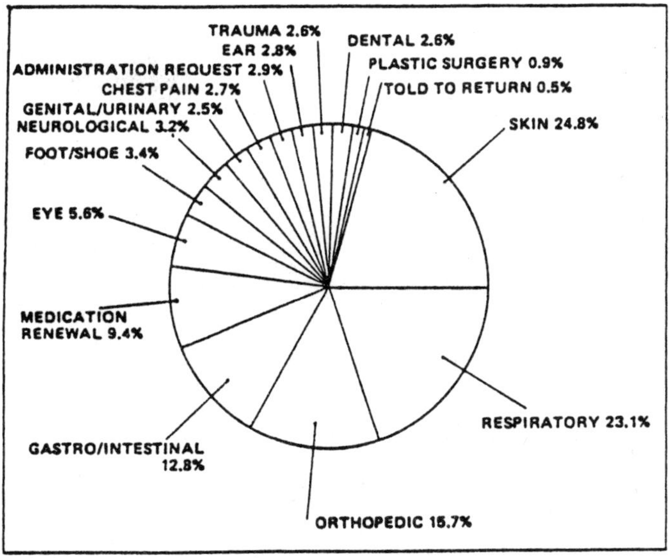

CHART 1. Complaints and Reasons Given for Sick Call Attendance

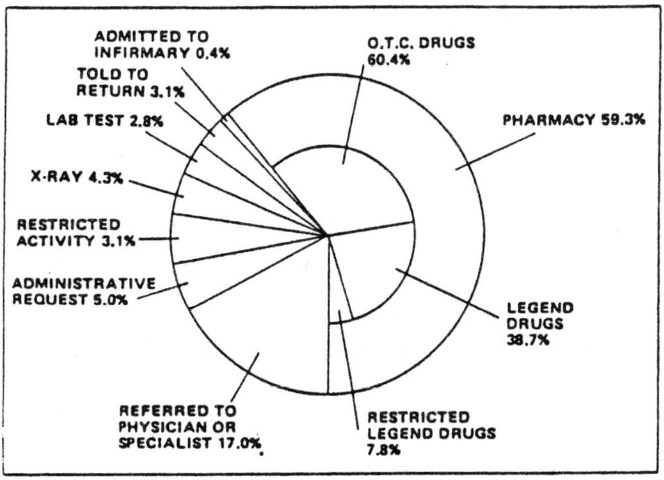

CHART 2. Services Generated by Sick Calls

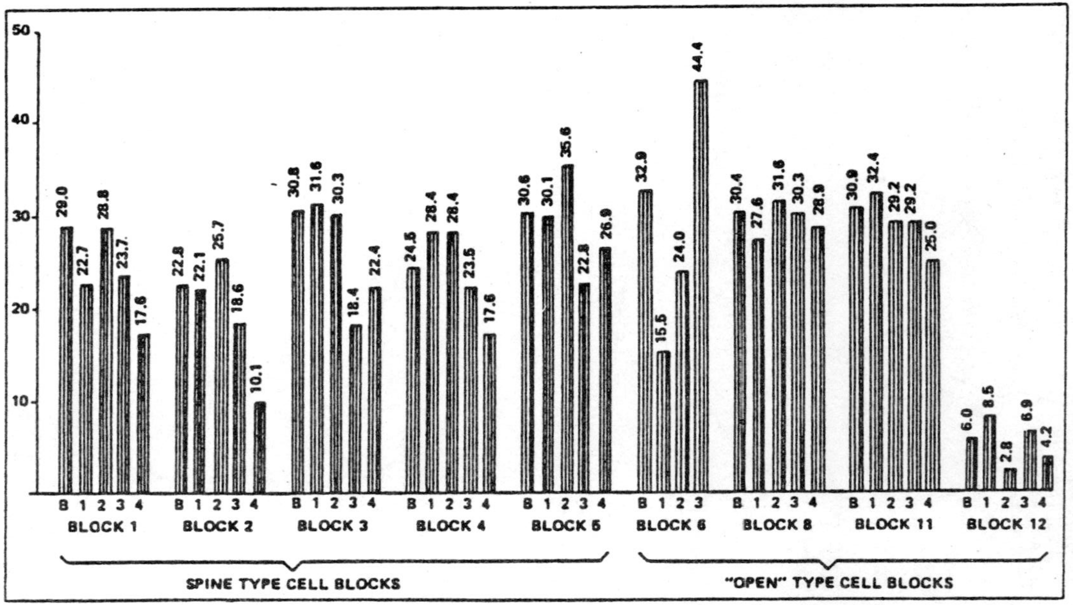

CHART 3. Percent of Prisoners Coming to Sick Call at Least One Time on Each Gallery Level in Each Cell Block

quency of sick call. This seems to indicate that self-determination and the amount of control over one's life, has some direct relationship to the amount of stress that people experience. Throughout this study, attendance at sick call was utilized as an indirect measure of stress.

Chart 4 indicates the noise level in this large prison in each cell block. The graph represents the percentage of time over 24 hours that the decibel noise level remained above the indicated levels. From the graph it becomes evident that the spine type cell blocks are noisier over longer periods of time than the open cell blocks. The segregation cell block number 5 is the noisiest of all the spine blocks. Noise in prisons is amplified by the typical hard surfaces of concrete and becomes an uncontrollable nuisance and source of stress. The research by D. C. Glass et al. (1973) has demonstrated some of the detrimental effects of loud uncontrollable noise which are probably at work in this prison.

Table 1 shows the odds of not coming to sick call within the spine blocks relative to the orientation of the cell block. It is notable that prisoners on the side of the cell block which overlooked the farmland were less apt to come to sick call than those who lived on the side facing inward, toward the prison yard. This suggests that the open land, field, hills and greenery are preferred environments and have a soothing effect on prisoners (Kaplan and Kaplan, 1978). It is with this background on the S.P.S.M. environment that we now turn to the older prisoner study.

THE OLDER INMATE AT IONIA

From the prison population at S.P.S.M., a group of older men were selected to be relocated in a different facility in Ionia, Michigan. This group served as a follow-up to examine the health care needs and demands as well as the influence that the environmental change had upon these older relocated inmates.

Many elderly persons have chronic health problems requiring special and ongoing pharmacy services, special diets, and more supportive environments. When one examines the typical prison management and environmental systems the mismatch between the systems and the needs of the elderly inmate is vividly evident. We

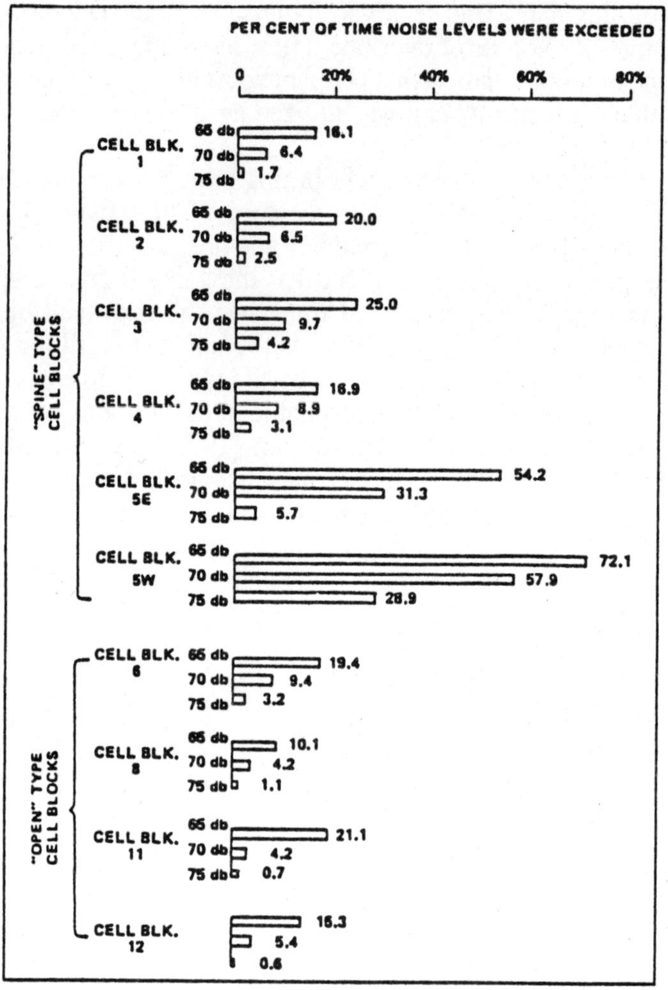

CHART 4. Percent of Time in 24 Hours that Noise Levels Were Exceeded in Each Cell Block

have found that the older prisoners are integrated with the general prison population in most state departments of correction. There are very few states which have instituted ongoing formal programs specifically aimed at care and housing for the elderly prisoners. Michigan, however, is one state in which such a program was initiated.

TABLE 1. Odds Prediction of *Not* Coming to Sick call by "Inside" vs. "Outside" Cell Orientation (Cell blocks 6, 8, 11, and 12 are excluded.)

	Change in Odds Multiplier	*Std. Err.*	*Significant Level*	*Predict. Odds No Sick Call*	*% Coming to Sick Call*
Inside	.843	-2.6505	0.8	2.52	28.4
Outside	1.178	+2.6505	0.8	'3.52	22.9

The Michigan Department of Corrections obtained from the Department of Mental Health a facility in Ionia, Michigan. This former mental hospital complex was modified to serve as a correctional facility. The Department of Corrections had three major goals in mind with the acquisition of this property. The overall strategy was to house prisoners with special needs in one location more conducive to serving their unique needs. Three major goals directed the acquisition of this property. The first objective was to move all acute and chronic psychiatric patients from various prisons in the state to the Ionia facility, resulting in better care and treatment. The second objective was to provide a reception and classification center for the younger prisoners under age 21. This procedure would remove the more vulnerable young men from mixing with the populations of the major prisons. Provisions were also made for protective custody for younger inmates unable to function in a general prison population for one reason or another. The third goal was to establish an age segregated facility to house and care for those older men with special problems and/or inmates with unique physical or medical problems such as paraplegia, blindness, heart problems, etc.

In contrast to the large S.P.S.M. prison facility previously described, the Ionia facility is a converted mental hospital facility consisting of individual two-story building, housing from approximately 80 to 112 men. The men who participated in this study, lived in a building that housed 30 men in double bunks located in a dorm room on each floor. There were 20 men in individual rooms on each floor. Each room had a window which was under the control of the inmate and each room had a heating radiator, also controlled by the inmate. Toilet facilities were centrally located on each floor. Each room had a solid door. Food was prepared by civilian cooks with some support service by inmates. The food was brought to each housing unit where it was served to the inmates in the dining room located on each floor. Each dining room seated approximately 50 men at tables and chairs. An outside view was available from the dining room.

A fenced yard was adjacent to the building which housed the older prisoners, and it was for the exclusive use of these men. They were also able to use the general prison yard if they wanted to do so.

Dayrooms were provided on each floor, equipped with pool tables, card tables, and TV viewing area. Laundry facilities and store facilities were provided in each building for inmate use.

Construction of the Ionia building was concrete masonry, brick, and concrete. Floors were covered with resilient tile. In general, the buildings were very well maintained since they were built in about 1950.

DATA GATHERING

The time schedule set by the Department of Corrections for the start of relocating the older men did not permit a pre-move test of the men involved. Relocated inmates were notified of the study and volunteers were sought for interviews. Fifty two men who were over fifty years old volunteered. Structured interviews were conducted in private with only the author and the inmate present. These interviews took place either in the inmate's room or in a private office provided. In addition, the author ate lunch with the inmates on days in which interviews were conducted. This offered an opportunity to meet other inmates who were not being interviewed, as well as to experience the food quality and eating environment in which the subjects ate. Incomplete or unreliable data from eleven men had to be discarded due to a mental impairment of the inmates.

Demographic information obtained included age, race, marital status, and number of children, if any. In addition, information was collected concerning length of sentence, time served, crime of conviction and location of residence within the Ionia facility and while confined at S.P.S.M.

Attitudinal questions tapped the inmate's feelings about the move; his prison job (if any), his degree of satisfaction before and after the move regarding food, friends, activities, religion, staff, visitors, coping strategies, fears, personal possessions, the cell, privacy, home range and typical day activities, and the perception of physical health.

Health records were then reviewed for service demands before and after the relocation for a period equal to the prisoner's time of stay at the Ionia facility.

ANALYSIS: CHARACTERISTICS

It is interesting to note that of all the men housed in the Ionia facility who were over 50 years of age, 51% of them were in prison for the first time in Michigan. Of all the men over 50 years of age 72% of them had been in prison less than 5 years. This indicates most of these men were not "long time" prisoners who had grown old in prison. Many of them had grown old outside of prison and through some criminal act were now living out their late years behind the fence and lock. The average age of the elderly residents in the building studied was 60.5 years.

We observed that this group of men required rather intensive medical services. These ranged from pharmacy, infirmary, dietary, x-ray, surgery to skilled nursing care.

Approximately 46% of these men were involved in a crime which resulted in the death of the victim and consequently we found approximately 46% of the men are sentenced to a 10 year or more term in prison. With 83% of the men having at least one chronic health problem, the magnitude of potential health-care required while they are in prison becomes evident.

Other characteristics of the 41 men who participated in the study are as follows:

1. *Age range* = 50 yr. to 80 yr.
2. *Age-mean* = 61.93 yr.
3. *Race* = 20 white, 21 non-white

4. *Marital Status*

9.8%	married
48.8%	unmarried
19.5%	divorced
22.0%	widowed

5. *Children*: 32 of the men had children

6. *Sentence Length* / *Time Served to Date*

Sentence Length		Time Served to Date	
1 to 2 years	= 40.0%	Less than 1 yr	= 24.4%
2 to 3 years	= 2.4%	1 to 2 years	= 31.7%
3 to 4 years	= 7.3%	2 to 3 years	= 14.6%
4 to 5 years	= 2.2%	3 to 4 years	= 0.0%
5 to 10 years	= 12.2%	4 to 5 years	= 2.4%
10 years & over	= 46.3%	5 to 10 years	= 14.6%
Life	= 4.99%	10 years & over	= 14.6%

7. Average time at Ionia at time of interview = 2 months

8. *Crimes Committed*

Assault	= 7.3%	Sex-related	= 19.5%
Armed Robbery	= 9.8%	Non-Violent	= 4.9%
Homicide	= 22.9%	Other	= 12.2%
Murder	= 24.9%		

9. *Chronic Health Problems*
   83% had at least one chronic health problem
   49% had three or more chronic health problems

10. *Types of Chronic Health Problems*

Vision	= 17.0%	Gastro Intestinal	= 9.0%
Cardiac	= 25.9%	Urinary	= 2.2%
Hearing	= 4.5%	Internal Med.	= 7.9%
Dental	= 7.9%	Orthopedic	= 3.6%
Lung	= 14.8%		

ANALYSIS OF THE IMPACT OF THE CHANGE IN ENVIRONMENTS

The data collected at Ionia was analyzed by the author and Ruth Phillips, a doctoral student in the College of Architecture, for factors or attributes of the environment related to the change in inmate welfare. Three major areas were considered:

1. Changes in inmate welfare
2. Inmate perceptions of environmental changes; and
3. Open ended question responses which helped explain influences on inmate perceptions of change.

FINDINGS

1. Changes in Inmate Welfare

a. Self perceived mood levels;
   (1) an *improvement* in mood level was experienced by 69% of the men after the move.
   (2) Only 9% experienced a *decrease* in mood level.

b. Confrontations and/or incidents:
   (1) 25% of the men experienced *fewer* incidents or confrontations after the move.
   (2) 9% experienced *more* incidents of confrontations.

c. Establishment of friendships:
   (1) 36% of the men indicated they had a good friend at Ionia but they previously had *no* good friends while at S.P.S.M. (This was particularly interesting since they had spent an average of 2-3 years at S.P.S.M. and only an average of 2 months at Ionia.)

d. General Satisfaction:
   (1) 75% of the men were generally more satisfied after the move to Ionia.
   (2) 17% were less satisfied after the move.

e. Health Status Change:
   (1) There was a 100% increase in health care demands, among inmates who were placed in rooms at Ionia after the move from S.P.S.M.
   (2) There was no significant increase in health care demands by those housed in the wards at Ionia.

2. Inmates Perceptions of Changes in Environment

a. Jobs: no significant change in job situation satisfaction.
b. Food: a significant *improvement* in satisfaction with food after the move.
c. Activities: no significant change in activities.
d. Spare time usage: no significant change.
e. Religious Activity: a significant *negative* change in attendance of religious activities after the move.
f. Satisfaction with staff: no significant change.
g. Medical care: no significant change.
h. General relationship with others: some *improvement* was noted but not at a significant level.
i. Satisfaction with cell/room/ward: some *improvement* was noted but not at a significant level.
j. Privacy satisfaction: some improvement noted but not significant.
k. Number of visits: significant negative change noted after the move.

3. Open Ended Question Responses

The inmates responses quite candidly identified what they preferred and why. The following examples give a broad overview and perhaps explain some of our conclusions.

a. Responses to "What do you like *most* about Ionia?"
   (1) 63% of the responses related to physical environment such as *cleanliness* and physical arrangement (ward, room, windows, doors).
   (2) 17% responded to food improvement.
   (3) 14% responded to staff improvement over S.P.S.M.

b. Responses to "What did you like *most* about Jackson, (S.P.S.M.)?"
   (1) 38% liked their trustee status and privileges.
   (2) 23% said they liked *nothing* about S.P.S.M.
   (3) 14% preferred the food at S.P.S.M.
   (4) 11% liked their job at S.P.S.M.

c. Responses to "What do you like *least* about Ionia?"
   (1) 55% disliked loss of trustee status and privileges or changes in security measures at Ionia.
   (2) 21% said they did not *dislike* anything at Ionia (except being in prison).

d. Responses to "What did you like *least* at S.P.S.M.?"
   (1) 36% disliked factors related to physical environment such as: cell, filth and rats, excessive noise.
   (2) 19% disliked fellow inmates at S.P.S.M. who were described as racists, racketeers and young punks.

When inmates elaborated on their reasons for preference in all areas the most significant answers related why they felt more comfortable with the men in their unit. Responses to those inquiries were as follows:

1. 45% liked being with men of similar age
2. 16% said they were less hassled and felt they were in a safer place
3. 16% liked the quieter environment at Ionia.

CONCLUSIONS

Though the move to Ionia seemed to cause what we believe to be a temporary increase in illness or health care demands among the more elderly and aged inmates, all other measures of inmate welfare showed significant improvement. Both the statistical analysis and verbal responses of the inmates support our conclusions that the policy of age segregation along with improvements in the physical environment are responsible for these improvements in welfare. These findings were strongly reinforced in conversations with administrators at the Ionia facility. We were told of the study group's sense of community, low incidence of aggressive hostile actions, and reduced need of security personnel.

The planning for a prison facility for accommodating the needs of older prisoners requires a different approach. Understanding the aging process will give insight for design solutions which can achieve financial savings while making the environment more humane.

Simply putting older prisoners together into a typical prison cell block is not sufficient. Joseph Ham's report on the "Limited Duty Unit" in the Columbus, Ohio correctional facility vividly points out the short-comings of such an approach (Ham, 1979).

The needs of the elderly inmate are the same as any other prisoner but more critical. Their reduced ability to cope and have those needs met in the typical prison setting is the crux of the problem. The close relationship of coping ability and health or perceptions of well-being is discussed in A. Antinovsky's (1979) extensive exploration of this subject.

Based upon our analysis and observation, a number of design implications are suggested:

1. To accommodate the physical limitations resulting from the various chronic health problems, one story living areas would be desirable. This would provide an element of safety in the event of fire as well as reduce the effort required to go to the yard for exercise and diversion.
2. Provisions for a minimal examination room and space for certain health care delivery services would be desirable near or in the housing unit.
3. Rooms with doors for all elderly prisoners would provide privacy and quiet for resting, as well as adding a measure of security for the elderly. When the activities in the dayroom were such that the elderly weren't interested or they were too noisy, their room could provide a retreat. Many times those men with rooms were in them writing letters or watching their personal TV set. Privacy needs for prisoners tend to be overlooked or ignored in many existing prisons when in fact it is a critical issue in many situations. The discussion of privacy by Leon Pastalan and Daniel Carson (1970) explains the aspects of privacy that are so important to older persons. Undoubtedly, these older prisoners are utilizing their new found privacy to its maximum.
4. Provisions for gardening appears to be a very desirable feature. Several men at Ionia became interested in the flower gardens which were ultimately provided at Ionia. The research of Dr. David Guttman of role changes in the aging process has

indicated a tendency for older men to become more interested in gardening.

5. Security measures such as heavy duty prison hardware and building construction can be reduced in many units housing elderly prisoners, who are not considered hostile or aggressive.
6. Age segregated housing units can give an added measure of security to the older prisoners.
7. A reduction in the number of inmates in any one housing unit or in any one prison will also reduce internal crime and the perception of danger. Several inmates spoke of the relief in being with all older men instead of with all "those young punks."

BIBLIOGRAPHY

Antinovsky, A., *Health, Stress, and Coping*, Jossey-Bass Publications, San Francisco, California, 1979.

Glass, D.C., J.E. Singer, and J.W. Pennebaker, Behavioral and Physiological Effects of Uncontrolled Environmental Elements, *Representative Research in Social Psychology* 4: 165-183, 1973.

Gunderson, E., R. Rahe, and R. Arthur, The Epidemiology of Illness in Naval Environments: II. Demographic, Social Background and Occupational Factors, *Military Medicine* 135: 453-458, 1974.

Ham, Joseph N., Ph.D., Evaluation of Conditions at the Limited Duty Unit, Columbus Correctional Facility, Columbus, Ohio, prepared for the U.S. Department of Justice 1979.

Kaplan S., and R. Kaplan (eds.), *Humanscape: Environments for People*, Duxbury Press, North Situate, Massachusetts, 1978.

Moore, Ernest O., D. Arch, A Prison Environment's Effect on Health Care Service Demands, *Journal of Environments Systems* Volume II, No. 1, 1981-82.

Pastalan, Leon A. and Daniel H. Carson (eds). *Spatial Behavior Of Older People*, The University of Michigan 1970.

Selye, H., M.D., *The Stress of Life*, McGraw Hill Book Company, New York, New York, p. 178, 1976.

Twaddle, A. C., Utilization of Medical Services by a Captive Population: An Analysis of Sick Call in a State Prison, *Journal of Health and Social Behavior*, 17: 236-248, 1976.

Health Status of the Incarcerated Elderly: Issues and Concerns

Dorothy E. Booth

The events preceding incarceration for committing a crime are stressful experiences for most individuals. Prior to incarceration, processes such as the arrest, arraignment, exam, trial, conviction and sentencing are likely to produce a high level of anxiety in the elderly with outcomes that may be very detrimental to their health. Bergman and Amir (1973) found that the strain of incarceration produces an accelerated deterioration in both the physical and mental health status of the elderly.

Persons in older adulthood who are caught, convicted, and sentenced to a correctional facility for white collar crimes or for acts committed while intoxicated often respond first with shock and/or disbelief. This is especially true for those who have not pursued a long life of criminal activities and/or who do not view themselves as criminals (Booth, 1987). Accepting the grim realities of their situation can be an ego shattering experience, and destructive to the elderly offenders' self-image. The chronic grief and state of depression which may ensue can precipitate or contribute to other health problems in the elderly, especially when feelings of deep remorse are not resolved following incarceration.

The elderly are a small minority group in the prison system (Bachand, 1984). For this reason, extra effort must be made to ascer-

---

Dorothy E. Booth is Assistant Professor of Nursing at the University of Michigan. She has an MSN in teaching community health nursing from Wayne State University (1974), a PhD in education from the University of Michigan (1985). She has taught at Wayne State University.

tain that their special mental and physical health needs are not overlooked. Although the cost of medical care for the incarcerated elderly can be high, and has been known to place tremendous strain on correctional facility budgets, once persons are incarcerated, the correctional system is responsible for making the provisions necessary to maintain and promote their health.

Bachand (1984) has described the concerns of correctional facility administrators related to the general health status of elderly inmates. Excessive mental worry and feelings of disgrace, as well as a monotonous diet and environment, and the lack of work that is stimulating to the mind are only a few of the many factors that can have a negative effect on inmates (Allen and Simonsen, 1981). These same factors can be even more harmful to the health of the incarcerated elderly because these persons are usually in a compromised state of health as a result of age related changes and in most cases they will have one or more chronic illnesses that require ongoing medical attention. Older inmates, then, have more stressors to contend with than younger inmates who have not experienced ill health or major changes in strength, vitality, endurance, and/or problems in functioning effectively in their respective roles.

The incarcerated elderly may also have experienced other major changes. For example, they may have lost some of their closest family members and friends to death and may not have been able to maintain a supportive social network. In some cases, they may have become isolated or estranged from significant persons in their lives as a result of their criminal activities and for incarceration. The lack of a supportive social network can adversely affect the incarcerated elderly because social support from significant others is one of the key factors that can serve to buffer the effects of continuous stress. Elderly residents in community settings who were under stress and who had inadequate social support were found to be at increased risk for both morbidity and mortality as compared to elderly persons who received adequate support (Berkman and Syme, 1979).

As members of the fastest growing aggregate in our population, the elderly require special consideration because they have experienced the effect of numerous age related physical and physiological changes. In addition, they have experienced psychosocial changes and often have lost meaningful life roles. Income levels and exchanges of social support may have dwindled for the elderly as compared to what they had in the earlier years of their lives. Major changes in work roles, death of parents, spouse, siblings, and mandated relocation are other factors that can serve to increase the elderly's feelings of loss. The exchanges of social support will be less than adequate for elderly inmates who are incarcerated in facilities which are geographically distant from friends or relatives. Law enforcement and jail personnel (LEJP) who introduce measures to promote a sense of community within the correctional facility will increase the elderly inmates' sense of security and opportunities for choosing new family ties within the facility (Carr, 1988).

Whether age associated changes, ill health, and losses experienced by the elderly contributed to the acts they committed which led to their incarceration, or were precipitated by the stress of incarceration, those elderly inmates who view their situation negatively or as hopeless, are at high risk for developing depression. Elderly inmates who become depressed may attempt suicide without warning, or with only subtle verbal or nonverbal messages relayed to others. This is especially true of elderly male inmates who have experienced abandonment and who have not been provided the benefits of psychological counselling.

Health conditions in the incarcerated elderly may be difficult to detect and manage within many of the nation's correctional facilities. LEJP who are responsible for monitoring the health status of those elderly who are being held in detention centers or small correctional facilities as compared with the incarcerated elderly in federal institutions with well-staffed health units will have different types of responsibilities and dilemmas (Carr, 1988). Carr also pointed out that when incarcerated elderly feign illness, this is a situation that will pose a problem for LEJP in any of these settings. In addition, it may increase risks for those elderly who develop a reputation as malingerer because they may not get the attention they need when they require immediate assistance with a health problem.

The early detection and the management of chronic illnesses known to occur with increased frequency in our aged population (e.g., arthritis, cardiac, and hypertensive disorders, diabetes mellitus, and cancer) present multiple challenges for health professionals in our traditional health care settings. Similarly, with increasing percentages of elderly inmates in some facilities, LEJP will have additional responsibilities which include observing and reporting changes in the health status of the elderly inmates, and assisting and encouraging them to better manage their health problems. For example, those incarcerated elderly who have cognitive impairments may not be able to provide accurate information about their health status and LEJP will need to monitor and report changes in their health status. Even those elderly inmates that require attention who are cognitively functional may be unaware of changes in their health status, or they may be reluctant to disclose health information about themselves to law enforcement and jail personnel (LEJP) until they have learned to trust them. It is important, then, for LEJP to recognize the need to modify the assessment protocol used with incarcerated elderly as compared with younger persons and carefully select and use strategies which will motivate and to actively participate when possible in the management of health problems they have incurred.

One of the issues central to the thesis of this writing is that LEJP in a majority of correctional facilities must assume some responsibility for obtaining selected assessment data about their elderly prisoners. This is necessary because (1) health care services are not readily available in many facilities or may only be provided for prisoners when they are requested by LEJP, and (2) the health status of elderly prisoners can deteriorate rapidly, and death may ensue if observations of the early signs and symptoms of an impending health crisis in the elderly are not noted and/or when appropriate care is not given in a timely manner. A systematic health assessment needs to be conducted when elderly persons are first incarcerated to obtain a baseline of data about their health status and at regular intervals thereafter until their release from the correctional facility. Monitoring for any changes in the elderly's health status is a responsibility that should be assumed by those LEJP who have daily or weekly contact with the inmates.

Another issue of concern regarding the assessment and maintenance of the health of the incarcerated elderly is the need for the correctional system to provide training for LEJP in the assessment of the elderly. The costs involved in the training of personnel is a third issue of concern. These issues will present challenges for county, state and federal systems with limited resources. However, it is clear that the elderly have a right to health services and there rights cannot be ignored any more than the possibility that massive expenses might be incurred by a prison system if it can be demonstrated that elderly prisoners' death is attributable to some treatable health condition which was neglected, ignored, or not reported in a timely manner by LEJP. It is imperative, then, for law enforcement and jail personnel to become knowledgeable about the physical and psychological changes associated with normal aging. They also need to be able to identify early signs and symptoms of health conditions known to occur with increasing frequency as persons age.

Many LEJP have already developed skill in observing and documenting pertinent facts about suspected and convicted criminals, their behaviors, and their appearance. It is important that they expand their skills by developing a knowledge base about the normal aging process, and by learning to differentiate between normal and pathological changes that they observe in elderly prisoners. Relevant learning experiences would also provide LEJP the opportunity to learn about and practice following an assessment protocol and using an assessment tool which would assist them in systematically observing, collecting, and documenting essential information about the incarcerated elderly's health status. In these learning sessions, LEJP should also be provided information which would enhance their ability to make appropriate medical referrals and other recommendations related to the health care needs of the elderly persons who are incarcerated in their facility. If approved by the facility, referrals could be made to clinical nurse specialists, physical therapists, and other health professionals who are skilled in providing many of health services needed by elderly persons.

Other content and practice experiences offered to the LEJP in the training sessions should be focused on the use of health assessment questionnaires specifically designed for application in prison settings with elderly populations. Well-designed questionnaires can assist LEJP to make relevant observations, collect other needed information, and systematically document important observations about the health status of the elderly incarcerated who are in their units. Sample health assessment questionnaires designed for use in correctional facilities are provided in the Appendix. One of the questionnaires is designed to be completed by the LEJP and the second questionnaire is designed for self-completion by the elderly inmates. This assessment approach encourages the collection of both subjective and objective information about the inmates' health. These questionnaires can be modified as needed for use in specific facilities. One additional learning objective and related content is recommended for the training sessions. This objective would be to assist LEJP to develop an appreciation for the benefits that can be derived by the incarcerated elderly and the correctional system by supporting the development of selective health promotion activities within the system. Identifying strategies which could be used by LEJP to involve the population in activities to enhance their health status would be essential content to include in the training sessions.

The early recognition and response to changes in elderly prisoners' health status is important for reasons other than those that have been previously discussed. For example, the elderly's reserve capacity for handling rapid changes in the cardiovascular or respiratory system is diminished, and pathophysiological changes that are reversible in younger adults, if not attended to early, may become life-threatening or irreversible in the elderly. Pain, elevated temperature, redness, and swelling, which are the classical signs and symptoms of infection in younger persons, do not necessarily present with the same intensity in the elderly, and an early infection may go unnoticed by untrained LEJP until the condition has become too far advanced to treat effectively. Similarly, changes in cognitive status, such as the decreased ability to remain oriented to time, place, or person may signify the presence of anemia, depression, or a hypothyroid condition in the elderly and should be referred promptly for treatment. Any other changes in cognitive function, whether the onset is gradual or sudden, should also be referred for medical evaluation.

Rogers (1980), a nurse theorist, and Butler and Lewis (1982), who are recognized as expert gerontologists, concur that adults become increasingly diverse and complex as they age. Individualized health assessments of the incarcerated elderly, then, are necessary if their unique health care requirements are to be identified. The myth in our society that all older persons are just alike should be dispelled among those LEJP who work with the incarcerated elderly. Chronological age is certainly not the best predictor of age related changes or specific health conditions. In fact, wide variances are found in the functional abilities and overall health status of persons who are of similar chronological ages. Elderly prisoners are likely to present with varying health needs or problems which in part, may be attributable to genetic differences, environmental influences, previous life styles, personal habits, patterns of response to stress, and previous health care and multiple other factors.

There are many normal age related changes that need to be considered whenever law enforcement and jail personnel are working with the incarcerated elderly. A discussion of all of the changes is not feasible in this writing. However, some of the important changes that could be introduced in LEJP training session will be identified in the remainder of this paper, as well as the implications of these changes for law enforcement and jail personnel.

Sensation: The elderly have decreased sensitivity to both heat and cold. With decreased subcutaneous fat tissue and sweat gland activity, they do not adapt well to environmental extremes. Warm, light, loose clothing, moderate environmental temperature (e.g., 70-72°F.) and activities that require frequent movement are advised measures.

Pain: The elderly respond more slowly to heat and pain or not at all. They may exhibit nonverbal signs of discomfort (e.g., restlessness, withdrawal, or reduced level of activity) rather than complaining about pain.

Smell and Taste: There may be a decreased sense of smell and taste with aging, which affects the elderly's appetite. They may demand more sugar, and condiments to make their food taste palatable. Weight loss may become a problem, especially for older males. With diminished salivary gland response, dry mouth, and diminished muscle strength, elderly persons are more vulnerable to choking.

Receding gum lines can contribute to ill-fitting dentures, another problem that can aggravate choking spells and create eating problems. Soft, easy-to-chew foods are recommended.

Touch: Pressure injuries and falls are more likely. Carpeted, highly waxed floors become hazardous. Sensible shoes (rather than nonsupportive loafers) are advised. Velcro closures on shoes will help the prisoner with arthritis in hand joints to remain independent.

Cardiovascular Changes: Heart tissue enlarges and becomes less elastic. Valves and blood vessels become thicker, more rigid, less compliant. Blood flow meets more resistance, thus less blood is pumped by the heart per minute. The decrease in cardiac output leads to slower heart rate and pulse, and subsequently, less oxygen is delivered to the tissues. Slower rates and decreased oxygen will not adversely affect older prisoners *unless* they exercise strenuously or are under great stress. A pulse rate of 100 or greater at rest, or 120-130 after activity, puts undue stress on the heart. Shortness of breath with exertion (rather than pain) should be used as an indicator level of an older person's tolerance. Digitalis preparations used to strengthen the heart contractions have a small margin of safety between therapeutic and toxic levels. Thus, monitoring for sign/symptoms of toxicity is essential. Age-related changes or kidney failure intensifies the elderly's risk for toxic responses to heart drugs. The increased resistance of blood flow against hardened vessels may lead to a rise in blood pressure. This is a phenomenon that is prevalent in our society but not in persons from societies with vegetarian food patterns. Persons on blood pressure medications also require careful monitoring. Distention observed in the neck vein(s) when the person is upright, or at a 45 degree angle, is a serious sign and requires immediate attention.

Respiratory Tract: With increased age, there is reduced lung capacity. Persons 80 years of age get only one third the amount of oxygen as compared with young adults. Lower portions of the lungs do not expand well; these along with other changes predispose older persons to lung infections such as pneumonia. Marked fatigue, confusion, persistent and productive cough, fever, and/or general chest discomfort may indicate infection and should be explored. Wheezing from emphysema may be aggravated by anxiety, fear, cold, exertion, or smoke. Prevention of exposure to infections and administration of influenza vaccines are important.

Nervous System: Reaction time is decreased, thus the elderly respond more slowly to stimuli, and it takes an increased level of stimuli to excite a response. Use of high speed machinery by the elderly can be dangerous.

Tremors: The elderly may develop fine intention tremors or shaking in hands and body which may be aggravated by extremes in temperature, exertion, fatigue. This contrasts with coarse rhythmical tremors of limbs (e.g., arms, trunk) when the person is at rest and which subside with deliberate movements. This second type of tremor is associated with Parkinson's Disease, which also presents with increased muscular rigidity which leads to changes in gait (e.g., shuffling, short steps, or running steps), slow movements and weakness.

Sights: Pupils are decreased in size and the eyes are less able to accommodate for sudden changes in the intensity of the lighting; this change is a result of the eye lenses losing their elasticity. There is decreased accommodation to near objects requiring corrective lenses (bifocals). Peripheral vision is reduced, as is depth perception. Cataracts may form (yellowing, thickening, and opacity of one or both lens). With extremely bright lights or glare from waxed floors, persons with cataracts will have difficulty seeing clear images. Accidents can be prevented by reducing glare, and increasing intensity and constancy of lighting. Surgery for cataracts, eye exams every third year to determine the need for corrective lenses, and providing contrast of colors in the environment (e.g., differentiating edges of steps and the steps themselves with contrasting colors), should enhance the elderly's vision and prevent falls and other accidents.

Hearing: Three common hearing problems are seen with increased frequency as persons age. A higher percentage of men as compared with women are affected. These problems include:

1. Degeneration of the auditory nerve (Presbycusis): This is a common hearing problem which results in loss of ability to hear high frequency tones and discriminate between consonant sounds (e.g., S and F).
2. Ostosclerosis: Excess bone cells are laid down and the movable bones which conduct sound to nerves become fixed. Surgery can be used to correct this condition in many cases.
3. Build-up of ear wax (cerumen): This condition will also affect transmission of sound, and can be remedied.

The elderly with hearing losses may become withdrawn and irritable and/or less communicative. Hearing aids need to be checked for proper fit, for battery changes, and turned on for those elderly who are forgetful. Touch and visual stimuli can be used to communicate with hearing impaired prisoners when verbal communication is ineffective.

Sleep and Rest: Patterns of sleep and rest may change as persons age. The deepest stages of sleep (third and fourth stages) may be absent or reduced in length from ones earlier life patterns. If unable to sleep well at night, the elderly may require naps during the day. Sleep apnea presents a problem for some older adults with greater risk for those who are obese. With this condition, they stop breathing, which may or may not wake them from their sleep, or they may die of respiratory arrest during sleep. Weight control is important. Elderly persons with sleep disorders need to be referred to determine related underlying problems that may be correctable.

Skin: The outer layer (dermis) of skin thins, wrinkles, and appears more transparent, dry, and is easily irritated. There is an increased incidence of skin cancer, especially in those who have had repeated exposure to the sun. Skin conditions need to be observed over time and changes in size and color of lesions, which might include a raised appearance or irregular edges which seem to be spreading out like feelers on the skin should be evaluated. Many skin and nail changes seen in elderly persons are non-malignant, but they still may be problematic, such as fungus infections which attack the nail beds. Ingrown nails are common, a result of an overgrowth and thickening of the nails. Foot infections are often preventable with good foot care; the skin should be kept clean and dry. Good nutrition, adequate amount of fluids, and lotions used for dry skin surfaces, treatment of systemic conditions, such as diabetes, are important measures for promoting healthy skin, as is the protection of the skin from strong sun (e.g., middle of the day exposure) which contains ultraviolet light which is injurious to both the skin and eyes.

Extremities: Loss of hair and shiny pale skin on lower legs may be related to circulatory problems. Persons with poor circulation will complain that their feet feel cold all the time. It may be necessary for elderly inmates to wear warm, lightweight stockings that are nonbinding year round and elevate their legs every two hours to improve circulation.

Muscle and Bone: Despite exercise, there is decreased muscle strength and some depletion of calcium salts from persons' bones as they age. With inadequate calcium intake, lack of regular exercise, and/or changes in estrogen level, bones are more likely to fracture, and elderly persons may also experience severe muscle cramping. Cartilage at the ends of long bones become brittle and often will break off into joints, resulting in painful and stiff joints. The elderly should avoid jolting movements and hazards which have the potential for causing falls should be eliminated.

Rest can relieve joint pain associated with osteoarthritis, a condition affecting most persons over the age of 70. The cartilage pads or discs between the vertebrae thin; similarly, kyphosis which resembles a "hump" on the upper back develops in many older persons. These changes are associated with postural changes and decreased muscle strength which impair normal expansion of the lungs and reduce the exchanges of air and carbon dioxide in the elderly's lungs. The rib cage becomes fixed which also affects breathing. A barrel-shaped chest may indicate the presence of emphysema; breathing problems and increased risk for infection are likely outcomes for inmates with emphysema. Smoking should be discouraged, and preventive measures instituted (e.g., vaccines) so that inmates with emphysema are protected from influenza and pneumonia and not exposed to others with upper respiratory infections.

Gastrointestinal Changes: The esophageal sphincter relaxes; hence, elderly persons should always eat in an upright position to prevent the aspiration of fluid or foods from their stomach into their lungs. Digestion is slowed; there are changes in enzyme and peristaltic activity in the gastrointestinal tract. Elderly persons also develop intolerance to certain foods, including foods high in fat. The liver is 50% smaller, which has the effect of slowing food and drug metabolism. Constipation is a common problem in elderly persons, especially those who are physically not very active. Increased fluids and bulk-forming foods and exercises that are tolerated should be encouraged to correct the problem. The use of laxatives should be avoided. Over 40% of the elderly who have achieved the age of 80 have gall stones, but their problem may not become symptomatic unless certain foods are eaten. Prolonged vomiting and diarrhea in the elderly presents a serious situation because they can dehydrate more quickly than younger persons and develop a fluid and electrolyte imbalance. Early referral is important.

Pancreas: The pancreas produces insulin when sugars are ingested and metabolized. With age, the pancreas becomes less efficient. Large intakes of the foods containing simple sugars, such as pastries, are not handled well by older persons' systems.

Urinary Tract: Kidneys are decreased in size with age, and as a result the ability to filter waste products is decreased 46% in elderly persons. Thus, those drugs excreted by kidneys (and most are) will take longer to be eliminated from the system. For this and other reasons, including an age associated increased risk for adverse drug reactions, elderly persons on medications bear close watching for toxic effects or adverse reactions.

In males, an enlarged prostrate gland is common over the age of 60. It has been estimated that 80% of the males over age 80 are at high risk for prostatic cancer. The enlarged prostate gland and the decreased bladder capacity result in increased frequency of urination, difficulty in starting and stopping the stream of urine, nocturnal frequency, and greater potential for infection in elderly males. Persons placed on diuretic preparations also will experience increased frequency.

Females may also experience increased frequency with reduced bladder capacity. Incontinence, more prevalent in females, should always be evaluated; many cases can be improved with treatment. Decreased vaginal acidity with aging makes the older female more susceptible to vaginal infections from a number of organisms that thrive in less acidic environments. It is important to encourage good hygiene, report symptoms of infection (i.e., itching, burning or unusual discharge) and provide yearly physicals and pap smears. The aging process also increases the female's risk for breast cancer. Older female inmates should be taught to do self-breast examinations on a monthly basis.

Cognition and Psychology: Unless there are pathological changes in the brain which result in Alzheimer's Disease or other dementias, elderly inmates will be able to continue to learn new information. They may, however, continue to use old solutions and past experiences which may not be useful to them as they try to solve new problems. Elderly persons have to learn to adjust to declining functions and work through their feelings of loss and grief, reviewing their life and putting it in perspective in terms of their remaining strengths and achievements and the legacy they have created. The incarcerated elderly may have difficulty doing this, depending on how they view their situation. Reminiscence and life review may be very painful for them. Some elderly will become preoccupied with body functions and/or be less accepting of age related changes than their peers. Some will find comfort in religious or spiritual activities. Counselling for those who are not successful in resolving feelings about their life may be of great value.

A number of mental status tests have been developed which can be used to determine the older adult's overall level of functioning, and problems they may be having in terms of their behavior and orientation, memory, recall, comprehension, calculation and judgment. Butler and Lewis (1982) have described some of these tests, but caution that none of the mental status tests have received full acceptance for standard use. Other mental status tests have been described in very recent research literature and may be of great clinical value when their reliability and validity are better established. It might be useful to use one of the mental status tests, as well as an assessment tool such as the one provided in the Appendix of this paper to identify health needs and problems among elderly prisoners.

A well-designed assessment tool will assist law enforcement and jail personnel who are knowledgeable about age associated physical and psychological changes to make relevant observations and recognize changes that are not a normal expectation of the aging process. The assessment tool provided in the Appendix is divided into two sections, with the first section structured to guide LEJP in the assessment and the documentation of their own observations. The second section contains open-ended questions and other items that will guide prisoners in performing a self-health assessment. The tool is designed so that changes in the prisoner's health over time will be easily identified by LEJP.

From many years of experience, and from his vantage point as a Senior Correctional Supervisor in a facility with 25% of the population age 65 or older, Carr (1988) believes that all incarcerated elderly need to have a thorough evaluation of their health status and a two week orientation to the correctional facility before they are given a work assignment. This is an important suggestion, in that within that two week period, physical and psychological strengths and limitations of elderly inmates can be determined and appropriate treatment instituted when necessary. Carr suggests that the concept of unit management, where correctional officers and case managers work together as a team, is especially useful on units with elderly inmates. With this approach, the team develops professional rapport with the elderly inmates, and all members of the team assume responsibility for monitoring and reporting changes in the health status of the incarcerated elderly. Their suggestions may also be very relevant for smaller correctional facilities and detention centers.

SUMMARY

The age-related changes and the maintenance of health and wellbeing of elderly prisoners require special management skills. The literature and persons experienced in the field of law enforcement and/or corrections suggest that it is necessary to provide environments for the elderly prisoners that are different and apart from the environments provided for younger prisoners. This is an important consideration in assisting the elderly to survive the combined stressors of incarceration and the increased health risks inherent with the aging process. Law enforcement and jail personnel who are provided opportunities to develop a knowledge base about the normal aging process and age associated health problems and who learn assessment skills will be able to make accurate assessments and appropriate referrals. They will also recognize and support the need for special programs, focusing on nutrition, exercise and health education, which are designed to maintain and promote the health of the elderly prisoners. Protecting and promoting the health of the elderly, as a primary preventive intervention, will serve as a cost-containment measure for correctional facilities, as well as enhance the quality of life for the elderly during their term of incarceration. By assuming responsibility for activities which promote health of the incarcerated elderly, law enforcement and jail personnel will also reflect one of the professional components of their roles as correctional officers.

REFERENCES

Allen, H.E. and Simonsen, D.E. (1981). *Corrections in America: An introduction*. New York: Macmillan Publishing Co., Inc.

Bachand, D.J. (1984). *The elderly offender: An exploratory study with implications for continuing education of law-enforcement personnel*. Doctoral dissertation, University of Michigan, Ann Arbor, MI.

Bergman, S. & Amir, M. (1973). Crime and delinquency among the aged in Israel. *Geriatrics*, January.

Berkman, L.F. and Syme, L. (1979). Social networks, lost resistance, and mortality: A nine year follow-up study of Alameda County residents. *American Journal of Epidemiology, 109*, 186.

Booth, S.M. (1987). Personal interview. Patrolman. West Bloomfield Township, MI.

Butler, R. and Lewis, M. (1982). *Aging and Mental Health*, 3rd ed. St. Louis: Mosby Co.

Carr, R.C. (1988). Telephone interview. Senior Correctional Supervisor. Federal Correction Institution, Milan, MI: U.S. Dept. of Justice, Federal Bureau of Prisons.

Rogers, M. (1980). Nursing: A science of unitary man? In Riehl, J. and Roy, C. (Eds.). *Conceptual Models for Nursing Practice*. New York: Appleton-Century-Crofts.

OTHER RECOMMENDED READINGS

Carnevali, D.L. and Enloe, C. (1986). Assessment in the elderly. In Carnevali, D.L. and Patrick, M. (Eds.), *Nursing Management for the Elderly*, 2nd ed. Philadelphia: J.B. Lippincott, 26-49.

Elipoulos, C. (ed.) (1984). *Health assessment of the older adult*. Reading, Massachusetts: Addison-Wesley Publishing Co.

Malinchak, A.A. (1980). The elderly as criminals? *Crime and Gerontology*. Englewood Cliffs, NJ: Prentice Hall, 140-165.

Shrock, N.M. (1980). *Holistic assessment of the healthy aged*. New York: James Wiley and Sons.

APPENDIX

LEJP ASSESSMENT TOOL

NAME: ______________________
I.D. NO.: _________________
SEX: __
LEJP I.D.: _________________

DIRECTIONS: Document <u>your</u> observations about the prisoner in each of the categories on pages 1-3. Have the prisoner complete the self-assessment sheet on pgs. 4-5. Enter N.O. (not observed) and D.N.A. (does not apply) where applicable.

DATE:	DATE:
TIME:	TIME:

A. Overall general appearance: i.e., neatly dressed, unkempt, inadequate clothes for climate

---

B. Weight versus height: i.e., thin, normal, overweight, appears emaciated, bloated

---

C. Symmetry: Face, lips, head, body, extremities: i.e., shape, missing digits, etc., swollen joints, i.e., fingers, ankles, wrists, distended abdomen, barrel chested

---

D. Skin and Nails: Color, condition: i.e., pale, jaundiced, swelling, rashes, bruises, lesions, scars, needle marks, infected areas, perspiration, nevi or moles (color location); identify any discoloration of skin

---

E. Hair condition: Color, amount: i.e., cleanliness, infestations, balding, etc.

F. Corrective devices/appliances:
1. Vision: eye glasses, contact lens (one or two), artificial eye(s)
2. Hearing: Aid
3. Heart: Pacemaker
4. Teeth: Upper, lower, partial or complete dentures, loose teeth, infected or capped teeth
5. Artificial limbs
6. Ambulation: Crutches, cane, wheelchair

APPENDIX (continued)

		DATE: TIME:	DATE: TIME:
G.	Gait: Limping, shuffling; i.e., difficulty sitting, standing, walking, etc.		
H.	General posture; evenness of movements; uncoordinated, rigid, tremors (describe)		
I.	Complaints and Observations: (Describe location) Pain, redness, swelling, feels hot, cold, has drainage, palpitations, sensation of pressure, numbness, throbbing, bleeding, tingling, etc.		
J.	Breath Odor; Body Odor: i.e., rancid, sweet, fruity; odor of alcohol, urine, feces, etc.		
K.	Breathing pattern: i.e., even, uneven, unable to catch breath or short of breath with or without exertion, rapid, shallow, slow, noisy sounds when inhales or exhales		
L.	Coughing, blowing nose, spitting up: i.e., describe pattern, color of sputum, nasal drainage or bleeding from mouth or nose		
M.	Distended veins: neck, legs, anal area: i.e., neck veins are distended when prisoner is at 45o or 90o angle-sitting position		
N.	Eyes: Pain, drainage, complaint of vision: i.e., change, reads news-print at one foot; pupils respon-sive to light, dark and are equal in response. Lid changes.		
O.	Hearing: Responds to normal voice: i.e., reads lips, hears only loud, low sounds. Ears: appear normal, red, complains of ear pain, etc.		
P.	Legs: Color, swelling (location): i.e., pain in calf with or without walking		

APPENDIX (continued)

	DATE: TIME:	DATE: TIME:
Q. Speech Pattern: Normal, slurred, i.e., hoarse, etc. (describe). Quiet or babbling, etc.		
R. State of Tension: Shaking, relaxed, i.e., restless, pacing, withdrawn, sleeping, quiet, coarse or fine trembling, assaultive to self or others, etc.		
S. State of Continence: i.e., unable to control urine, feces (describe); unable to urinate, defecate (describe)		
T. Other Complaints: i.e., headache, dizzy spells, (describe), nauseated, stomach pains, vomiting, diarrhea, abdomen appears distended		
U. Comments made by prisoner during interview: i.e., threats to own life, threats to others		
V. State of Consciousness: i.e., no response to stimuli, difficult to arouse (requires strong, repeated stimuli), eye contact but unable, unwilling to speak, lethargic, responds slowly		
W. State of Cognitive Ability: i.e., oriented to time, place, person. Can count by 7's backward, short-term memory (can recall three items after rehearsal of items); affect dull, sad, euphoric, flat, etc.		
X. Any drugs/medications/alcohol in prisoner's possession? (describe)		
Y. Any hallucinations? (seeing things that are not there, etc.) Any paranoid ideas? (unprovoked suspicion), thinks people are talking about him/her, trying to poison, or otherwise harm him/her Any delusional (i.e., reports he/she is God)		
Z. Any other notable observations:		

Medical Referral Yes ____ No ____ Date _________

Referral for ____
(Identify the reason for referral)

APPENDIX (continued)

SELF-HEALTH ASSESSMENT TOOL

NAME: ____________________________ DATE: ______________

SEX: ___ I.D.#: _____________

Directions: **PLEASE RESPOND TO THE FOLLOWING QUESTIONS BY FILLING IN THE BLANKS OR CIRCLING THE APPROPRIATE RESPONSES.**

1. Name of physician/clinic you go to for care __________________
2. Your Weight _____ Your Height _____
3. When and where were you last hospitalized? ____________________ Date

   ____ Location
4. Circle and describe any of the following conditions you have been treated for in the last five years:

Allergies/Drug Reactions____________ Head Injuries _________________

Aneamia/Sickle Cell_________________ Headaches______________________

Angina Pain_________________________ Hearing/Ear Problems___________

Asthma/Emphysema____________________ Heart Problem/Murmur___________

Back Ailment________________________ Hemmorrhoids___________________

Bladder/Kidney Problem______________ Hepatitis______________________

Bone/Joint/Arthritis________________ High Blood Pressure/Hypertension

Bowel Problems______________________ _______________________________

Cancer/Tumors_______________________ Nervous/Unable to Sleep_________

Cataracts___________________________ Pain___________________________

Dental Problem______________________ (location)

Depression__________________________ Palpitations/Rapid Heart Beat___

Diabetes Mellitus___________________ Pneumonia/Influenza____________

Dizzy Spells/Blackouts______________ Prostrate/Urinary Problems______

Epilepsy/Seizures___________________ Psychiatric Problems___________

Falls/Fractures/Other Injuries______ Sinus Problems_________________

Foot/Leg Problems___________________ Thyroid/Goiter Condition________

Gall Bladder/Stones_________________ Tuberculosis___________________

Any other health problems:__________ Ulcers_________________________

____________________________________ Venereal Disease_______________

APPENDIX (continued)

Any surgery in last 5 yrs.__________ Food Allergies________________

__________________________________ ____________________________

5. What drugs/medicines are you allergic to?___________________

6. How often do you exercise: Never___ Occasionally ___ Every Week ___ Every Day ___

7. What is your usual pulse rate at rest? _____ When you are exercising? _____

8. What is your usual blood pressure? __________

9. Do you have a problem with constipation? Yes No

10. Describe your appetite: Poor Fair Good Excellent

11. Describe how much you smoke a day: None 1 pack 2 packs 3 packs Over 3 packs

12. How much alcohol do you normally consume in a day? __________

13. How many hours do you normally sleep at night? ________

14. List the names of each medication/drug that you use regularly at the times and dosage taken:

Time Taken Dosage

1.____

2.____

3.____

4.____

5.____

6.____

15. What laxatives, sleeping pills, antacids, aspirin or other over-the-counter drugs do you use on a regular basis?

____

____

16. Describe any other health problems that it would be important for us to know about: ___________________________________

APPENDIX (continued)

17. Females: Date of last Pap Smear __________

Date of last pregnancy __________

Instrument Developed by:
Dorothy E. Booth
Date Revised: 01/13/88

The Older and Long Term Inmate Growing Old in the New Jersey Prison System

C. Eamon Walsh

INTRODUCTION

Seven percent of New Jersey's resident prison population is growing old while incarcerated. As of January 1987, there were 8,669 individuals within the prison complex, 599 of whom will be fifty-five or older before they reach parole eligibility. By January 1990, the percentage should climb to 10%; 9,889 inmates being in residence within the prison complex, 981 of whom will not reach eligibility until they attain fifty-five years of age or older.[1]

This phenomenon is due partly to New Jersey's enactment of the 2C Criminal Code in 1979 which increased the volume of custodial terms imposed and more to the point, increased the duration of incarceration.[2] Enchancements to 2C, such as the Graves Act also prolonged the average length of stay.[3]

The impact of the new sentencing structure was felt in 1981, when a state of emergency in State and County institutions was promulgated by Governor Kean. The full weight of mandatory minimum terms without chance for parole was felt at this time. This prompted the Department to question whether the medical, psychological and social needs of this graying population was being met by the Department's traditional delivery of service geared to a younger offender.

C. Eamon Walsh is Executive Assistant to Adult Institutions, New Jersey Department of Corrections. He received his BA from Villanova University and an MA in Public Administration from Rider College and is presently writing his dissertation on older offenders at Rutgers School of Criminal Justice.

This report is an attempt to address several important questions about this group. It is intended to provide a descriptive overview of the number, offense characteristics, sentences, and length of stay of aging inmates in the New Jersey system. It also examines changes in the nature of the aging population over time. It is the first part of a long range study of aging inmates within the Department.

The second phase of the study will examine the socioeconomic characteristics of the group, their custody status, and reclassification potential. It will also tap the inmates' perspective of their needs. In addition it will assess management and line's perspective concerning the match between needs and services available. It will attempt to inventory the Department's potential to address the problem.

The final phase of the study will provide general recommendations concerning how needs can be met systematically as well as the ideal setting in which to provide these services.

SOURCES OF DATA

The report utilizes the Department's "Offender Based State Correctional Information System." This data base contains detailed information in a variety of areas such as committing offense, criminal history, racial and ethnic origins and some social and economic characteristics. The social and economic variables have not been programmed in summary format hence preventing us from addressing these issues thoroughly at this time. Some preliminary conclusions are reached in this area by our conversations with experts in the prison system. There is some unevenness in the classification of various age groups as displayed in the tables due to the summary format of the Department's information system and our secondary analysis of data classified to meet the purposes of this report.

The data used in conjuction with inmates in the state system from 1970 to 1975 was drawn from the New Jersey Correctional Master Plan, an effort on the part of a broad-based policy council in summarizing and describing the correctional population as well as defining needs and articulating policies to meet these needs.

DEFINING AND MEASURING THE OLDER POPULATION

Defining "Older"

There is no uniform cut-off age to measure when inmates should be called "elderly," "aged," "senior inmates" or "older."[4] The retirement age of 65 for Social Security purposes is the most frequent age used nationwide; however, many 65-year-olds would disagree that 65 marks the passage of middle age. "Old age" is a construct and it begins when a classifier declares it to begin (Rubenstein, 1984).

The Federal Bureau of Investigation uses 65 as a cutoff point, while some state jurisdictions, including the Federal system, use 45 as the passage to old age, other state jurisdictions use 60 or 55 (Rubenstein, 1984).

Between the years 1970-1973, in New Jersey, total *admissions* included 8% of the 50 and older inmate and 7% were 50 and older between the years 1974 to 1975.[5] Admissions for this group from 1978 to 1986 measured a total of 7.6%, evidencing that there has not been much change in the influx of inmates 50 years old and older from 1970.

The total number of inmates in *residence* age fifty-five and older from 1981 and their percentage of the total prison population is displayed in Table 1.

For purposes of this study we chose 55 as a cut-off for becoming old or "older" in prison. Almost 23% of prison admissions range from age 19 to 29 for a mean age of 24. Almost 70% range from age 30-49 for a mean age of 39, and a median age of 38. On the other hand, only 7.6% of admissions range from 50 to 70 for a mean age of 60 and a median age of 61.5. Table 2 displays these results.

If we choose 55 as the cut-off point, inmates entering at age 24 would need 31 years confinement to reach this age. This would call for a sentence of 55 years or a mandatory minimum of 31 years. Those entering at 39 would need 16 years of confinement, with a sentence of 80 years or a mandatory minimum term of 16 years.[6]

Of total mandatory minimums (as of 2/21/86) 59% received a

sentence in excess of twenty years from the years 1978 to 1986. Fifty-seven inmates during this time span received a mandatory minimum of 31 years or more, 108 received 30 years, and 153 received a minimum of 20-29 years. (See Table 3.)

Table 4 displays the catchment population reached by cut offs of 60, 55 and 50. Cut-off 50 would capture 533 inmates reaching this age prior to eligibility, cut-off 55 would capture 358 and cut-off 60 would theoretically capture only 318.

It is somewhat ridiculous however to talk of 50 as an entrance to old age. Available research shows that age 55 is the starting point of physical and mental deterioration; that most chronic illnesses begin at this age, and that many of the aged's social needs become accentuated at this age (Atchley, 1972).

THE "OLDER" POPULATION

Current Age and Distribution (In Residence as of 9/15/86)

Table 5 illustrates that the largest number of older inmates are age 55 to 59. There are 142 inmates 60 and older, representing 51% of the total. Those over 70 constitute 13.7% of this total.

Present Age and Future Parole Eligibility Dates

Of the 277 inmates displayed in Table 6, 71 or 26% are past initial parole eligibility. Sixty-five or 24% will become eligible in 1988. Of the 55-59 group, 14% are past initial eligibility. The 60 to 70 and older group has 11% past eligibility. The medium group, numbering 8 inmates, will become eligible between 1995 to 1999. A majority of inmates or 79% will become eligible by 1994.

Figure 1 displays the relative number of inmates becoming eligible for parole from "past initial eligibility" to 2000 plus.

Table 7 shows *age at date of parole eligibility* (totals only). Three hundred twenty-two cases have been added to the 277 inmates already age 55 or older, representing the "Long Term Offender Growing Old." Trenton Prison is a recently reconstructed, maximum security facility with the largest number of cases (50%). Over 50% of long term inmates will not reach eligibility until 2005 to 2009 (see Table 15). Twenty-nine cases at the State's sex offender institution lack eligibility dates at this time and are not reflected in the total.

The total number of inmates who will mature to age fifty-five in coming years will constitute an older group than their counterparts, who were fifty-five at sentencing. They will also capture more inmates in age brackets 65-69 and 70 up (5%). Thirty-one percent of all inmates will be sixty-five and older at parole eligibility, contrasted to 23% of the group who reach 55 at sentence.

OFFENSE DISTRIBUTION BY AGE

Approximately sixty-six percent of the "older" population in residence were convicted of personal offenses, contrasted to thirty-four percent of their number being convicted of property, drug and public order offenses. Table 8 lists the offense distribution by age.

Sixteen percent of this group were convicted of Murder or Homicide charges. Sexual Assault, however, accounted for 19% and Robbery 4%. Property offenses show Theft at 5% and Drugs at 13%. Among the property/other offenses, Drugs made up the majority at 38% of the total.

Nineteen seventy-four to 1975 showed an average of 52% of the total admissions were for property and drug offenses versus 48% for personal offenses.

LENGTH OF SENTENCE BY AGE

Table 9 demonstrates that the largest number of this group, 93 inmates or 34%, received maximum sentences of 5 to 9.9 years. An inspection of Table 10, which displays average length of stay with modal offense committed, suggests that the majority of the cases receiving 5 to 9.9 years were convicted of Sexual Assault. The average time to parole eligibility for a 5 to 9.9 year sentence would be 1 to 2 years.

Seventy-one percent of this cohort received sentences of one to twenty years, which would make them eligible for parole as early as 1982 (sentencing for the group started in 1978) and no later than 1990. This is verified by Table 6, which shows that on average, 68% of the group would become eligible for parole by 1989.

Eight percent received a Life sentence and 38% received mandatory minimum sentences with an average of 8.3 years without parole.

AVERAGE LENGTH OF STAY BY CRIME COMMITTED WITH MODAL OFFENSE

The modal length of stay to parole eligibility for older offenders (displayed in Table 10) is 5 years. The average length of stay for persons convicted of personal offenses is 11.2 years. The average for property offenders is 1.6 years.

The New Jersey Correctional Master Plan reports the average length of stay for all *departures to parole* from 1970 to 1973 totaled 26 months and from years 1974 to 1975 averaged 24 months.

The older cohort is now spending an average of 60.2 months to parole *eligibility*. This does not factor in the additional length of stay to actual parole release. Preliminary studies by the Department suggest that the stay could be as long as 235 months for a number of inmates.

During 1970 to 1975 the average length of stay to parole for offenders against persons was 35.5 months and for offenders against property, the average was 16 months.

Offenders against persons among the older group are now serving 41% more time to eligibility and property offenders are serving 20% longer to become eligible for parole.

Thirty-three percent of all offenses by the 55- to 59-year-old inmate were property offenses receiving terms of 10 years or less with an average length of stay of 1 to 4.9 years. This group had the highest percentage of cases past eligibility (56%). It is a high movement group from admission to parole, exiting faster than any other subgroup.

ADMISSIONS AND RELEASES

Table 11 displays all admissions into the prison system from years 1978 to 1986. The 30- to 34-year-old group make up the highest percentage (28.1%) and showed an proportionate increase over the years from 6.5% to 15.3%. Although the 18 to 20 group represented a mere .3% of all admissions to the prison system, their number increased from 0 to 38 displaying a large influx into the system in 1985.

The 50- to 59-year-old group represented 5.3% of all admissions with a modest proportionate increase of 12.9% in 1978 to 14.3% in 1985. The 60 and older group captured 2.3% of total admission showing a proportionate increase from 14.8% in 1978 to 10.4% in 1985.

Table 12 displays admissions and releases for the older cohort, by offense. Total admissions outpaced releases by 32%. Bed space deficits for the total prison population are pictured in Table 13. Bed space deficits are likely to rise continuously in future years as predicted by the New Jersey Administrative Office of the Courts. This presents more serious problems for older inmates who often wait more than a year in County jails to come in to the state system. County jails are notorious for providing few or no amenities to provide for the needs of the elderly. Deficits have increased 19.8% from 1980 to 1985.

Property offenders admissions rose proportionately from 14% in 1980 to 19% in 1985 of all total admissions during this period. Personal offenders declined from 18% in 1980 to 17% in 1985. Property offenders made up 51% of all admissions with personal offenders making up the balance. In sheer numbers, property offenders increased 23% from 1980 to 1985 and personal offenders declined 8.8%.

Personal offenders releasees ranged from 18% of the older population in 1980 to 15% in 1985. In numbers, releases decreased 17% from 1980 to 1985. They made up 54% of the total release population. Property releasees made up the balance, declining from 15% in 1980 to 14% in 1985. In numbers they declined 9%.

THE LONG TERM INMATE GROWING OLD

Table 14 displays the number and percentages of younger inmates incarcerated by age category, who will reach 55 years or older prior to eligibility.

The number of incarcerated, older inmates goes up progressively as age increases, which is intuitively correct, as it takes less time to reach 55, as one advances in age. The 50 to 54 group contains the largest number of inmates (23.6%), because of this, and despite their small share of admissions, (less than 5.3%), since 1978 30% of their offenses carried a maximum sentence of 5 to 9.9 years, which is due partly to 39% of their offenses being property crimes. Sixty-one percent of their group however were convicted of serious personal offenses. Fourteen percent of these offenses carried a sentence of anywhere from 10 years to Life, partially accounting for their larger share of inmates in residence.

PRESENT AGE AND FUTURE ELIGIBILITY DATES

It could be argued that our use of the term long term offender growing old is a misnomer when applied to the upper row of inmates, 50-54 years of age in Table 15. This would be true if you use the definition of long term as continuous confinement for a period of seven years rather than five years; five and seven years being two commonly utilized points to distinguish long term inmates (Flanagan, 1980). With the 7 year definition, we would have to eliminate those cases who achieved 55 without spending seven years in confinement. Our intention in using "long term" was more descriptive than methodological, a distinguishing characteristic of the majority of younger inmates who will reach 55 before eligibility. Table 15 demonstrates this. The first significant group of inmates will not reach eligibility until 1990 to 1994. Assuming for purposes of argument that they were all sentenced at the latest point in time, 1986, they would have to be in confinement for 8 years to reach a 1994 eligibility date. In addition, 72% of this cohort will not reach eligibility until, at least, the year 2000. Again, using the latest point in time as a common sentence date, the earliest the majority would reach eligibility is the year 2000, which would place them in custody for a term of 14 years, having to serve a sentence of 42 years or a 14 year mandatory minimum. When one notes that 50% of the group will not reach eligibility until 2005 to 2009, "long term" would appear to be an apt description.

Thirty-five percent of this cohort will turn 55 to 59 prior to eligibility, 24% will turn 60 to 64 prior to eligibility and 24% will reach

70 and above before eligibility. There are 8.2% more in this group reaching 55 at eligibility than the average for the total population.

OFFENSE DISTRIBUTION BY AGE

Table 16 shows that 58% of this younger cohort were convicted of Murder contrasted to 16% of the older group (compare with Table 8). The younger group committed only 8% Sexual Assault offenses contrasted to 19% by the older group. The relative absence of property offenses among the Long Term Inmate Growing Old is due to these offenses carrying shorter sentences and by definition, we would not capture many property offenders in this cohort who would turn 55 prior to eligibility. Another point of contrast is the 13% incidence of drug offenses by the older group contrasted to 3.4% by the younger group. We suspect that a large percentage of the serious offenses committed by the younger offenders were drug related, but our research has not covered this issue yet.

LENGTH OF SENTENCE

In Table 17, the first point of comparison with the older offender is the 52.2 percentage of Life sentences among the younger group compared to an 8% incidence with the older inmates (compare with Table 9). Long Term Inmates Growing Old also have 79.8% mandatory minimums in their sentencing pattern compared to 37.5% for the older inmate. The average mandatory minimum was 25 years as illustrated in Table 18.

Table 16 demonstrates that 58.1% of the younger cohort were convicted of Homicide charges, which would account for the 52.2% of Life sentences.

Sixty-two percent of the younger group either received a Life sentence or a term in excess of 50 years. Only .3% received a sentence under 5 years.

AGE AND AVERAGE LENGTH OF STAY BY NATURE OF CRIME AND MODAL OFFENSE

The modal length of stay for long term offenders growing old, as displayed in Table 18, is 25 years. The average length of stay for persons convicted of personal offenses is 22.7 years and the average stay for property offenders is 17.9 years. The medium length of stay for personal offenders is 25 years and for property offenses it is 9.9 years (compare with Table 10).

For crimes against persons within the older group there is an inverse relationship between age and length of sentence and an inverse relationship between age and volume of sentencing. On the other hand, with the Long Term Inmates Growing Old there is a direct relationship between age and length of sentence and a direct relationship between age and volume of sentencing up to age 35 to 39. Generally speaking, among the older group the older you are, the less your sentence and length of stay, however, with the younger group, the older you are, the more likelihood you are serving a longer sentence and length of stay.

Older inmates were convicted of 11% more sexual offenses than their younger counterparts.

There were 74% offenders against person among the older group compared to 95.3% of the younger group and 26% property offenders among the older group versus 4.6% with the younger group.

ADMISSIONS

Both admissions for personal and property offenses increased for the younger group over the years 1980 to 1985 as illustrated in Table 19. Admissions for crimes against person outnumbered property offenses by 94% in the year 1985. This stands in sharp contrast to admission for the older cohort at 49% for personal offenses versus 51% for property offenses.

Admissions for personal offenses increased 82% (in numbers) from 1980 to 1985 compared to 80% (in numbers) for property offenses for the same time period. Total admissions for the group increased 82% from 1980 to 1985.

FUTURE POPULATIONS

A simple formula was used to project the future populations for the older group: P = P{l} + A – R, where P is the projected end year population for the year, P{1} is the population in the previous year, A is the number of admissions during the year in question and R is the number of releases during this year.[8] Working from a base line population in 1986, simple linear regression was used to project admissions and releases for each year. Of course, the long term inmate growing old had no releases to parole. The results are illustrated in Tables 20 and 21.

The long term inmate growing old increased in population size from 53.7% of the total in 1986 to 63.1% in 1990.

The Department is presently working on another modal which will disaggregate admissions and releases by offenses. Average lengths of stay for each offense group will be multiplied by the projected admissions to arrive at releases for each future year.[9]

SUMMARY AND DISCUSSION

As of September 1986, the Department housed 350 inmates 55 years of age or older. This figure includes 73 released to parole during the year. Approximately 51% (118) were 60 or older, 13.7% (38) were 70 or older. In 1986 the percentage of inmates 55 and older to the general prison population averaged 4% and the total 60 and older averaged 2%. This ratio has not changed substantially since 1981.

As of the same date, the Department housed 322 inmates who will turn 55 and older prior to eligibility. This group called the "Long Term Inmate Growing Old" represents 3.7% of the total prison population. This ratio grew incrementally from 2.6% in 1981 to its present size in 1986. In 1990 there should be 362 inmates 55 years and older. This would represent 3.6% of the total projected prison population of 9,889. In the same year, there will be 619 inmates who will turn 55 and older prior to eligibility. This represents 6.2% of the projected prison population.

This younger cohort will go from a resident population of 87 in 1980 to 619 in 1990, increasing seven fold over the years with a net increase of 2.6% from 1980 to 1981 to 18.7% in years 1989 to 1990. At this rate, by the year 2000, *ceteris paribus*, the ratio of this younger group to the older inmate could exceed 3 to 1.

Admissions for the older group showed a decrease over the years of 2.8%. All other things being equal, past trends would suggest no substantial increase in their numbers to year 2000.

Although the general population is experiencing a large demographic increase in its older population, it is problematic whether this will be affected by the commitment rate of the older group.

Research with long term offenders suggest that there is no significant relationship between rates of incarceration and measures of population (Flanagan, 1980), however the Steffensmeier's study of age specific index crimes below.

Fifty percent of older inmates are past eligibility by 1987 contrasted to 2.5% of the Long Term Inmate Growing Old. Approximately 80% of the older group will be eligible for parole by the year 1994, whereas only 12% of the younger cohort will be eligible. Over two-thirds of the younger group will not be eligible for parole until 2010 to 2014. Twelve percent of the younger cohort will not reach eligibility until well after the year 2020, contrasted to 1.4% of the older group. The total number of inmates who will mature to fifty-five in coming years will constitute an older group at parole eligibility compared to the present older cohort. At present there are 38 (14%) of the older inmates who have reached 70 or older; 26 (9%) are between 65 and 69 and 78 (28%) have obtained 60 to 64. When total inmates reach eligibility there will be 106 (18%), 70 years and older; 78 (13%) between 65 and 69 and 140 (24%) between 60 and 64.

Fifty-eight percent of the younger group were convicted of Murder or Homicide contrasted to 16% of the older group. The younger group committed only 8% Sexual Assault offenses contrasted to 19% by the older group. Personal offenses accounted for 66% among the older group versus 34% property offenses. The Long Term Inmate Growing Old had an incidence of 93% personal offenders versus 7% property offenders. The older group outranked the younger group by a 13% incidence of drug offenses contracted to 3.4 by the younger group. All offenders had an average of 10.5% prior arrests and 8% prior convictions[11].

The average length of stay to parole eligibility for the older group was 5 years and for the long term inmate 25 years. The average length of stay for all offenders during 1970 to 1975 averaged 35.5 months for offenses against person offenders and 16 months for property offenders. Personal offenders among the older group are now serving 190% more time to eligibility and property offenders are serving 8% more time.

For total admissions into the prison system, from 1978 to 1986, the age group 30 to 34 made up the highest percentage at 28%. The 50 to 59 group represented 5.3% of the total and showed a net increase of 1.4%. The 60 and older group constituted 2.3% of the total and showed a decrease of 3.5% over the years. Admissions for the long term inmate growing old increased 64% from 1980 to 1985 including a 93% rise for person offenses and a 7% rise for property offenses. For the older group, admissions outpaced releases by 56%. The younger group, of course, had no releases.

The profile that emerges for the older inmate is man of 57 years of age, who is a resident of Rahway State Prison and has been convicted of Homicide, Manslaughter, or Sexual Assault. He has received a sentence between 10 and 15 years with a manadatory minimum of 5 years. His average length of stay is 5 years and he was eligible for parole in 1986, having been sentenced in 1981. He has had 5 prior arrests with 4 previous convictions, one of which was for a property offense for which he served a previous incarceration in the reformatory system.

The Long Term Inmate Growing Old is 37 years old; is a resident of Trenton State Prison and has been convicted of Homicide. He has received a Life sentence with a mandatory minimum of 25 years. He will be eligible for parole in 2010 having been sentenced in 1985. He has had 8 prior arrests with 6 prior convictions, 2 of which lead to a reformatory term for a property offense and a prior prison term of Armed Robbery.

The "older inmate" in New Jersey can be classified into three categories: one who was 55 or older at age at sentence and is institutionalized for the first time or who is in the above age category but has been in and out of prison previously or who is younger when sentenced but by the nature of his sentence will reach 55 or older before eligibility. This latter group could also be subdivided into first time and repeat offenders.

New Jersey has had a slightly higher percentage of inmates 55 and older, (4%) contrasted to the national average of 2.3% for 1981. During that year state and federal prisons held an estimated 8,853 person aged 55 and older (Newman, 1984).

Teller and Howell report that arrests for those 55 years of age and over for Index Crimes increased 77 to 89% from 1970 to 1980 (Teller et al., 1981). Arrest rates by age for the years in question were not available as of the date of this report, however rates of *admissions* to the prison for the same age group for a comparable term of years are as follows. The prison system showed 38% property and 42% crimes against person admissions for base year 1975. These admissions, per the Master plan included all index offenses.[11] From 1981 to 1986, prison admissions averaged 32.2% for property offenders and 48% for versus person offenders. Although we have no data on missing years 1976 to 1980, a reasonable interpolation could be made that property admission declined 5.8% and versus person admissions increased 8% between the years 1970 and 1986 for the total prison population.

The 55 year and older group displayed a 176% increase for property admissions and 64% increase for versus person admissions from years 1980 to 1985. The younger cohort showed an 400% increase for property offenses and a 461% increase for versus person offenses. These percentiles are misleading because of the small numbers involved.

In a recent article, Steffensmeier et al. reports that a sizeable portion of the reported drop in the nation's crime rate (Index crimes) is due to demographic changes (Steffensmeier, 1978). Adjusting UCR rates to reflect age specific rates they report a 9% decline for all Index crimes.

National forecasters are recording a 12% increase for all index arrests from 1970 to 1980 for the older group. In New Jersey we are showing an increase of *admissions* for all index crimes of 114% for years 1970 to 1985.

The Bureau of Justice Statistics' Survey of the Inmates of State Correctional Facilities, 1979 study showed a larger proportion of elderly inmates (55 and older) were serving time for a violent offense (70.03%) than were younger inmates (55.92%).

In New Jersey for years 1980 to 1986, the percentages are as follows: for the older group; 66%, for the Long Term Inmate Growing Old, 93% and for their younger counterparts (reformatory inmates, ages 18 to 26) 39.8%.

Among our older cohort, one subgroup stands out by its size and makeup. Experts at the prison report that the majority of 55 to 59 year olds are repeat offenders, having served at least one previous institutionalization. They also make up 22.5% of our total older population. They have the largest percentage of property offenses (42.3%) committing more diversified offenses than any other subgroup. They also have the largest percentage of people past parole eligibility (53%) and have the largest percentage (30%) having the shortest length of stay—1-4.9 years.

A national profile of the older defender defines one subgroup as the "geriatric delinquent," who has a history of repeat offenses and more closely resembles the younger offender than the older inmate in prison for the first time (Newman et al., 1984). This is a high activity inmate who passes in and out of the system faster than any other member of our population. It is a picture of the younger, repeat offender grown old.

GLOSSARY OF OPERATIONAL TERMS

Older Inmate is any individual sentenced to the Commissioner of the Department of Corrections for a year or more who was fifty-five years of age at sentencing or achieved fifty-five at date of this study, September 15, 1986.

Long Term Inmate Growing Old is any individual sentenced to the Commissioner of the Department of Corrections who will reach fifty-five years of age prior to reaching parole eligibility.

Admissions include:

—Commitments from the court who may be on probation or Intensive Probation Supervision.

- Commitment from Parole by the court of offenders for a new offense.
- Commitment from Parole or technical violations.
- Transfers in from another state correctional institution.
- Returns from escape status.

Departures or Release include:

- Releases to parole supervision or parole to a detainer.
- Discharges from custody without supervision at expiration of maximum status.
- Release to Intensive Probation Supervision Release to halfway houses, alcohol and drug programs.
- Discharges by court action Escapes from the prison system.

Average Length of Stay to Parole:

- The time measured from date of sentence to day of release on parole.

Average Length of Stay to Parole Eligibility:

- The time measured from date of sentence to day of parole eligibility. Parole eligibility is calculated by dividing the maximum sentence by three and subtracting compensatory (good time), work and minimum credits.

NOTES

1. Total prison population projections are based on A Report on Correctional Population Projections submitted to the Governor's office of Policy and Planning by The Task Force on Prison Overcrowding Population Projections Subcommittee, February, 1987.

2. N.J.S.A. TITLE 2C, 1979.

3 The Graves Act limits the discretion of the sentencing judge by requiring that a mandatory sentence be imposed for a certain percentage of the total term in all cases in which it is proven a gun was involved.

4. The very terms we use should be approached with caution to avoid labeling and stereotyping. "Older inmate" seemed less offensive to us than any other label.

5. The data used here and in subsequent references to years 1970 to 1973 and

1974 to 1975 are derived from the New Jersey Correctional Master Plan, New Jersey Department of Corrections, 1977.

6. A convenient rule of thumb for figuring actual time served from a total sentence is to divide by five or in this case, multiply years of confinement by five.

7. This is a simulation method of projecting prison population. In order to simulate the process which leads up to projecting P{1}, two parameters must be estimated: admissions and releases up to the date(s) for which the projections are made. Admissions and releases used here up to 1990 were projected by linear regression. For a review of the various methods of projecting prison populations see: Prison Population Projections Methods, Illinois Department of Corrections, Bureau of Policy Development, 1981.

8. The correlation coefficients for older inmate admissions was $r = .87$, $r\{2\} = .76$, younger inmate admission, $r = .82$, $r\{2\} = .67$, older inmate releases, $r = .79$, $r\{2\} = .62$.

9. The goal of disaggregation is to isolate divergant impacts on the system so they can be identified and measured. The Department is disaggregating by type of crime, i.e., Homicide, Sexual Assault, etc. Average lengths of stay will be established from past patterns and multipled by projected admissions for each year to determine rates of releases.

10. These averages are derived from Arrest and Convictions Data, Adult Offenders, New Jersey Department of Corrections, 1985.

11. Not counted are Narcotic offenses and uncoded offenses.

REFERENCES

Atchley, Robert C. (1972). The Social Forces in Later life, *An Introduction to Social Gerontology*, Calif.: Wadsworth Pub. Co.

Flanagan, Timothy J. (1980). *Long Term Prisoners: A Description Analysis,* Albany, N.Y.: Criminal Justice Research Center.

Illinois Department of Corrections (1981). *Prison Population Projection Methods*, Bureau of Policy Development.

New Jersey Correctional Master Plan Policy Council (1977). *New Jersey Correctional Master Plan*.

Newman, Evelyn S., Donald J. and Mindy L. Gervitz (1984). *Elderly Criminals*, Cambridge, Mass.: Gelgeschlager, Gunn and Hain, Pubs.

Steffensmeier, Darrell J. and Harer, Miles P. (1987). "Is the Crime Rate Really Falling?" *Journal of Research in Crime and Delinquency*, 24.

Teller, Fran E. and Howell, Robert J. (1981). "The Older Prisoner: Criminal and Psychological Characteristics", *Criminology*, 18, Feb.

Rubenstein, Dan (1984). "The Elderly in Prison: A Review of Literature" in Newman, Evelyn, et al. (eds.), *Elderly Criminals*, Cambridge, Mass.: Gelgeschlager, Gunn and Hain, pubs.

TABLE 1. Percentage of Total Prison Population

1981	174	4%	(4351 prison population)
1982	203	4%	(5384 " ")
1983	274	4%	(6341 " ")
1984	301	4%	(7391 " ")
1985	333	4%	(8004 " ")
1986	350	4%	(8597 " ")

TABLE 2

Age	Percentage of Total Admiss.	Mean and Medium Age
19-29	23%	24/24
30-49	70%	39/38
50+	7.6%	60/62.5

TABLE 3. Mandatory Minimum of Admissions

Man/Min.	Number	% of Man/Min.
31+	57	1.10%
30	108	2.09%
20-29	153	2.96%
16-19	40	.77%
15	175	3.39
	533	

TABLE 4. Catchment Population

60	318
55	358
50	533

TABLE 5

55-59	60-64	65-69	70+	Total
135 (48.7%)	78 (28.2%)	26 (9.4%)	38 (13.7%)	277 (100%)

TABLE 6. Present Age and Future Eligibility Dates—Older Inmates

Age	Past. Elig.	1987	1988	1989	90-94	95-99	2000-04	05-09	10-14	15-19	2020+	Total (n=)
70+	17%	9%	13%	14%	12%	25%		14%	33%			38 (4)
65-69	6	14	3	7	18				17			26 (4)
60-64	21	29	38	29	24	25	25%	29	17	100%		78 (11)
55-59	56	48	46	50	46	50	75	57	33			135 (8)
Total	100%	100%	100%	100%	100%	100%	100%	100%	100%	100%	100%	
(n=)*	71	65	37	14	33	8	4	7	6	1	4	277 (27)*

* 27 cases at Avenel have no eligibility dates.

TABLE 7. Age at Date of Parole Eligibility

Age	Totals
70+	106 (18.6%)
65-69	78 (13.7%)
60-64	140 (24.5%)
55-59	246 (43.2%)
Totals	599 (100.0%)

TABLE 8. Offense Distribution by Age—Older Inmates

Age	Murd.	Mans.	Asslt.	Sex Asslt.	Kidnap	Robb.	Weap.	Arson	B&E	Theft	Checks	Gamb.	Drugs	Other	Total (n=)
70+	9%	23%	12%	22%		33%	17%		11%	15%			5%		38
65–69	9%	10%	8%	11%				13%		8%	25%		11%	23%	26
60–64	24%	37%	40%	22%		17%	33%	25%	33%	23%		40%	34%	42%	78
55–59	58%	30%	40%	45%	100%	50%	50%	62%	56%	54%	75%	60%	50%	62%	135
Total	100%	100%	100%	100%	100%	100%	100%	100%	100%	100%	100%	100%	100%	100%	
(n=)	43	30	42	54	2	12	6	8	9	13	4	5	36	13	277

TABLE 9. Length of Sentence by Age – Older Inmates

Age	1- 4.9	5.9- 9.9	10- 14.9	15- 19.9	20- 24.9	25- 29.9	30- 34.9	35- 39.9	40- 44.9	45- 49.9	50+	Life	Man Min. (Avg. 8.3 yrs.)	Total (n=)
70+	27.8%	13.9%	15.1%	12.1%	0.0%	11.1%	25.0%	0.0%	0.0%	0.0%	0.0%	13.0%	10.6%	38
65-69	27.8	6.4	7.5	6.1	23.5	0.0	18.8	0.0	33.3	0.0	0.0	4.4	10.6	26
60-64	11.1	38.8	34.0	18.2	17.6	22.2	31.2	0.0	33.3	33.3	25.0	13.0	35.5	78
55-59	33.3	40.9	43.4	63.6	58.9	66.7	25.0	100%	33.3	66.7	75.0	69.6	43.3	135
Total	100%	100%	100%	100%	100%	100%	100%	100%	100%	100%	100%	100%	100%	
(n=)	18	93	53	33	17	9	16	5	3	3	4	23	104	277

TABLE 10. Age, Average Length of Stay by Nature of Crime with Modal Offense—Older Group

	vs. Person						vs. Property/Drugs						
Age	1-4.9	5.9.9	10-14.9	15-19.9	20-24.9	25+	1-4.9	5-9.9	10-14.9	15-19.9	20-24.9	25+	Total (n=)
70+	9.1%	23.2%	6.2%	19.1%	25.0%	10.0%	13.5%						38
	S/M	S/R	R	H	SO	H	T/D						
65-69	9.1%	5.8%		14.3%		5.0%	15.4%	21.4%					26
	S/D	H/R		H/S		H	T/D	D					
60-64	28.6%	33.3%	18.8%	9.5%	25.0%	20.0%	34.6%	28.6%	33.3%				78
	S/H	S/H	H	S	M	H	D	D	D				
55-59	53.2%	37.7%	75.0%	57.1%	50.0%	65.0%	36.5%	50.0%	66.6%	100%			135
	S	S	H	H	S	H	D/T	D	A	D			
Total	100%	100%	100%	100%	100%	100%	100%	100%	100%	100%			
(n=)	77	69	16	21	4	20	52	14	3	1			277

A= Arson; S= Sexual Assault; H = Homocide; M = Manslaughter; D = Drugs; T = Theft; R = Robbery; SO = Sodomy

TABLE 11. Total Admissions by Age

	18-20	21-24	25-29	30-34	35-30	40-49	50-59	60+	Total (n=)
1986*	5.7%	3.4%	2.0%	1.2%	1.0%	.1%	.7%	.2%	276
1985	71.7	27.5	21.0	15.3	13.1	12.7	14.3	10.4	3,248
1984	15.0	23.0	20.4	17.6	16.8	15.5	15.2	12.9	3,576
1983	3.8	20.6	17.8	18.9	15.9	15.4	13.7	15.8	3,486
1982	0	14.2	13.5	12.5	12.5	12.4	12.4	10.4	2,583
1981	0	7.6	10.6	12.0	12.7	11.3	8.4	9.0	2,290
1980	3.8	2.8	7.0	9.0	10.0	10.6	13.1	13.8	1,873
1979	0	.6	4.5	7.0	9.6	10.9	9.3	12.7	1,598
1978	0	.3	3.2	6.5	8.4	11.1	12.9	14.8	1,516
Total	100%	100%	100%	100%	100%	100%	100%	100%	
(n=)	53	954	3,680	5,749	4,581	3,856	1,093	480	20,446

* Only first quarter figures for 1986 are illustrated

TABLE 12. Admissions and Releases for Older Inmates by Offense

Year	Admissions vs. Person	vs. Property	Total (n=)	Releases vs. Person	vs. Property	Total (n=)	Grand Total (n=)
1985	17%	19%	197	15%	14%	66	263
1984	19%	21%	244	16%	18%	80	302
1983	19%	25%	224	22%	23%	104	348
1982	16%	9%	138	15%	13%	66	204
1981	11%	12%	126	14%	17%	74	200
1980	18%	14%	181	18%	15%	76	257
Total	100%	100%		100%	100%		
(n=)	549	568	1,108	230	236	466	1,574

TABLE 13. Bed Space Deficits

1985	131	(20.4)
1984	142	(22.1)
1983	140	(21.8)
1982	72	(11.2)
1981	52	(8.1)
1980	105	(16.4)
Total	642	(100%)

TABLE 14. Ages of Long Term Inmate Growing Old

19-24	25-29	30-34	35-39
11 (3.5%)	43 (13.4%)	49 (15.2%)	59 (18.3%)

40-44	45-49	50-54	Total
42 (13.0%)	42 (13.0%)	76 (23.6%)	322 (100%)

TABLE 15. Present Age and Eligibility Dates—Long Term Inmates

Age	Past Elig	1987	1988	1989	90-94	95-99	00-04	05-09	10-14	15-19	2020+	Total (n=)
50-54	100%	100%	100%	100%	66,6%	31,2%	11,1%	25,5%	5,2%	1,6%	2,5%	76
45-49					30,8	46,9	16,7	9,1	5,1	4,9	2,5	42
40-44					2,6	21,9	38,9	14,5	14,1	16,1	2,5	42
35-39							27,8	32,7	28,1	21,0	17,5	59
30-34							5,5	18,2	28,1	21,0	22,5	49
25-29									17,6	33,8	30,0	43
19-24									1,8	1,6	22,5	11
Total	100%	100%	100%	100%	100%	100%	100%	100%	100%	100%	100%	
(n=)	1	7	3	8	39	32	18	55	57	62	40	322

TABLE 16. Offense Distribution by Age—Long Term Inmates

Age	Murd.	Mans.	Asslt.	Sex Asslt.	Kidnap	Robb.	Weap.	Arson	B&E	Theft	Checks	Drugs	Other	Total (n=)
50-54	11,8%	42,1%	41,6%	26,9%	11,8%	30,8%	100%	100%	100%	100%	100%	81,8%	100%	76
45-49	11,2%	36,8%	16,7%	11,6%	5,9%	17,9%						9,1%		42
40-44	11,8%			15,4%	41,2%	23,1%								42
35-39	20,3%	5,3%	16,7%	26,9%	23,4%	17,9%								59
30-34	20,8%	10,5%		11,6%	5,9%	7,7%						9,1%		49
25-29	19,8%	5,3%	8,3%	3,8%	11,8%	2,6%								43
19-24	4,3%		16,7%	3,8%										11
Total	100%	100%	100%	100%	100%	100%	100%	100%	100%	100%	100%	100%	100%	100%
(n=)	187	19	12	26	17	38	2	1	2	2	2	11	3	322

TABLE 17. Length of Sentence by Age – Long Term Inmates

Age	1–4.9	5.9–9.9	10–14.9	15–19.9	20–24.9	25–29.9	30–34.9	35–39.9	40–44.9	45–49.9	50+	Life	Man Min. (Avg.25 yrs)	Total
50–54	100%	100%	90.9%	77.8%	77%	0.0%	10.5%	0.0%	35.7%	0.0%	5.9%	14.9%	19%	76
45–49			9.1	22.2	18	85.7	15.8	50.0	21.5	11.1	2.9	9.5	11	42
40–44						14.3	28.9	25.0	7.1	22.2	20.6	11.3	13	42
35–39					5		10.5	25.0	21.5	33.4	23.5	23.2	19	59
30–34							13.2		7.1		17.7	22.0	17	49
25–29							21.1		7.1	22.2	20.6	14.9	17	43
19–24										11.1	8.8	4.2	4	11
Total	100%	100%	100%	100%	100%	100%	100%	100%	100%	100%	100%	100%	100%	
(n=)	1	5	11	9	22	7	38	4	14	9	34	168	258	322

TABLE 18. Age, Average Length of Stay by Nature of Crime with Modal Offense – Long Term Inmates

	vs. Person							vs. Property/Drugs/Other							
Age	1-4.9	5-9.9	10-14.9	15-19.9	20-24.9	25+	Total (n=)	1-4.9	5.99	10-14.9	15-19.9	20-24.9	25+	Total (n=)	Grand Total (n=)
50-54	100%	72.7%	55.0%	42.8%	25.09%	6.9%	62	100%	100%	66.%	100%		100%	14	76
	S	M	R	H	H	H		D	D	D	D				
45-49		27.3%	45.0%	45.8%	18.7%	4.6%	41				33.3%			1	42
		M	H	H	H	H					D				
40-44				8.6%	18.7%	16.7%	42								42
				H	H	H									
35-39				2.8%	37.6%	24.1%	59								59
				H	H	H									
30-34						22.7%	49								49
						H									
25-29						19.9%	43								43
						H									
19-24						5.1%	11								11
						H									
Total	100%	100%	100%	100%	100%	100%	100%	100%	100%	100%	100%		100%	100%	100%
(n=)	9	11	20	35	1	216	307	2	8	3	1		1	15	322

D = Drugs; H = Homicide; M = Manslaughter; R = Robbery; S = Sexual Assault

TABLE 19. Admissions for Long Term Inmates by Crime

Year	vs. Person	vs. Property/Drugs/Other	Total (n=)
1985	36.0%	31.4%	78
1984	25.1%	25.0%	55
1983	20.7%	25.0%	46
1982	8.4%	6.2%	18
1981	3.4%	6.2%	8
1980	6.4%	6.2%	14
Total	100%	100%	100%
(n=)	203	16	219

TABLE 20. Total Populations at End of Each Calendar Year

	1986	1987	1988	1989	1990
Older	277 (46.3%)	299 (43.5%)	320 (40.9%)	341 (38.6%)	362 (36.9%)
Younger	322 (53.7%)	388 (56.5%)	462 (59.1%)	542 (61.4%)	619 (63.1%)
	599 (100%)	687 (100%)	782 (100%)	883 (100%)	981 (100%)

	In Puts	Out Puts	In Puts	Out Puts	In Puts	Out Puts	In Puts	Out Puts	In Puts	Out Puts
Older	104	73	118	96	120	99	123	102	126	105
Younger	31	0	66	0	74	0	80	0	89	12

TABLE 21. Projected Total Populations

Year	Total
1987	687
1988	782
1989	883
1990	981

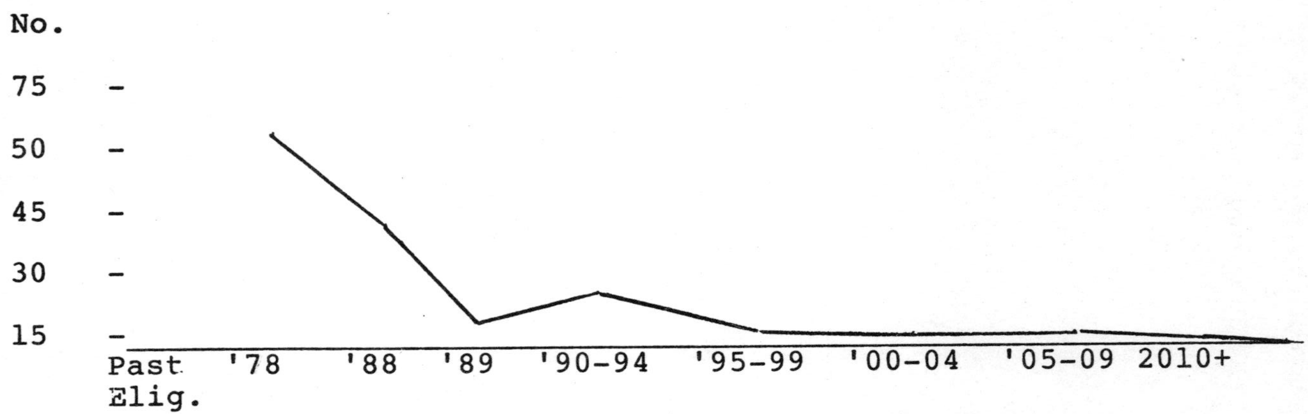

FIGURE 1. Graph of Total Number of Inmates Becoming Eligible by Year of Eligibility